COGNITIVE DEVELOPMENT IN MUSEUM SETTINGS

Researchers in cognitive development are gaining new insights into the ways in which children learn about the world. At the same time, there has been increased recognition of the important role that visits to informal learning institutions plays in supporting learning. Research and practice pursuits typically unfold independently and often with different goals and methods, making it difficult to make meaningful connections between laboratory research in cognitive development and practices in informal education. Recently, groundbreaking partnerships between researchers and practitioners have resulted in innovative strategies for linking findings in cognitive development together with goals critical to museum practitioners, such as exhibit evaluation and design.

Cognitive Development in Museum Settings offers accounts of how researchers in cognitive development partner with museum practitioners. The chapters describe partnerships between academic researchers and museum practitioners and details their collaboration, the important research that has resulted from their partnership, and the benefits and challenges of maintaining their relationship. This approach illustrates cutting-edge developmental science, but also considers how researcher-practitioner interactions affect research outcomes and influence educational practice. Each partnership discusses how their interaction affects the goals both researchers and practitioners have, and to what extent researchers and practitioners benefit from their collaborations.

David M. Sobel is a professor in the Department of Cognitive, Linguistic, and Psychological Sciences at Brown University. His research examines how children represent and learn causal knowledge and make inferences about their own and others' mental states.

Jennifer L. Jipson is an associate professor in the Department of Psychology and Child Development at California Polytechnic State University in San Luis Obispo. Her research investigates preschool children's developing understandings within the domains of science, health, and technology, with a focus on how everyday interactions in informal settings contribute to children's learning.

COGNITIVE DEVELOPMENT IN MUSEUM SETTINGS

Relating Research and Practice

Edited by David M. Sobel
and Jennifer L. Jipson

Routledge
Taylor & Francis Group

NEW YORK AND LONDON

First published 2016
by Routledge
711 Third Avenue, New York, NY 10017

and by Routledge
2 Park Square, Milton Park, Abingdon, Oxon OX14 4RN

Routledge is an imprint of the Taylor & Francis Group, an informa business

Library of Congress Cataloging-in-Publication Data
Cognitive development in museum settings : relating research and practice / [edited by] David M. Sobel, Jennifer L. Jipson.—1st Edition.
      pages cm
   Includes bibliographical references and index.
   1. Cognition in children.   2. Cognitive learning.   3. Museums—Educational aspects.   I. Sobel, David M., editor.   II. Jipson., Jennifer L., editor.
   BF723.C5.C6342 2016
   155.4'13075—dc23
   2015019517

ISBN: 978-1-84872-488-4 (hbk)
ISBN: 978-1-84872-489-1 (pbk)
ISBN: 978-1-315-66755-3 (ebk)

Typeset in Bembo
by Apex CoVantage, LLC

Printed and bound in Great Britain by
TJ International Ltd, Padstow, Cornwall

CONTENTS

SECTION 3
General Discussion   **209**

PREFACE

Researchers in cognitive development and practitioners in children's museums have been engaged in productive working relationships for several decades. Recently, however, interest in the potential value of such partnerships has become increasingly visible in both academic and applied circles. In 2005, Museum of Science, Boston, launched the first Living Lab (described in Corriveau et al., this volume), in which researchers and museum practitioners work together to pursue and share child development research. This model influenced many researchers and efforts to establish research–museum partnerships proliferated. In 2012, a timely "Tools of the Trade" article describing different partnerships and styles of researcher–practitioner interaction came out in the *Journal of Cognition and Development* (Callanan, 2012). Shortly thereafter, the Presidential Symposium at the 2013 Biennial meeting of the Cognitive Development Society was entitled *Science at an Exhibition: What We Learn from Studying Children in Museums*, and highlighted the relation between researchers and museum practice. In 2014, the Association of Children's Museums developed the *Learning Value of Children's Museums Research Agenda*, a document that described ways in which museum practitioners can broaden their participation in research and create "a field-wide research agenda for children's museums" (ACM, 2014). This agenda is beginning to be implemented in research networks around the country. As evidenced by these activities and others, many professionals perceive clear value in establishing partnerships between researchers in cognitive development and museum practitioners.

This led us to think about the value of providing additional resources to guide, inform, and inspire others curious about this increasingly popular approach to bridging research and practice. We also identified merit in documenting the recent past and emerging future of researcher–practitioner partnerships. Our desire to pursue these issues form the basis of this book in which we ask: *How do participants currently engaged in researcher–practitioner partnerships describe how their partnerships were formed and are maintained? How would they characterize the value of the research being done in museum settings to the field of developmental science? How would they discuss the potential impact of this research on the everyday practice of museum educators? And how might they convey the ways that working with practitioners affects research activities?*

To launch our inquiry into these topics, in the summer of 2014, we organized a small workshop, with 16 of the 37 authors in this book participating. Critically, we asked several of our partnerships to have at least one researcher and one practitioner attend and *together* describe their partnership process, the research outcomes, and the implications for both research and practice. We then asked some of the discussants in this book to give their thoughts on the overall goals for collaboration between researchers and practitioners. One of the outcomes of that workshop was agreement by both the researchers and practitioners who were present that more and better communication between fields was needed and desired. This strengthened our resolve to produce a foundational book that highlights existing collaborations and addresses core considerations in establishing and maintaining productive partnerships.

Asking researchers and practitioners to present at a workshop together is one thing; asking them to write chapters collaboratively is another. We think the final product is remarkable; each chapter is well-crafted, honest, and informative. We hope that readers will get a better sense of the varied research on cognitive development being done in museums, and at the same time gain insight into how researchers and museum practitioners can partner in ways that benefit both research and practice endeavors. By sharing stories of existing partnerships, this book will be particularly valuable for researchers who want to start collaborations with a museum in their area, and practitioners who want to establish research connections. We also think the book presents cutting-edge scientific findings as well as valuable lessons for the ways research influence practice and practice influence research.

We are deeply indebted to all of our authors; both our partnerships who constructed chapters that potentially went outside of their comfort zones in writing, and our discussant chapters who took on the challenging task of being fair to others' work while bringing in their own perspectives and voices (not to mention working on a rather strict timetable). We are also grateful to Michelle Ross, who took on the role of organizing the logistics of the initial workshop. The National Science Foundation (1223777 to DMS) and the Department of Cognitive, Linguistic, and Psychological Sciences at Brown University supported the workshop. NSF also funded both of our research programs during the last few years, and we are grateful for the support. We thank Georgette Enriquez at Psychology Press for her enthusiasm for the project and guidance through the publishing process, and also for her patience when there were delays. We also thank Lisa Faille and

Michael Hardy whose encouragement and understanding were indispensable as we navigated the process of crafting this book. Finally, we thank our children, Paulina, Nate, Josie, and Bixby. We are inspired by their sense of wonder and enthusiasm for learning. They remind us every day of what is important in life.

—Dave Sobel and Jennifer Jipson

References

ACM (Association of Children's Museums) (2014). *Learning value of children's museums research agenda.* http://childrensmuseums.org/images/learningvalueresearchagenda.pdf

Callanan, M.A. (2012). Conducting cognitive development research in museums: Theoretical issues and practical applications. *Journal of Cognition and Development, 13*(2), 137–151.

1

THE INTERACTION BETWEEN RESEARCH AND PRACTICE IN MUSEUM SETTINGS

An Introduction and Synthesis

Jennifer Jipson

CALIFORNIA POLYTECHNIC STATE UNIVERSITY, SAN LUIS OBISPO

David M. Sobel

BROWN UNIVERSITY

These are exciting times for those interested in better understanding and supporting children's learning. University researchers in cognitive development are steadily gaining new insights into the intricacies of children's reasoning about the world. At the same time, there has been increased recognition of the important role that visits to informal learning institutions (e.g., museums, science centers, zoos, botanical gardens) play in supporting learning. Traditionally, pursuits in research and practice typically unfold independently with different goals and methods. The disconnect between these endeavors can make it difficult to identify meaningful intersections between laboratory research in cognitive development and educational practice in informal settings. In this book, we document and discuss a diverse set of pioneering partnerships between university researchers and museum practitioners that have resulted in innovative strategies for linking investigations of children's cognitive development with goals critical to museum educators, such as evaluation and design.

The primary focus of this book is on the partnerships themselves, with the contributors sharing multiple perspectives on the complexities, challenges, and rewards of establishing and maintaining productive working relationships. Of particular interest is consideration of how engaging with informal educators influences the research process, and how engaging with researchers influences the work of informal educators. A complementary focus is on the cutting-edge cognitive developmental science being done by researchers working in museum settings. The researchers who locate their work in museum settings report that by doing so they reap more robust research findings and recognize more direct implications for practice.

This book includes chapters that reflect a variety of forms of research–museum partnerships. For example, some partnerships can be described as newly emerging, whereas others are long-standing collaborations. Some researchers work at large public research universities, whereas others are situated in smaller private colleges and universities. Some partner museum sites are children's museums, whereas others are science centers. Some researchers are invested in studying children's learning in situ, whereas others are pursuing topics not directly related to the exploration and learning that occurs in museum settings. Through an overview of the topical and organizational structure of the book, this introductory chapter tracks key issues upon which contributors focus with regard to their experiences at bridging historical divides between research and practice. We then concentrate on core issues that arise across the chapters, with the goal of providing readers with some context for the individual perspectives shared in the partnership chapters.

Organization of the Book

Our goal for this book is to provide current examples of groundbreaking approaches to research–practice partnerships that will serve as models and inspiration for others who also strive to engage in work that redefines the boundaries between research and practice. We also examine fundamentals of how children learn about and engage with the world around them, and explore age-old questions of how to better connect developmental research with educational practice and public awareness of the importance of the science. Throughout the book, authors consider how research in cognitive development can affect practice in informal learning settings, and how practitioners can influence novel and fruitful lines of research. These topics are examined across three major sections. The first section comprises principal partnership chapters. The second and third sections are discussion chapters. In one set of discussion chapters, outside scholars and museum practitioners provide their insights into the value of the highlighted partnerships. In the next set of discussion chapters, leaders in the fields of cognitive development and education provide a critical examination of how the increasingly popular approach of developing research–practice partnerships between university scholars and museum practitioners may have broad implications for understanding and supporting children's learning and development.

Partnership chapters. We used our professional networks to identify seven ongoing partnerships between university researchers in cognitive development and museum practitioners. We invited these research and practice partners to contribute to this book by reflecting on the nature of their collaboration, describing some of the research that has emerged from that collaboration, and providing insights into how research and practice intersect in their approach to partnership. We asked each partnership to describe the history of their collaboration and some of the research that had emerged from that collaboration. To offer further structure to our authors, we suggested topics they could consider in their chapters. One suggestion was to include what each partner's expectations were in terms of both shared and individual goals. Another was to describe any benefits of the collaboration, with attention to both individual and mutual benefits. For example, we wanted to know what advantages motivate continued pursuit of the partnership by each participant. We also wanted to know whether and how research informs any of the activities taking place in the museum and whether and how engagement within the museum influences the researchers' ideas and activities. Finally, we asked all of the contributors to comment on their perceptions of the value of the collaboration to their respective fields.

We also tailored questions specific to each member of the partnership. For example, we asked researchers whether and how their research activities have been affected by interaction with skilled practitioners. This way, we could document the broader benefits to the research community that these partnerships provide. Similarly, we asked practitioners whether and how exposure to the scholarly expertise offered by researchers has been helpful and to consider ways in which it can bring additional advantage. This way, we could describe the ways in which having basic researchers partner with museums affects the visitor experience.

We wanted to provide models for both researchers and practitioners who might be interested in constructing such partnerships, but who are not currently connected with the appropriate partner. Some researchers might not pursue partnerships because they do not currently conduct research that focuses on the appropriate age group, or because they perceive that their research interests are not aligned with the activities that take place within museums, or because they simply have never explored the possibility of doing research in museum settings. Similarly, some practitioners might not pursue partnerships because they do not know who among researchers would be interested in this type of partnership, or because they are concerned about how visitors and staff might react to have researchers on premises, or because they simply have never explored the possibility of having researchers come to their setting to conduct research. We wanted to describe ways in which each of these concerns is addressable, and offer ways to navigate the process of establishing such relationships for both parties.

By focusing the content of each chapter on some common questions, we encouraged contributors to explore certain foundational issues of broad relevance. At the same time, we were sensitive to the possibility that by suggesting topics, we were setting up a frame that might limit the range of possibilities for the contributors' chapters. We were happy to find that our instructions were not taken as prescriptive; the content we desired for this book is evident in the partnership chapters, yet not every partnership responded to all of these questions, and many of the partnerships introduced additional topics that surprised and intrigued us. Thus, throughout the partnership chapters, there is both consistency and variability, resulting in a book that will help researchers imagine how their work could benefit from engaging with museum partners, and help museum practitioners recognize the value in establishing research partnerships.

Each partnership starts their chapter by providing brief descriptions of the researchers and practitioners who interact on a regular basis to form the partnership. Because all of the research reported in this book takes place in museums, we also asked each partnership to describe the museum setting in some detail. These descriptions provide context for the research questions and procedures, as well as support consideration of how research activities might influence the museum visitor experience. Review of partnership biographies and museum settings reveals that the partnerships differed in a variety of ways. Some partnerships, like the one at the San Jose Children's Discovery Museum (Callanan, Martin, & Luce, Chapter 2), are long-standing, and have evolved in many ways over the course of the relationship. Other long-standing partnerships, such as the one at NY Hall of Science (Evans, Weiss, Lane, & Palmquist, Chapter 3), are more singularly focused on a particular set of goals, research questions, and exhibition design. Still others, such as the one at Chicago Children's Museum (Haden, Cohen, Uttal, & Marcus, Chapter 5), seem more of a hybrid between these two approaches.

The other partnerships described in this book are more recently established, each with different foci and goals. At Museum of Science, Boston (Corriveau, Kipling, Ronfard, Biarnes, Jeye, & Harris, Chapter 4), the Living Laboratory model emphasizes dissemination of research and seeks to help museum visitors gain insight into the importance of developmental science. At the Children's Museum of Manhattan (Rhodes & Bushara, Chapter 6), researchers pursue cognitive development topics through experiments, the findings of which often end up inspiring the development of novel programs within the museum. Although the partnership at Providence Children's Museum (Sobel, Letourneau, & Meisner, Chapter 7) started in a similar manner to the Living Lab model, the authors of this chapter describe ways in which the collaboration has affected questions the researchers ask—research that would not have been done in the absence of the collaboration. Finally, at the Thinkery (Legare, Gose, & Guess, Chapter 8), a new partnership with exciting potential is forming; although this partnership is still developing its identity, important contributions are already being made to the fields of cognitive development and museum education.

Discussion chapters. The final two sections of the book focus on discussion of issues that emanate from critique of specific partnerships, consideration of the overall value in cultivating professional relationships between researchers and museum practitioners, and insights into the broader impacts that such partnerships can have on multiple stakeholders (children, families, researchers, educators).

In the second section of the book, four discussants, each with different areas of expertise and professional backgrounds, consider different subsets of the partnership chapters. We asked them to examine and analyze the approaches that the partnerships take in their work together, but also to highlight the ways that their own specific expertise informs thinking about researcher–practitioner partnerships in general. Consequently, the discussion chapters in this section feature insightful critique of the various partnership endeavors, and describe additional models of collaboration between researchers and practitioners.

We assigned partnership chapters to discussants based on intersections that we anticipated might result in provocative commentary. We asked Suzanne Gaskins (Chapter 9), an expert in the ways that cultural experiences shape child development, to reflect on the approaches taken by Callanan et al. and Evans et al. to better understand learning as it unfolds in the context of everyday interactions on the museum floor. Helen Hadani and Caren Walker (Chapter 10) are currently engaged in developing an innovative new distance model for collecting research data in museum settings; we capitalized on their recent experiences by soliciting their views on Corriveau et al.'s description of the Living Lab approach as a broadly scalable mechanism to facilitate research–museum partnerships. The recency of Hadani and Walker's ongoing effort to develop new partnerships also positioned them to provide insights into Legare et al.'s description of the burgeoning collaboration at the Thinkery. Bronwyn Bevan (Chapter 11) provides a rich theoretical and experiential frame of reference to her critique of the ways that Sobel et al. and Rhodes and Bushara engage research for the benefit of practice, and vice versa. Finally, Sue Allen and Josh Gutwill (Chapter 12) use their vast experience working at the crossroads of research and museum practice to examine the intersections among research, practice, and evaluation, as they consider Haden et al.'s partnership.

In the third section of this book, we invited two sets of recognized experts in children's learning to comment on the full set of discussion chapters. Our goal here was not to offer further examination of the inner workings of any specific partnership, but rather to solicit reflections on how the process of navigating the challenges and promises of research–museum partnerships opens new possibilities in both research and practice. In addition to addressing the integration of academic and applied benefits, these chapters serve to emphasize points of critical importance that situate this work within broader conversations about approaches to integrating research and practice in formal educational settings (Grotzer & Solis, Chapter 13) and about public outreach about children's learning (Hirsh-Pasek & Golinkoff, Chapter 14).

In sum, our approach to organizing the book seeks to emphasize a range of perspectives on research–practice partnerships. We hear first from those actively engaged in focal partnerships. We then consider specific analysis of those partnerships from the perspectives of discussants who have experience with research–practice endeavors themselves but who are not involved in these particular partnerships. Finally, we examine key takeaways offered by another set of discussants that situate the topics addressed in the partnership chapters within a larger set of theoretical, social, and practical issues. The content of this book presents key issues that promote a reconceptualization of research and practice relationships for the good of both cognitive developmental research and informal educational practice.

Core Issues

We take this opportunity to highlight and discuss certain focal concerns that are prevalent in both the partnership and discussion chapters. Specifically, we noted that many contributors provide insights that inform such questions as: What are the patterns of interaction that describe researcher–practitioner partnerships? What practical issues both promote and constrain the perceived success of these partnerships? And, what unique opportunities do researcher–practitioner partnerships provide for education and public outreach?

Patterns of partnership interaction. One dominant issue that we identified after reading the chapters relates to how researchers and museum practitioners structure their partnerships. Variability in the ways that the researcher and practitioner partners engage one another requires careful consideration of the language used to describe their partnerships. Throughout the chapters, readers will notice that the authors use a variety of verbs to describe their interactions, such as "collaborate," "communicate," "cooperate," "contribute," "jointly negotiate," and "support." Bevan (private communication) describes *cooperative* research as similar to a "handshake" between agreeable partners, *collaborative* research as one that engages the partners in productive transactional dialogue, and *jointly negotiated* research as one in which research and museum partners constitute a unified team. A similar taxonomy of researcher–practitioner relationships is offered by the Chicago Children's Museum, an institution that provides clear guidelines for researchers seeking *cooperative*, *supported*, and *collaborative* partnerships with the museum (see Haden et al., this volume).

Each of the above descriptors of partnership processes suggests different modes of interaction that may reveal something about partner goals, may reflect the developmental stage of the partnership, and may predict the ways that research and practice are likely to shape one another. These elements are not unrelated. Our reading of the chapters leads us to conclude that partnership's goals often become more and more aligned the longer the partnership is in place. This convergence of goals seems to result from two mechanisms promoted by time and contact. First, the experience of working in a museum can shape an authentic research direction for the researcher. Second, research results can shape new programs, exhibits, and facilitation strategies at museums. Throughout the volume, the authors emphasize the critical process of cultivating trust and respect for one another, regardless of the form of the partnership.

In several chapters, the authors provide evidence of clear and natural alignment between the researchers' empirical questions and the goals that the practitioners have for collaborating with researchers (e.g., exhibit design or evaluation). This is visible in the relationships described in the chapters authored by Callanan et al. and Evans et al. The convergence of goals experienced by these authors is not surprising given that the authors are engaged in long-standing partnerships; however, their descriptions of the trajectories that led to their current interaction modes tell a story of progressive appreciation of one another's viewpoints and expertise. For example, Callanan et al. describe an initial relationship process that was more cooperative than collaborative. Catalyzed by a serendipitous research finding that surprised both the research team and museum practitioners, the relationship began to shift and the team started to craft jointly negotiated research–practice goals. A similar process seems to be unfolding in the relationships described by Haden et al. at Chicago Children's Museum, as well as by Rhodes and Bushara at Children's Museum of Manhattan. In both of these partnerships, initial interactions were based on each party offering cooperative assistance with independent goals until a provocative practice-relevant question and compelling research finding sparked a more collaboratively defined set of research and practice goals, including co-development of new programs and exhibits.

In other chapters, the researchers' and practitioners' goals at the beginning of the partnership reflected authentic shared interests, and the authors describe an ongoing exploratory process wherein they are navigating whether and how to pursue collaborative, or even jointly negotiated, goals. Specifically, Sobel et al. and Legare et al. describe partnerships in which partners' roles and relationships are evolving and have yet to reach full potential. Sobel et al., for example, describe an early relationship characterized by independent goals that are becoming more aligned, aided in part by a model for partnership in which a hybrid researcher/practitioner position was created to help bridge the two sets of activities. The partnership described by Legare et al. is the newest partnership reflected in this volume; negotiation of goals, communication pathways, and strategies to address practical considerations are in the early stages. Much can be learned by using Legare et al.'s experiences as a guide for how to initiate collaborations, and how to set the stage for a relationship that may eventually provide mutual benefit.

Another interesting case is the Living Lab model, described in the chapter by Corriveau et al. This approach to researcher–practitioner partnerships is unique in that, from the museum perspective, the research topics themselves are secondary to the goal of disseminating research findings and communicating the importance of developmental science to the general public. Upon establishing partnerships under the Living Lab model, researchers commit to engaging in outreach and public education. The authors of this chapter seem to embrace this opportunity. Thus, the Living Lab model promotes the development of a shared outreach goal between researchers and museum practitioners, yet much of the core work of researchers and practitioners remains independent.

It is our hope that examination of the variety of partnership models will inform those who are considering initiating researcher–practitioner relationships in the future. There are multiple lessons to be learned from reading the chapters in this book. Our own experiences lead us to suggest a few additional points consistent with the topic of partnership interactions. First is the issue of institutional endorsement. Although academic researchers enjoy a great deal of autonomy, they are nonetheless employees of universities and colleges wherein research is only one expected professional activity. Similarly, museum educators hold positions that are embedded in the formal and informal structures of their particular institutions. Thus, productive partnerships rely not only on individual vision and commitment, but also on institutional buy-in and support. Hints at the potential for tension in this regard are peppered throughout the chapters in this volume, although none of the authors raise this concern as one that seriously limited the development of their partnership. It is possible, however, that there is something akin to a selection bias at play here in that the partnerships included in this volume have reached a certain level of professional visibility. Conversations with members of partnerships that failed to flourish might reveal the critical role of institutional support.

A second open question concerns the presumed advantage of collaborative (or jointly negotiated) relationships over other forms of interaction. Privileging the status of relationships characterized as collaborative may discourage some emerging researcher–practitioner partnerships that might otherwise find that partner cooperation and support are sufficient for their goals. Some researchers might find it ideal to participate in a model that emphasizes access to onsite data collection, opportunities for research dissemination, and engagement in communicating the importance of developmental science in general. Such researchers would be well matched to practitioners who seek benefits that come with opportunities to connect with researchers, such as access to a differing perspective and knowledge base. Other researchers and practitioners may strive to engage in a relationship in which they can collaboratively explore ideas for exhibits, jointly define approaches for evaluating the efficacy of programs, and co-construct research questions. What we see in the chapters in this volume is that cooperation tends to cultivate collaboration. Open questions that invite further exploration are: Is it the rare or common case for partnerships to grow mutually over time? Do those that do not evolve in this manner have diminished potential to help partners meet their goals and develop new goals? Finally, do all attempted partnerships have the potential to take on a collaborative form if core practical matters are addressed effectively?

Practical matters. A second issue, one that recurred throughout all of the chapters, is the influence of seemingly mundane practical concerns on the perceived benefits and challenges of researcher–practitioner partnerships. When we asked our contributors to think about how they have benefitted from their ongoing partnerships, they mentioned many common advantages. Similarly, when reflecting on the challenges of forming and maintaining their partnerships, almost everyone brought up some of the same issues. The list of benefits is long, with museum educators often mentioning improvements in evaluation processes, opportunities for staff professional development, and inspiration for new exhibit topics and design approaches. Researchers frequently highlighted issues of participant access and diversity, opportunities for student training, and inspiration for new research directions. Collectively, the authors also expressed jointly appreciated benefits, such as pathways toward improved communication of scientific understandings to the public and access to differing funds of knowledge. One benefit that was not shared in a majority of the chapters, but that was of primary importance to a few researchers, relates to access to environments in which learning in situ can be readily observed.

Practical concerns also dominated discussion of challenges to efficient and effective partnerships. Several issues relate to the relationship between museum activities and the research process itself. Multiple contributors had stories to tell about their experiences navigating the disparate paces of the work of researchers and the work of museum practitioners. Museums and universities, for example, tend to have conflicting calendars. The times of the year when researchers want to collect data are exactly the times when museums do not want extra bustle on the floor. Likewise, the times most convenient for museums to have researchers engage their visitors often correspond to times in the academic calendar when teaching and service commitments are at their highest, or when undergraduate or graduate student assistants are not able to work. The seemingly ordinary concern over timelines and schedules appeared to present serious challenges for some partnerships, as evidenced by the number of partnerships that chose to mention this issue. More specific to researchers exploring learning in situ was the issue of adapting to novelty in the museum environment, as exhibits may be modified and sometimes even removed from the museum floor before researchers have completed their investigations.

These examples, as well as many others introduced in the chapters that follow, highlight a critical distinction between the goals of researchers and museum practitioners that did not go unnoticed by the contributors to this volume. Namely, museum practitioners are primarily focused on the visitor experience, whether that be the learning of exhibit content, engaging in modes of thinking that emanate through play and family interaction, or simply offering parents a place to relax for an hour while children are engaged. Friction can occur when researchers' efforts to ensure and maximize the integrity of their data intrude upon visitor experience. As Bevan points out in her chapter, bridging this gap can be difficult given that research and practice take place amid historically unequal power relations. To this end, the contributors to this volume emphasize the importance of regular face-to-face communication between partners for advancing mutual understanding and appreciating one another's work. A powerful message that emerged from their advice is that establishing intentional communication protocols early on in a developing partnership can have long-lasting consequences for both successful research and practice, and that relying on spontaneous, unsystematic, or absent communication pathways might not allow the partnership to grow to its full potential.

Education and public outreach. Multiple authors examined the issue of education and public outreach. One clear benefit of locating research in museum settings is the potential for researchers to interact with the public by demonstrating scientific methodologies, describing findings, and discussing the implications of their work. Direct access to scientists, particularly those who provide good accounts of their research, can facilitate scientific literacy in museum visitors. As Corriveau et al. report in their chapter, many museum visitors are eager audiences because the specific area of scientific study under consideration has to do with children's development and learning. Consequently, it is incumbent upon researchers to generate explanations of their work that are accessible to general audiences while still accurately reflecting their research procedures and results. In some partnerships, this work is delegated to trained undergraduate and graduate students working on research projects within museums. In other partnerships, this is left to practitioners because they often have experience communicating complex academic content to their visitors. The daily check-ins required under the Living Lab model (described in Corriveau et al.), the design of the Mind Lab space (described in Sobel et al.), and the public education programs at Children's Museum of Manhattan (described in Rhodes & Bushara) are all examples of explicit attempts at outreach.

Although communicating with visitors who stumble upon research being conducted in museums is important, Hirsh-Pasek and Golinkoff ask both researchers and practitioners whether they can do more. They push the researchers and their museum partners to consider other spaces as settings for informal learning, such as grocery stores and community events. Their Ultimate Block Party, for example, represents a way in which informal learning and the importance of developmental science can be communicated to the community in general, not just visitors to a museum. Grotzer and Solis take a different approach by considering how these researcher–practitioner relationships can inform both research and practice in formal educational settings. Thus, there are varied opportunities for researchers and practitioners to move beyond their comfort zones and integrate education and public outreach into broader community contexts.

Concluding Thoughts

One striking final point that emanated from the partnership and discussant chapters was that there is a genuine commitment to professional activities that will result in better understandings of how children learn, and how to support their learning. The missions of the museums engaged in the researcher–practitioner partnerships featured in this book share an emphasis on promoting learning and, specifically, learning through play and discovery. The research programs of the researchers working within these museum settings complement and inform this objective by examining a wide range of variables that influence what and how children learn.

This interest in learning aligns with the research agenda of the Association of Children's Museums (ACM, 2014), in which efforts to engage research in service to practice are encouraged. Several questions posed by this agenda are relevant to the issues addressed by the contributors to this book. For instance, "What kinds of learning are effectively facilitated and supported in children's museums (e.g., cognitive learning, emotional growth, social skills, mastery of the physical environment, attitude formation)?" and "What type of early learning experiences lead to foundational knowledge and skills needed for success?" (ACM, 2014, p. 4). Insights into each of these questions can be offered independently by researchers and practitioners, however, the contributors to this book show us that the potential to generate richer understandings of how children learn increases when academic and applied experts join together.

In sum, by highlighting a range of flourishing research–practice partnerships and discussions of the utility and challenges of initiating and maintaining these relationships, we wish to demonstrate that opportunities to establish partnerships between researchers and museum practitioners are readily available regardless of individual circumstances. An important caveat, however, is that for the partnerships described in this book, a variety of elements cohered to support stable frameworks for productive and mutually beneficial research–practice relationships. Attention to these elements is critical for new investigators and informal educators who hope to develop similarly successful partnerships. It is our hope that the lessons learned from contributors' critical examination of their own partnerships will inspire new collaborations that will streamline pathways to productive research programs, promote evidence-based educational practices, and allow for better understandings of how learning unfolds within everyday settings.

Acknowledgements

During the writing of this chapter, the first author was supported by NSF (1217441), and the second author was supported by NSF (1223777).

Reference

Association of Children's Museums (ACM). (2014). *Learning value of children's museums research agenda.* http://childrensmuseums.org/images/learningvalueresearchagenda.pdf

SECTION 1

Researcher–Practitioner Partnerships

2

TWO DECADES OF FAMILIES LEARNING IN A CHILDREN'S MUSEUM

A Partnership of Research and Exhibit Development

Maureen Callanan, Jennifer Martin, and Megan Luce

The Team

Maureen Callanan is a professor of psychology at University of California, Santa Cruz. Her research takes a sociocultural developmental approach, focusing on cognitive and language development in young children, as well as children's informal science learning in the context of family conversations and activities.

Jenni Martin is director of education and programs at Children's Discovery Museum of San Jose in San Jose, CA. Jenni has been PI on several National Science Foundation full-scale development projects. She has a background in project management and research partnerships, and has served on national committees, including the Learning Value of Museums Advisory Committee for the IMLS-funded research agenda project of the Association of Children's Museums and University of Washington.

Megan Luce is a research associate at Stanford University in the Graduate School of Education. She earned her Ph.D. in developmental psychology from the University of California, Santa Cruz. She has research interests in cognitive development and informal science learning, and design interests in supporting families in collaborative scientific sensemaking. Information about her current project can be found at www.playfulscience.org.

The Museum Setting

Children's Discovery Museum of San Jose's mission is to inspire creativity, curiosity, and lifelong learning so that today's children become tomorrow's visionaries. Located in downtown San Jose, CA, the museum opened in 1990 and serves over 325,000 visitors each year. San Jose is a minority majority community (29% Latino, 26% Asian, 3% African American, and 44% Caucasian), and the museum's visitors mirror the community's demographics. Children's Discovery Museum designs and builds most of its original exhibits onsite and incorporates a rigorous prototyping process with new exhibits designed to gather feedback from visitors.

Within the field of cognitive developmental psychology, the sociocultural perspectives of theorists such as Rogoff (2003) and Cole (1996) have built on Vygotsky's (1978) ideas and broadened the focus of developmental research from the individual child to the child in social context. Studying children in natural contexts, rather than only in laboratory settings, can support new insights about development. Gutiérrez and Rogoff (2003) see culture as involving "repertoires of practices" (p. 19) that children learn in the midst of everyday social activity. Research on how children learn through family conversation has yielded important findings about similarities and differences in the "habits of thinking" to which children are exposed (Callanan & Jipson, 2001; Callanan & Valle, 2008; Eberbach & Crowley, 2009; Gelman, Coley, Rosengren, Hartman, & Pappas, 1998; Palmquist & Crowley, 2007). Our approach in this chapter combines this sociocultural perspective with the more traditional constructivist perspective (Callanan & Valle, 2008). Our research team argues that children's causal and conceptual reasoning cannot be fully understood without embedding it in the broader context of their social and cultural lives, and yet, that children actively construct their understanding of the world within these social settings.

For many children, museums are a particular natural context where collaborative action and thinking can happen with family members and friends. This makes them a potentially rich site for the study of children's thinking in context (Callanan, 2012; Haden, 2010; Knutson & Crowley, 2005). The body of research exploring children's learning in museums has been growing in recent years and has focused on a variety of issues, from characterizing diverse motivations of museum visitors to designing museum exhibits in light of learners' content knowledge and interaction styles (Allen & Gutwill, 2009; Atkins, Velez, Goudy, & Dunbar, 2008; Borun et al., 1998; Ellenbogen, 2002; Falk & Dierking, 1992; Spiegel, Evans, Gram, & Diamond, 2006; Szechter & Carey, 2009; Zimmerman, Reeve, & Bell, 2009). Our research partnership has been particularly interested in exploring the ways that adults and children interact together in a variety of ways to accomplish the goals intended in the exhibit and to make sense of phenomena together. For example, children who engage in explanatory talk with parents at exhibits are likely to explore more deeply and gain better conceptual understanding of relevant concepts than children visiting the same exhibits on their own (Crowley, Callanan, Jipson, et al., 2001; Fender & Crowley, 2007). Variation in children's experiences at exhibits has also been demonstrated in studies exploring gender

(Crowley, Callanan, Tenenbaum, & Allen, 2001), cultural background (Gaskins, 2008; Siegel, Esterly, Callanan, Wright, & Navarro, 2007; Stein, Garibay, & Wilson, 2008; Tenenbaum & Callanan, 2008), and parents' epistemologies (Luce, Callanan, & Smilovic, 2013). Viewing family conversations as a setting where developmental change happens makes these findings crucial pieces of the puzzle of how children's thinking develops. In addition to research documenting various types of family interactions observed in museums, other studies offer evidence-based suggestions for strategies that increase parents' tendencies to engage in explanatory or elaborative conversations (Allen & Gutwill, 2009; Gutwill & Allen, 2010; Jant, Haden, Uttal, & Babcock, 2014), or children's tendency to engage in exploratory play (van Schjindel, Franse, & Raijmakers, 2010).

Through a partnership spanning almost twenty years between Children's Discovery Museum of San Jose (CDM) and University of California, Santa Cruz (UCSC), we have discovered considerable overlap between the goals of a group of researchers and a group of museum practitioners. Understanding how children's thinking develops in everyday settings requires being able to listen to and analyze family conversations that are natural and spontaneous; a children's museum is an ideal environment for such observational research. Through our partnership we have found that these same analyses of family conversations can also provide extremely informative feedback to museum designers and developers whose focus is on creating settings where children and families can explore interesting ideas and collaborate on new understandings. Our partnership has evolved over multiple projects and studies, and in addition to published research findings and successful exhibit designs, we have uncovered core insights about how research and practice can often support one another in unexpected ways.

Through our partnership, we have investigated research questions such as: How do children develop ways of reasoning in family conversations (e.g., in museums)? How are children exposed to explaining and using evidence as "cultural practices"? How and why do families vary in conversational patterns or practices? Do these differences have impact on the ways that children reason or on their interest in STEM (science, technology, engineering, & mathematics) fields?

In this chapter we introduce the nature and history of our partnership, considering both mutual benefits and interesting challenges that have arisen. Next, within a section on changing perspectives, we discuss several particular studies and findings as illustrations of how research and museum practice have influenced and informed one another throughout this collaboration. Finally we draw some conclusions that may be helpful to those considering embarking on a research–museum partnership.

Nature of the CDM–UCSC Partnership

History of the Partnership

Children's Discovery Museum and Callanan's UCSC lab began working together in 1995 when Maureen Callanan and then-postdoctoral scholar Kevin Crowley approached the executive director of the museum, Sally Osberg, proposing to do unobtrusive research focused on children's engagement in explanatory family conversation (see Osberg, 1998). The timing was right and the request overlapped well with Osberg's submission of a proposal to the National Science Foundation (NSF) for the *Take Another Look* project, which needed an evaluation component. While the researchers' goal at the time was basic research, the data collected throughout that project became the basis for the museum's evaluation needs for NSF as well.

The distinction between evaluation and research is something that has become more familiar to all of us as our partnership has developed. And yet, the dividing line between the two is not as clear as we would have thought. The goals of the museum team were to better understand how particular exhibits were supporting rich thinking and deep conversation among children and their families. While the research team's focus was not on particular exhibits, they were interested in capturing and characterizing those same conversations. In that early work, we found a way to meet both needs by collecting video data that could be used in two ways. In what Kevin Crowley named "blitz coding," researchers developed a method for giving quick feedback to the museum team by answering specific questions with a subset of the data. For example, in an exhibit focused on the movement of cars down a track, the research team was able to quickly report back to the museum team such things as the number of different types of cars that children were sending down the ramp, whether families were talking about the attributes of cars that seemed to make them go faster, and whether these behaviors and utterances varied by children's age and gender. This information helped museum designers and developers make decisions about potential changes to exhibit design, materials used, and additions that might better serve a particular age group. Subsequently, and over a much longer period of time, those same videotapes could be studied using the kind of painstaking coding, inter-rater reliability, and statistical analysis required for publication in academic journals.

The pursuit and evolution of mutual goals has become the cornerstone of this successful partnership. This began when the initial collaboration on *Take Another Look* yielded an interesting and unexpected finding from our first study: a strong gender difference in parents' explanatory talk at science-related exhibits. Our research team coded parents' explanations to children in 298 interactions, with children ranging in age from 1 to 8 years. The results showed that parents provided many more explanations to boys than to girls across ages (Crowley, Callanan, Tenenbaum, et al., 2001), despite the fact that girls and boys were equally likely to ask questions, approach, and engage with exhibits. Researchers hypothesized that parents may unknowingly talk differently to girls because they do not expect their daughters to be interested in science domains. CDM staff responded to this finding in a new grant proposal to the National Science Foundation, for which Jenni Martin was PI, for the exhibition *Alice's Wonderland*, presenting STEM content in the context of an exhibit clearly intended to be relevant to girls. For the *Alice's Wonderland* project, researchers were invited to play the dual role of researcher/

evaluator. At the time this was a new idea, but the reviewers and program officers were convinced that it constituted a positive collaboration, and the inclusion of researchers on the museum's exhibit development team was a productive next step in deepening the museum–research partnership. Discussions at biweekly project meetings, participation in exhibit conceptual development from start to finish, articulation of learning goals and experiences for exhibit prototypes, and periodic presentations of quick blitz coding feedback to the broader exhibit team all contributed to a greater understanding of theory and practice in both fields by research and museum team members.

Findings from the *Alice's Wonderland* project revealed that the gender gap in family explanatory talk was not present in this STEM-focused exhibition (Callanan, Frazier, & Gorchoff, 2015). Parents explained equally to boys and girls in the new exhibit, which supported the idea that parents' differential talk to boys and girls may be influenced by aspects of the activity context. In addition, the research helped to document success for the museum's goals of creating exhibitions that promote both STEM learning and gender equity.

Subsequent projects shifted the focus from gender differences in parent–child conversations to other areas of mutual interest for both researchers and museum staff, especially exploration of family talk with parents from different cultural and linguistic backgrounds (specifically Mexican- and Vietnamese-descent families), and parents with different epistemologies or guidance styles. Our focus also narrowed to specific STEM-focused exhibition development projects—mathematics in *Secrets of Circles* and paleontology in *Lupe's Story* (later renamed *Mammoth Discovery!*)— affording additional opportunities for this museum–research partnership to explore children's reasoning within rich domains in the context of family engagement.

Mutual Benefits

Research Perspective

The benefits of museum research for researchers may seem too obvious to require mentioning. Families in museums are an accessible population of potential participants, and traveling to a museum to ask families to participate is a very efficient recruitment strategy. And yet, there are many benefits that go well beyond access to research participants.

Access to Spontaneous Interaction

For anyone taking a sociocultural theoretical approach, there are much deeper reasons to consider museums as a research site. It is quite difficult to capture spontaneous interactions between parents and children. Museums are, in some ways, an ideal balance between the more artificial setting of the lab and the very familiar, but private, home setting. Families attending museums are in a public place where it may seem less intrusive to be observed, compared to having a researcher in their home. At the same time, while being videotaped arguably makes interactions less natural, families who attend museums are engaged in a familiar activity setting rather than an unfamiliar lab. Another aspect of the research that may increase participation is the opportunity to help the museum design better exhibits. Families that may be reluctant to participate in "basic research" may find themselves more willing to participate if it also "helps the museum."

Exposure to a New Knowledge Base

For developmental researchers, exposure to both the research literature on informal learning and to the practical expertise of museum practitioners is a clear benefit. Much of the knowledge base in museum fields is difficult to access (Bell, Lewenstein, Shouse, & Feder, 2009); evaluation studies are often not published, or are available in venues that are unfamiliar to developmental psychology researchers. For this reason, the Center for the Advancement of Informal Science Education maintains the website informalscience.org, where project updates and findings can be communicated. More recently, another website, relatingresearch topractice.org, connects practitioners in informal science learning with research findings from both the formal and informal learning fields.

Through our partnership, our research team has learned a great deal from our museum team, whose professional practices often involve sharing knowledge and ideas through conferences and advisory board meetings. As part of our *Mammoth Discovery!* project, we formed a cohort group of children's museum professionals whose questions and reflections have generated new research projects that we are now pursuing.

Valuable Experiences for Student Researchers

Another benefit that might seem less obvious involves the experiences of student researchers, both undergraduate and graduate, as well as postdoctoral researchers. Undergraduate student researchers learn skills for interacting with families and children, and have the professional experience of representing the university, as well as the research process, in a public place outside of academia. Graduate students and postdoctoral scholars, especially those who have joined the exhibit development team, as for example Jennifer Jipson did for *Take Another Look* and Megan Luce did for the *Mammoth Discovery!* project, have the advantage of learning about the workings of another type of institution beyond the university. There are opportunities, through project meetings and informal conversations, to learn what aspects of developmental research are informative for designing learning environments. These opportunities have led to additional research questions not only about how children's thinking develops, but about how to design naturalistic family experiences that might elicit the kinds of interactions and conversations that support children's science reasoning skills. Graduate students and postdocs gain insight into the gaps in developmental research from the museum's family learning design perspective; when presenting research findings to the museum staff, they learn from the questions and ideas of this group of professionals with practical experience about children's learning. Graduate students and postdocs also get valuable experience talking about the research topics, including theoretical perspectives, with families who ask many and varied questions. Many parents make (well-reasoned) assumptions that developmental researchers are knowledgeable about many aspects of child development, and they often ask for parenting advice and pose questions about whether they are doing things "correctly" or whether their child did well on the research tasks. Student researchers get valuable experience in learning how to handle these types of questions, for example, learning to draw appropriate boundaries between offering information versus speculating, and developing strategies for directing parents to appropriate expert sources. Students also gain skill in thinking about how various tasks or interview questions might be perceived by parents, given their concerns about parenting and child development.

Communicating Research to Non-Researchers

As has been articulated well by the Living Lab project at the Museum of Science, Boston (see www.livinglab.org; Corriveau et al., this volume), researchers have a great deal to gain by learning from museum staff about how to clearly communicate research findings, without jargon, to parents and other interested parties. Improving these skills in researchers can have several important impacts. While we have always communicated with parents about the research while it is underway, we are currently exploring ways that both the research team and the museum team can better connect with parents in our audience about the research discoveries made at CDM, even at times when research projects are not being conducted. We see this as an important strategy for visitors to have more personal connections with science, and hence a chance to improve public understanding of science. Further, the skills being developed in our research team members serve them well in their future ability to communicate research findings to broad audiences, including funders, policy makers, parents, and educators. Conversations with museum professionals and parents can even lead researchers in new research directions, causing them to consider future research questions they might not have thought of if discussing research only with those within their field.

Museum Perspective

For museum staff, the partnership with researchers has yielded many benefits beyond the obvious benefit of access to collection and presentation of data on family conversations and learning.

Articulating Goals and Interpreting Data

As our team works together, researchers ask museum staff to articulate the goals, or what we have come to call the "hoped-for experiences" of specific exhibits or programmatic activities. This process, which can sometimes be challenging, is an important step in exhibit development that is sometimes skipped. Inviting the development team to articulate goals clarifies the purpose of the activity, helps the team to understand what it is possible to document and measure, and ensures better alignment within the exhibit development team. Although some staff initially resisted this process, preferring to keep prototype exhibits more open-ended and responsive to ideas from individual visitors, museum staff ultimately agreed that this is a helpful step.

Generating and Interpreting Data Together

Researchers have brought a new voice to the museum's internal development team discussions. This has proven very helpful both in the idea generation phase and in assessing exhibit prototypes. As Osberg (1998) discussed, the presentation of data collected from an outside perspective can help to moderate between different perspectives within the museum. In the *Mammoth Discovery!* exhibition development, our team needed to know more about how children think about deep time and fossils, and their ideas about the coexistence of humans with now-extinct animals from the last Ice Age. While the existing cognitive development literature was helpful, the museum staff had more specific questions. The researchers conducted focused studies on these questions with children of varying ages at the museum and helped identify more specific developmental trajectories for children on certain topics.

Exposure to a New Knowledge Base

Museum practitioners, while educated and interested, do not always have the time to keep up-to-date on the latest research on children's cognitive development. Researchers have easy access to research studies and can find articles that would be difficult to find or too expensive for museum staff to access directly. For many topics that have been discussed in our team meetings, the researchers were aware of relevant research findings regarding developmental trajectories. For example, in the *Take Another Look* project that included aerial photographs of local landmarks, our research team summarized some of the developmental research on children's understanding of maps and other representations. A benefit of having in-person biweekly meetings was that topics of interest to the museum team could be conveyed as they arose, and research findings could be discussed in subsequent meetings, contributing greatly to progress on ideas and directions for exhibit design.

Deepening Rigor and Participation in National Discussions

Working with learning sciences researchers has increased the museum team's understanding of the cognitive sciences, while also affording the opportunity to tell visitors and funders about the deep partnership. Their perception of our work together is that it adds a sense of rigor to our exhibit and program development process. Indeed, when researchers are present on the museum floor, many adults take an interest in the research process and seem to enjoy talking about child development and learning with university students. The research partnership has also led our museum team to engage in different aspects of national discussions in the museum learning field. Our partnership positions us as players in recent discussions regarding the intersection between evaluation and research, and the delineation of a research agenda for children's museums.

Interesting Challenges

Just as in any human relationship, the researcher–museum relationship requires trust and compromise to achieve success. For museum practitioners, one of the highest priorities will always be ensuring a smooth and positive experience for visitors. So whatever requests researchers might have will always be viewed by museum staff through the lens of "How will this affect the visitors? How can we make this process pleasant and unobtrusive for visitors?" For researchers, the integrity of the data collection process is critical. Sometimes these competing goals can lead to conflicting plans, and compromise is needed.

Practical Matters

When developing consent forms for families, our research team has always worked to find a good balance between legalistic language and more everyday language emphasizing the importance of the work. In the fast-paced environment of the museum, asking parents to read a lengthy consent form while their child waited seemed unreasonable. Our research team addressed this problem by negotiating approval from UCSC's Institutional Review Board (IRB) to use a shorter single-page consent form that could be shown to parents on a clipboard, along with a business card that we could hand to parents with more information about the research and contact information for the researchers as well as the campus Office of Research Compliance.

We learned early on in our work together that inviting families to participate in a study as they were about to engage with a particular exhibit often seemed intrusive and off-putting. Instead, we found that approaching families just after they entered the museum, near the admissions desk, led to much greater participation and more relaxed responses from parents. Once parents have given permission, and children give verbal assent, the researchers ask children to wear a sticker, coded for age, which signals to our video camera operators that the child has consent to be videotaped. Both researchers and museum staff were pleased with this compromise, and families responded with a very high participation rate (usually approximately 90% of parents have given consent with this approach).

Other practical concerns involve finding ways to coordinate the very different schedules of museums and universities. Our data collection depends on student researchers doing research for credit. The museum team has often had to modify their original schedule because prototyping lab dates must be arranged around the academic calendar to ensure researcher availability. Special events and busy days at the museum raise another set of issues. For example, holidays and other busy days can be very successful in terms of recruiting many participants, and yet the needs for these special events can conflict with research recruitment, so care must be taken. Despite the best intentions, misunderstandings occur on occasion, and the best advice we can give is to be patient and continue to find ways to improve communication channels.

Visitor Perceptions of Research

A more substantive issue that quickly became apparent was how to deal with preconceived ideas about research that visitors, advisors, and funders bring to the experience. Much of our research involves using video cameras to capture conversations between parents and children. We learned how to quickly reassure visitors and others that the video cameras are very visible, and camera operators are present to turn cameras on or off depending on whether a child is wearing a sticker denoting signed IRB permission. Parents are also reassured to know that only the researchers will view the videotapes and that the videos will never be posted online, unless they give explicit consent otherwise. Not surprisingly, in recent years parents seem to be increasingly concerned about security and anonymity of the video; we have worked to ensure that we communicate the seriousness with which we take these security issues as well.

Another set of perceptions involves how the research experience might disrupt visitors' experience of the museum. In some of our studies, researchers invite families to leave the visitor floor to engage in a one-on-one activity. When children and parents expect hands-on, free choice activities in a museum setting, inviting them off the floor to do experimental tasks or an interview may seem disruptive (even though the research team takes care to make these activities enjoyable). The amount of time that visitors are willing to spend away from the highly engaging exhibits seems to be less than they might be willing to spend in a university lab setting or in their homes. Children's Discovery Museum has often made it possible for the research team to offer participants incentives in the form of a free family pass for a future visit. This has been welcomed by many families and has made them more comfortable participating in our studies. Many visitors are, in fact, very positive about their participation in the research and appreciative of the fact that the museum is interested in learning more about how visitors experience the exhibits.

Prototyping vs Final Exhibits

Children's Discovery Museum engages in an extensive prototyping process with visitors prior to building exhibits in their final form. The inclusion of researchers has meshed well with this exhibit development process and enhanced the documentation of learning from prototyping. Typically, the process looks like this: exhibit prototypes are built, the museum–research team identifies hoped-for experiences or learning goals for the exhibits, exhibits are put on the exhibit floor for visitors to enjoy, exhibit developers observe exhibits while researchers collect data via videotape, researchers bring blitz-coded data to team meetings, and the museum–research team discusses the ways in which "hoped-for experiences" are or are not being achieved. The exhibit team plans changes to the exhibits with suggestions from the research team. Challenges sometimes occur, however, when certain exhibits have been important for the research, and yet end up not being included in the final exhibition. Sometimes for reasons of practicality, researchers' recommendations cannot be followed. One example was in the *Secrets of Circles* exhibition, where prototyping included an extensive race track where cars with different shaped wheels could travel down the track, and children could keep track of how far the cars went and how bumpy the ride was. Our research team collected extensive data on families' interactions in this prototype exhibit (Callanan et al., 2013; Triona & Callanan, 2008), and hoped to do further data collection in the final exhibition. However, given the complex set of decision factors, including space configurations, tracking of materials, and other concerns, the decision was made not to include the race track in the final exhibition. The museum team addressed this potential problem, however, by agreeing to keep the prototype track on the museum floor for a few weeks after the prototype lab had closed so that further data could be collected.

Potential Mismatches in Expertise

One important challenge for collaborators is that researchers' expertise does not necessarily match the deepest interests of the museum staff with whom they are working. In some ways our team was lucky to have some overlap in interests from the start. We have heard of other cases where museum–research partnerships can be rocky because each side may have unrealistic expectations of the other. In isolated cases where the topics of interest are outside of our researchers' expertise, we have developed several strategies. For example, it is possible to assign students to do literature searches on topics of interest as part of their independent study credit. Importantly, our team also often consults with outside researchers and practitioners whose expertise is important to our projects, sometimes by inviting them to be part of grant advisory committees.

Working with Diverse Groups of Families

In all of our projects, engaging with diverse families has been a goal for the museum as well as for the research. Taking this goal seriously results in major challenges regarding cultural sensitivity at all levels. For example, in our work for the NSF-funded *Secrets of Circles* exhibition, focused on the math, science, and engineering of circles, we were particularly interested in engaging Vietnamese- and Mexican-descent families. While both the museum and research teams had worked with Mexican-descent families previously, we were newer to working with the Vietnamese community. There were many challenges to be solved from both the museum and research perspectives in order to engage with families of Vietnamese descent. Beyond the need to translate the consent form, workshops, and parent–child conversations, there were concerns from our Vietnamese advisors that the forms and procedures themselves might be off-putting to this community. We worked with the IRB again to adapt the form with more friendly language while also providing the content needed for informed consent. We learned that many of the Vietnamese-descent parents were reluctant to give critical feedback in a group setting, even though we were very clearly asking for changes that they might suggest to our exhibit prototypes. We also found that many of the Vietnam- ese parents preferred to let their children take the lead on activity engagement, while parents observed. This raised new challenges for finding ways to capture parent–child conversations, requiring us to find different strategies than we had used in other settings. Though both researchers and museum staff had worked with families from many different cultural communities previously, our work together on this project increased our understanding of this particular cultural community and caused us to do our work together differently.

Changing Perspectives: Research Findings and Reciprocal Influences

In this section we present some of our research findings in the context of a dis- cussion of how the research and museum practice have informed one another throughout the set of projects we have worked on together.

How Research Has Informed Museum Practice

Findings Lead to New Design Goals

Perhaps the best example of how research has influenced museum practice is the link from the unexpected gender difference already mentioned (Crowley, Calla- nan, Tenenbaum, et al., 2001) to the development of the full-scale NSF proposal to develop the new exhibit *Alice's Wonderland*. Even in a museum where exhibit staff spend a great deal of time observing families and children interacting with exhibits, this early finding demonstrated that there are patterns of data that require large numbers of participants and more observations than one can keep track of without statistics. The power of this initial finding was profound—both because it provided new data for the research field, and because it convinced some of the more skeptical museum staff that this research partnership could perhaps provide some unexpected value. For those skeptical staff members, there were some early moments when certain research findings seemed to provide a tipping point, suggesting that the researchers could in fact provide some information that would support the museum's goals. The gender difference raised a new question about how the museum could use exhibit design to counteract this "gender gap." The research became a much more integral part of the *Alice's Wonderland* project, and our partnership was strengthened as we pursued the joint goal of discovering whether a different type of exhibition could result in decreasing the gap. Indeed, we found that, unlike in the *Take Another Look* exhibit, parents' explanations to boys and girls did not significantly differ from one another in the *Alice's Wonderland* exhibit (Callanan, Luce, Martin, DeAngelis, & Kawaratani, 2015), suggesting that the strategy may have succeeded in counteracting parents' subtle gender biases. Children's Discovery Museum was honored with the American Association of Museum's Excellence in Exhibitions award for the *Alice's Wonderland* exhibition, in part because of the research partnership on the project and the compelling findings.

Opportunities to Systematically Test Assumptions

In our most recent project, *Lupe's Story* (aka *Mammoth Discovery!*), the museum was given the opportunity to build an exhibit around a set of fossilized mammoth bones found along the Guadalupe River near the museum. In this NSF-funded collaboration, a new group of science content experts were added to the partnership: paleontologists and science educators from the University of California Museum of Paleontology at UC Berkeley. The team faced the challenge of presenting fossilized mammoth bones that cannot be touched in a children's museum where the philosophy emphasizes hands-on activity as a productive way for children to learn. Building on their extensive experience creating developmentally appropriate hands-on experiences, the museum team worked with the researchers to explore family conversations around different types of presentations of the authentic bones.

One study from the *Mammoth Discovery!* project is illustrative of our pursuit of research questions that intersect developmental psychology and museum practice. In an early prototype phase of this exhibit development, we looked at family talk around authentic fossil bones—a femur bone and a large portion of the skull—presented in Plexiglas cases with signs identifying the bones and how they were found (see Figure 2.1a). We knew from the start that displaying objects in cases did not fit in with the hands-on nature of CDM. So we were disappointed, but not surprised, at the brevity of these conversations. We were also concerned that many visitors found the skull fragment difficult to understand; it was a fragment that was upside down and incomplete such that one is looking at the roof of the mammoth's mouth. Pulling together our combined expertise regarding young children's learning, the research team brought in research findings regarding children's spatial reasoning, and the museum exhibit staff came up with some clever ways to create "hands-on" versions of both exhibits.

FIGURE 2.1 How did families talk about the femur fossil with and without "hands-on" components?

a. Femur case

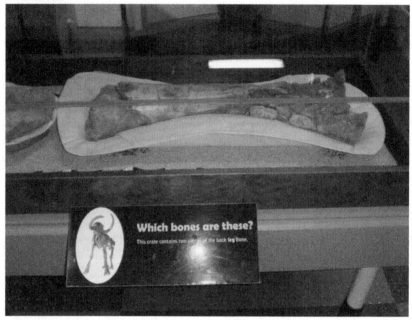

b. Femur chair

The "femur chair" exhibit included a chair attached to the case containing the mammoth femur, and the sign invited visitors to sit down and line up their femur with the mammoth's femur to compare their size (see Figure 2.1b). In the "rotating skull" version of the skull exhibit, a small replica of the mammoth skull could be rotated so that families could more easily orient themselves to this object that they could not directly manipulate. This allowed us to conduct a study comparing the new hands-on style exhibits with the parallel case style exhibits from the first prototype phase. The research team coded the labels/names used by visitors for the bones in both sets of exhibits. We found that families were significantly more likely to use the word "bone" in the Plexiglas case presentations than in the hands-on presentations. In contrast, in the hands-on exhibits, families were more likely to use a broader range of words to refer to the fossil (Callanan, Luce, Martin, DeAngelis, & Kawaratani, 2012, 2015). For example, Figure 2.2 shows an analysis of 28 families who visited the femur case exhibit and 27 families who visited the femur chair. We found a significant interaction between exhibit type and label types, $F(4, 51) = 8.79$ $p < 0.001$, $n_p^2 = 0.147$. As the figure shows, while families used the word "bone" more often at the femur case than at the femur chair, the word "mammoth" was used by more families at the femur case. This suggests that rather than merely labeling the object as a bone, families were engaging in deeper conversations about what they were viewing when the hands-on components were present. At the femur chair, preliminary findings showed more families also talking about analogies, for example, "This is a bone that's in your leg, too," and inferences, such as, "If that's just one leg bone, this must have been a huge mammoth!" These findings suggest that hands-on elements in exhibits may make it easier for children and their families to engage with the material in conceptual ways.

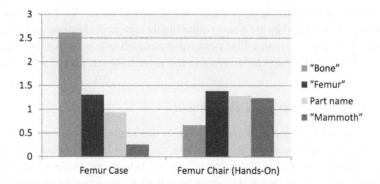

Families labeled femur as "bone" significantly more often at the femur case than at the femur chair; they used the word "mammoth" significantly more often at the femur chair than at the femur case.

FIGURE 2.2 Labels used by families for the femur bone at two versions of the exhibit.

How Museum Practice Has Informed Research

Reflecting back on the research emerging from this partnership, our research team is struck by the importance of the museum as a setting for observing "real life" family interactions. In this section, we discuss some examples of how this type of data has informed our research goals and our views about cognitive development.

Different Participant Pools

Working with families in museums involves a different kind of interaction than inviting them to a campus lab, and our research team has found that this setting can provide a different view of families. One striking feature of our museum participant pool is that it includes many more fathers than most of our studies in the labs or at home. In studies conducted in campus labs or in families' homes, "parents" are invited to participate, but almost all volunteers are mothers. In the museum, however, a large proportion of fathers are present and willing to participate in the research. This allows our research team to address questions regarding mothers' and fathers' interactions with children that might be much harder to address in other studies.

Some researchers argue that museums provide them with a more diverse participant population, and it may be true that visitors to museums are a different group than parents who travel to on-campus research labs to participate in research. However, our research team is cautious in our characterization of this diversity because the majority of museum visitors across the country tend be from high-income backgrounds and have high levels of formal schooling. Most museums engage in extensive outreach efforts to broaden their visitor population, and Children's Discovery Museum of San Jose is no exception. At the same time, it is not a given that museum research participant pools are diverse. In our studies together where we ask parents for demographic information, we find that our populations are extremely diverse in terms of cultural background and languages spoken at home, yet they are mostly quite highly educated. However, our research team often connects with CDM's extensive outreach events so that the research can include families from lower income and more basic schooling backgrounds.

Redefining Learning and Development

This partnership has led to deeper changes in our research than those already discussed. While our research team began with the sociocultural perspective in mind, engaging with families in the museum context helped our group to more fully appreciate what is entailed in this perspective. Rather than focusing on simply how adults *help* children to understand or learn, studying museum interactions helps to shift the focus toward how families make sense of phenomena *together*, and how they negotiate and renegotiate meaning in the moment of action and interaction. This shift in focus can, of course, occur with other sorts of interactions outside of museums, and our research team does study family interactions in other settings. However, the compatibility is striking between our research team's goal of uncovering family meaning-making, and our museum team's goals in creating a designed environment that can (to quote CDM's mission statement) "inspire creativity, curiosity, and life-long learning." Thus, in addition to designing learning experiences for children, CDM pays careful attention to the opportunities for adult caregivers themselves to learn, as well as supporting their roles as teachers, caregivers, and nurturers.

By observing adults and children playing and learning *together* in this unique setting, our research team has been able to expand our ideas about who is developing and how. Paying more attention to collaborative activity among families and making efforts to understand how to better capture the ways that families learn together in reciprocal and dynamic ways are valuable outcomes of this shift. Such a focus provides evidence for our research team to challenge the notion that it is only "individuals" who learn, and instead consider ways in which a dyad or group of people can be considered to have "learned" something. This is particularly relevant to issues of assessing and evaluating the learning that occurs in socially rich environments such as museums. More generally, this work potentially blurs the line between the notions of "learning" and "development" by emphasizing the ways that development happens in everyday settings in interaction with important other people.

New Research Questions and Directions

Finally, and most excitingly, as our partnership has grown, it has influenced the research directions taken. The best example of this is the development of a focus on families' use of evidence in talk and thinking in our work on the *Mammoth Discovery!* exhibition. Whereas our research team's earlier focus in family conversations had been on explanation, this broadened to include evidence talk as we worked together on this project. To explain this progression, we describe a bit more of the history of this project.

CDM was offered the opportunity to build an exhibit around a nearby mammoth fossil find. This was exciting, but also presented the great challenge of how to do paleontology in a hands-on children's museum. As PI on the project, Jenni Martin's insight was to find ways to encourage visitors to think of mammoth bones as evidence to answer questions. This meshed well with Maureen Callanan's previous work about children's "why" and "how" questions as an ideal setting for identifying children's interest and capturing moments when they might engage in explaining and revising their ideas. Paleontology experts were brought in from the UC Museum of Paleontology at UC Berkeley. As another co-PI on the project, Judy Scotchmoor's science education work became a focus; especially the *Understanding Science* website (http://undsci.berkeley.edu/), which supports teachers and students in thinking of science not as learning a set of facts, but as a complex, cyclical, and interactive process involving exploration and discovery (e.g., observing, asking questions), testing ideas (e.g., gathering and interpreting data), and understanding evidence in the context of the broader community (including scientific peers as well as the broader public). Inspired and energized by our overlapping interests, the motivating goal of this project became encouraging families to ask themselves and each other the question:"How do you know?"At the same time, Megan Luce was beginning to design her dissertation, which had a special focus on children's developing science practices and individual differences in families' habits of thinking. The synergistic merging of ideas from science education and informal science with cognitive developmental psychology gave us a different, and deeper, perspective on how to think about children's reasoning within a specific domain.

Because we wanted to understand more about how families vary in their approach to thinking about evidence, our final study in the *Mammoth Discovery!* project employed a new method, beyond our unobtrusive video of our earlier studies. We invited families to join us in our research room either before or after their visit to the exhibit; one member of the family wore a microphone throughout their exhibit visit, and a camera captured most of their movement around the exhibit. Through interviews and surveys we asked about parents' interest in and experiences with STEM subjects, attitudes toward science (using Szechter & Carey's 2009 scale), and the kinds of learning activities they engage in with their children. Our studies of evidence talk are leading to important new findings regarding the social context of cognitive development (e.g., Luce et al., 2013). Our research team is finding that children growing up in different families are learning different ways of talking about evidence. Understanding these variations in families' sense-making practices may have important impact for developing strategies to increase children's engagement in STEM fields. In Megan Luce's dissertation, she asked parents and children to discuss claims where there is conflicting evidence available (e.g., sugar leads to hyperactivity; global warming is caused by humans), and found that parents who discussed more evidence about these controversial claims had children who were more likely to override their own prior beliefs, and instead reason based on available evidence in a separate task (Luce, 2011, 2015).

It is not surprising that parents' science background is one factor that predicts their engagement in the museum. One analysis of family talk in the *Mammoth Discovery!* exhibit is showing that parents with more extensive science background were likely to ask more questions that invited their children to engage in critical thinking about the exhibits (Callanan, Castañeda, Luce, & Martin, 2015). Perhaps more surprisingly, the variations across families are sometimes linked to parents' characteristics beyond schooling or science background, such as personality or attitude measures. For example, in another part of the project, parents who scored high on a personality scale of "Need for Cognition" (indicating that they enjoy challenging tasks and figuring things out; Cacioppo, Petty, Feinstein, & Jarvis, 1996) were more likely to ask their children deeper questions about a set of fossils (e.g., "Which one feels heavier?" or "Does that look big enough to be part of a dinosaur?" or "Why do you think that's a bone?"). Intriguingly, this personality characteristic seemed to account for more of the variation in parents' talk than did measures of parents' schooling or science background. Parents who enjoy figuring out puzzling phenomena may engage their children in everyday practice with inquiry, while other families are using different kinds of sense-making practices.

Our research team has also explored potential variation in family conversations that may be related to families' cultural background (Tenenbaum & Callanan, 2008). Some patterns of difference have been uncovered across cultural groups. For example, in *Secrets of Circles* workshops, we found that Vietnamese-heritage families were more instructional with their children, while Mexican-heritage parents were more collaborative with their children (Callanan, Navarro, & Vu, 2015). Yet, it is often striking to see how much similarity is apparent across groups. For example, we found that while parents of Mexican heritage with fewer than 10 years of formal schooling explained less to their children in the museum than did Mexican-heritage parents with many years of formal schooling, in contrast, these two groups of parents were equally likely to explain to their children in a task conducted in their homes (Tenenbaum & Callanan, 2008). Often we see more individual variation *within* groups as opposed to across groups. Our research team is continuing to explore these data to learn more about links between parents' background and characteristics, family conversations about evidence, and children's developing reasoning skills and their beliefs about the nature of knowing.

Finally, Megan Luce is now drawing from her experience with the prototyping process to conduct design-based research on family science learning. It became clear that in addition to studying what families already do, it is important to design for varied learning experiences that can shed more light on what families *can* do and the conditions under which they do it, which helps to flesh out the kinds of family activity that contribute to cognitive development.

Conclusions

As we hope these examples have illustrated, our 20-year museum–research partnership has been extremely fruitful, productive, and beneficial to all parties involved. The opportunities that the partnership has afforded to influence both exhibit design and the field of cognitive developmental psychology have been sometimes serendipitous and always valuable. Members of both our museum team and research team have learned new perspectives on children's development and learning because of the opportunities we have had to connect in deep ways with professionals with very different experiences and perspectives.

References

Allen, S., & Gutwill, J.P. (2009). Creating a program to deepen family inquiry at interactive science exhibits. *Curator, 52,* 289–306.

Atkins, L., Velez, L., Goudy, D., & Dunbar, K. (2008). The unintended effects of interactive objects and labels in the science museum. *Science Education, 93*(1), 161–184.

Bell, P., Lewenstein, B., Shouse, A., & Feder, M. (2009). *Learning science in informal environments: People, places, and pursuits.* Washington, DC: National Academies Press.

Borun, M., Dritsas, J., Johnson, J., Peter, N., Wagner, K., Fadigan, K., . . . Philadelphia/Camden Informal Science Education Collaborative. (1998). *Family learning in museums: The PISEC perspective.* Philadelphia: The Franklin Institute.

Cacioppo, J.T., Petty, R.E., Feinstein, J.A., & Jarvis, W.B.G. (1996). Dispositional differences in cognitive motivation: The life and times of individuals varying in need for cognition. *Psychological Bulletin, 119,* 197–253.

Callanan, M. (2012). Conducting cognitive developmental research in museums: Theoretical issues and practical considerations. *Journal of Cognition and Development, 13,* 137–151.

Callanan, M., Castañeda, C., Luce, M., & Martin, J. (2015). *Family science talk in museums: Variations across families and impacts of exhibit design.* Manuscript under review.

Callanan, M., Frazier, B., & Gorchoff, S. (2015). *Closing the gender gap: Family conversations about science in an "Alice's Wonderland" exhibit.* Unpublished manuscript, University of California, Santa Cruz.

Callanan, M.A., & Jipson, J. (2001). Explanatory conversations and young children's developing scientific literacy. In K.S. Crowley, C. Schunn, & T. Okada (Eds.), *Designing for science: Implications from everyday, classroom, and professional settings* (pp. 21–49). Mahwah, NJ: Lawrence Erlbaum Associates.

Callanan, M., Luce, M., Martin, J., DeAngelis, S., & Kawaratani, L. (2012). Hands-on museum components shape family science talk about fossils. Presented at American Educational Research Association, Vancouver, BC, Canada.

Callanan, M., Luce, M., Martin, J., DeAngelis, S., & Kawaratani, L. (2015). *Hands-on museum components shape family science talk about fossils.* Unpublished manuscript, University of California, Santa Cruz.

Callanan, M., Luce, M., Triona, L., Rigney, J., Siegel, D., & Jipson, J. (2013). What counts as science in everyday and family interactions? In B. Bevan, P. Bell, R. Stevens, & A. Razfar (Eds.), *LOST: Learning about out-of-school-time* (pp. 29–38). Kluwer, Netherlands: Springer.

Callanan, M., Navarro, R., & Vu, L. (2015). *Cultural variation in Mexican-heritage and Vietnamese-heritage parents' guidance of children in a museum workshop setting.* Unpublished manuscript, University of California, Santa Cruz.

Callanan, M., & Valle, A. (2008). Co-constructing conceptual domains through family conversations and activities. In B. Ross (Ed.), *Psychology of learning and motivation* (Vol. 49; pp. 147–165). London, UK: Elsevier.

Cole, M. (1996). *Cultural psychology: A once and future discipline.* Cambridge, MA: Harvard University Press.

Crowley, K., Callanan, M., Jipson, J., Galco, J., Topping, K., & Shrager, J. (2001). Shared scientific thinking in everyday parent-child activity. *Science Education, 85*(6), 712–732.

Crowley, K., Callanan, M.A., Tenenbaum, H.R., & Allen, E. (2001). Parents explain more often to boys than to girls during shared scientific thinking. *Psychological Science, 12*(3), 258–261.

Eberbach, C., & Crowley, K. (2009). From everyday to scientific observation: How children learn to observe the biologist's world. *Review of Educational Research, 1,* 39–68.

Ellenbogen, K.M. (2002). Museums in family life: An ethnographic case study. In G. Leinhardt, K. Crowley, & K. Knutson (Eds.), *Learning conversations in museums* (pp. 81–101). Mahwah, NJ: Lawrence Erlbaum Associates.

Falk, J.H., & Dierking, L.D. (1992). *The museum experience.* Washington, DC: Whalesback Books.

Fender, J.G., & Crowley, K. (2007). How parent explanation changes what children learn from everyday scientific thinking. *Journal of Applied Developmental Psychology, 28,* 189–210.

Gaskins, S. (2008). The cultural meaning of play and learning in children's museums. *Hand to Hand, 22*, 1–11.

Gelman, S.A., Coley, J.D., Rosengren, K.S., Hartman, E., & Pappas, A. (1998). Beyond labeling: The role of maternal input in the acquisition of richly structured categories. *Monographs of the Society for Research in Child Development, 63*(1), Serial No. 253.

Gutiérrez, K.D., & Rogoff, B. (2003). Cultural ways of learning: Individual traits or repertoires of practice. *Educational Researcher, 32*, 19–25.

Gutwill, J., & Allen, S. (2010). Facilitating family group inquiry at science museum exhibits. *Science Education, 94*(4), 710–742.

Haden, C. (2010). Talking about science in museums. *Child Development Perspectives, 4*, 62–67.

Jant, E.A., Haden, C.A., Uttal, D.H., & Babcock, E. (2014). Conversation and object manipulation influence children's learning in a museum. *Child Development, 85*, 2029–2045.

Knutson, K., & Crowley, K. (2005). Museum as learning laboratory: Bringing research and practice together (Part 2 of 2). *Hand to Hand, 18*(5), 3–6.

Luce, M.R. (2011). *Mothers' speech to young children in conversations about conflicting evidence for science-related claims.* Unpublished doctoral dissertation, University of California, Santa Cruz.

Luce, M.R. (2015). *Mothers and children discussing conflicting evidence for science-related claims: Individual variation and links to children's reasoning.* Manuscript under review, Stanford University.

Luce, M., Callanan, M., & Smilovic. S. (2013). Links between parents' epistemological stance and children's evidence talk. *Developmental Psychology, 49*, 454–461.

Osberg, S. (1998). Shared lessons and self-discoveries: What research has taught Children's Discovery Museum. *Journal of Museum Education, 23*, 19–20.

Palmquist, S., & Crowley, K. (2007). From teachers to testers: How parents talk to novice and expert children in a natural history museum. *Science Education, 91*, 783–804.

Rogoff, B. (2003). *The cultural nature of cognitive development.* New York: Oxford University Press.

Siegel, D., Esterly, J., Callanan, M., Wright, R., & Navarro, R. (2007). Conversations about science across activities in Mexican-descent families. *International Journal of Science Education, 29*(12), 1447–1466.

Spiegel, A.N., Evans, E.M., Gram, W., & Diamond, J. (2006). Museum visitors' understanding of evolution. *Museums & Social Issues, 1*, 69–86.

Stein, J.K., Garibay, C., & Wilson, K. (2008). Engaging immigrant audiences in museums. *Museums & Social Issues, 3*, 179–195.

Szechter, L.E., & Carey, E.J. (2009). Gravitating toward science: Parent-child interactions at a gravitational-wave observatory. *Science Education, 93*, 846–858.

Tenenbaum, H., & Callanan, M.A. (2008). Parents' science talk to their children in Mexican-descent families residing in the USA. *International Journal of Behavioral Development, 32*(1), 1–12.

Triona, L.M., & Callanan, M.A. (2008). Science play: Comparing children alone, with peers, and with adults. In B.C. Love, K. McRae, & V.M. Sloutsky (Eds.), *Proceedings of the 30th Annual Conference of the Cognitive Science Society* (p. 1378). Austin, TX: Cognitive Science Society.

van Schijndel, T.J.P., Franse, R.K., & Raijmakers, M.E.J. (2010). The exploratory behavior scale: Assessing young visitors' hands-on behavior in science museums. *Science Education, 94*(5), 794–809.

Vygotsky, L.S. (1978). *Mind in society: The development of higher psychological processes.* Cambridge, MA: Harvard University Press.

Zimmerman, H., Reeve, S., & Bell, P. (2009). Family sense-making practices in science center conversations. *Science Education, 94*, 478–505.

3

THE SPIRAL MODEL

Integrating Research and Exhibit Development to Foster Conceptual Change

E. Margaret Evans, Martin Weiss, Jonathan D. Lane, and Sasha Palmquist

The Team

Evelyn Margaret Evans is an associate research scientist at the Center for Human Growth and Development at the University of Michigan. Her Ph.D. focused on the cultural and cognitive factors that influence the emergence of scientific concepts in children and adults from diverse U.S. communities. These studies have informed research projects and exhibit development for five different exhibits on evolution and related topics funded by the National Science Foundation and the National Institutes of Health. In this work, Evans and her colleagues have developed informal learning experiences for students of all ages, based, in part, on an analysis of participants' intuitive concepts of science, with a particular focus on evolutionary biology.

Martin Weiss is senior scientist at the New York Hall of Science and has been developing engaging interactive exhibitions since 1989. Prior to working at the Hall of Science, he did research at NYU Medical School on human malaria and then focused on cellular biochemical at Rockefeller University. At the Hall of Science, he has developed projects on microbiology, health, and the *Chemistry of Living Things*. His recent exhibits focus on evolution and include *Charlie and Kiwi's Evolutionary Adventure* and *The Evolution-Health Connection and Wild Minds—What Animals Really Think*.

Jonathan Lane is an assistant professor of psychology and human development at Vanderbilt University's Peabody College of Education and Human Development. His research is focused on children's social-cognitive development as well as their understanding of and belief in counterintuitive concepts. He helped to design the study assessing how effectively the *Charlie and Kiwi* exhibit facilitated children's understanding of biological evolution and also helped to coordinate the study at the New York Hall of Science.

Sasha Palmquist, of Palmquist & Associates, LLC, is a learning sciences researcher and professional evaluator of informal learning experiences. She has examined the impact of young children's interest and knowledge on family learning conversations in museums. Over the last ten years, her research and evaluation work has focused on understanding how prior knowledge, interest, engagement, and personal identity shape learning opportunities and experiences in out-of-school and informal learning environments.

The Settings
The New York Hall of Science (NYSCI) was founded at the 1964–1965 World's Fair and has evolved into New York's center for interactive science, serving a half million students, teachers, and families each year. NYSCI presents 450 exhibits, demonstrations, workshops, and participatory activities that explain science, technology, engineering, and math. It is particularly proud of its Career Ladder program, which trains high school and college students in science and prepares them for science careers. NYSCI offers professional development for teachers, produces curricula and resources for classrooms, and studies how technology, gaming, and play affect how we learn.

The University of Michigan Museum of Natural History, known locally as "The Dinosaur Museum," is situated on the University of Michigan's central campus in Ann Arbor, Michigan. The museum's 22,000-square-foot exhibit space consists of four floors, including a 9,000-square-foot "Hall of Evolution" fossil hall with three complete skeletons of dinosaurs. The Museum is also well known for its outstanding mastodon and whale evolution exhibits. Other displays include exhibits on current U-M science research, Michigan wildlife and ecology, Earth science, and anthropology.

Overview: An Evolving Relationship

This is the story of how the exhibit *Charlie and Kiwi's Evolutionary Adventure* came to be. This story has several themes, but the driving narrative was the pursuit of a single idea—making evolutionary theory accessible to the U.S. public, particularly children. By bringing research (Margaret Evans) and exhibit development (Martin Weiss) together, we hoped to create a learning experience that would prepare children's minds for the counterintuitive idea that humans are one lineage among many, part of the history of all living things on earth. We carefully avoided proselytizing, but instead opted for targeted persuasion. Along with a wonderful team of exhibit developers, designers, writers, evaluators, and researchers, we developed a compelling and exciting narrative that engaged a young audience (and their parents) in one of the most challenging ideas that the world has encountered.

Margaret Evans had spent many years investigating the development of scientific ideas that appeared to clash both with our basic intuitions and with cultural beliefs. In particular, she had chronicled the emergence of ideas about evolution in children and adults from religious and secular communities in the U.S. (Evans, 2000, 2001). On the basis of a chapter summarizing this research (Evans, Mull, & Poling, 2002), Judy Diamond, exhibit developer and informal science educator from the University of Nebraska Museum of Natural History, asked Margaret to use insights gained from these studies to help in the execution of a major NSF-funded exhibition on evolution. *Explore Evolution* (PI Judy Diamond) targeted an adolescent audience (Diamond & Evans, 2007) and was subsequently on permanent display in seven museums across the Midwest, including the University of Michigan Museum of Natural History (UMMNH), where Margaret collected much of her data. The exhibition and related research studies (Evans, Lane, Hetherington, & Weiss, 2010; Spiegel et al., 2012) provided the building blocks for Margaret's ideas about a new exhibition—this time focused on younger children.

Coincidentally, Martin Weiss was also interested in conveying ideas about evolution to children. After a career in biochemistry research on malaria and other parasites, Martin came to the New York Hall of Science as an exhibit developer. Once there he developed interactive and engaging exhibitions on complex topics in biology, especially evolution. These included the *Chemistry of Living Things*, which explored the common chemical pathways and molecules of bacteria, roses, fruit flies, and humans. Martin contacted Judy Diamond, whom he had known for many years from their early days as informal science educators, to see if she knew of a researcher who shared his interests. After introductions by Judy, Margaret and Martin decided to integrate their dual perspectives, exhibit development, and research, and apply for a grant to fund an exhibition based on the question: Could we build an informal learning experience that enabled elementary school children to learn about evolution? Moreover, we wanted to build an exhibition that could potentially serve the dual purposes of being a compelling informal learning experience and a laboratory for investigating science learning.

Joining the two of us on the grant proposal were museum partners Sean Duran (Co-PI; exhibits director, Miami Museum of Science) and Margie Marino (Co-PI; executive director, North Museum of Natural History), evaluators Martin Storksdieck and Judy Koke (Institute for Learning Innovation), exhibit designers Jeff Kennedy and Margie Prager, and writer Judy Rand. The grant was funded in early 2006 initially for four years and extended for an additional year to meet some unexpected challenges in the exhibition design. The team members fluctuated over the years; the original evaluation team, which carried out front-end and formative evaluations, was replaced by Sasha Palmquist, who carried out remedial and summative evaluations; Jon Lane joined the research team for the last three years of the grant and helped design and execute the final research project.

From the beginning, however, we (the team) faced two core challenges: the first was how best to integrate research findings into exhibit development, and the second was the content area itself. How does one present a complex theory like evolution in a manner that targets a young and diverse audience without seriously compromising the presentation of the scientific content? To solve the first problem we adopted, initially in an unsystematic manner and then more systematically, the spiral model of exhibit development, which we introduce next. To solve the content issue we applied this spiral model to the topic of evolution and grounded it in a series of key decision points, as described in subsequent sections. Finally we return to the core research question: "If we built it, would they learn?" Or, more specifically: "How do they learn?"

The Spiral Model: Integrating Research and Exhibit Development

The gap between research, theory, and exhibit development is often difficult to bridge. In the rest of this chapter, we will try to capture the way in which team members did bridge this gap over the years of exhibit development, from the initial research questions to working prototypes, which differed markedly from the original vision, to a finished traveling exhibition. In the process, we address the opportunities and challenges that were encountered during the project experience. First, we describe our fine-tuning of a model that represents the phases of this project, and then we describe a process of exhibit creation that exemplified this model.

Exhibit developers typically use content-matter specialists, often researchers, as advisors or consultants on projects. However, these researchers are rarely knowledgeable about or have much experience with exhibition development; further, they do not usually carry out research specifically for the project. In this chapter, we describe an iterative developmental process in which the phases of research, development, and evaluation were repeatedly revisited over the course of exhibit development (Evans, Weiss, Koke, Storksdieck, & Kennedy, 2008). To graphically represent this process, we have adapted the spiral model originally proposed for software development (Boehm, 1986) as a formalization (see Figure 3.1). This life-cycle model corrected some the inadequacies of earlier formalizations, such as stepwise models (Boehm, 1986) in which this kind of process is characterized as a series of stages in exhibit development; such a model is typically represented as a project work plan. The latter approach obscures the importance of feedback loops, a self-correcting mechanism that minimizes the repetition of earlier errors and includes a look-ahead element. From our perspective, a key outcome of the feedback was the articulation of revised goals and, based on these goals, the production of exhibit prototypes in a variety of configurations, ranging from a core idea to a working model. The goals were informed by the expertise of the exhibit development team and research on children's understanding of evolution. The output—the prototype—was then evaluated for efficacy and the results fed into the next cycle of the spiral. The novel aspect of this process is the integration of research into every cycle. Clearly evaluation and research overlap, but, at least in our project, evaluation tended to focus on the audience interactions and content knowledge, whereas research tended to

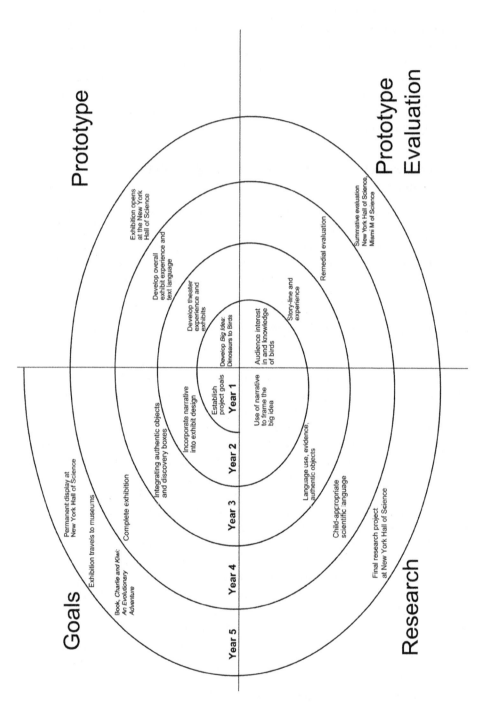

FIGURE 3.1 The spiral model of exhibit development. There are four iterative phases each cycle: exhibit goals, exhibit prototypes, prototype evaluation, and theoretical research.

focused on theory, particularly age- and experience-related changes in reasoning, which then fed into evidence-based practice—the exhibition.

Borrowing heavily from Boehm (1986), Figure 3.1 broadly captures the process. The quadrants represent four key phases that together complete one cycle of the spiral, which are repeated iteratively until the conclusion of the project: (1) Goals based on prior research and team expertise (upper left quadrant), (2) Prototypes (upper right quadrant), (3) Prototype evaluation with visitors (lower right quadrant), and (4) Research with the target population to inform new goals (lower left quadrant). With each successive iteration, one gets farther from the middle; thus the radial dimension (i.e., the distance from the middle of the spiral) represents increasing cost (Boehm, 1986). The quadrant markers may not be strictly observed as the phases often overlap. However, each completed cycle roughly represents one year in the life of the project (see Figure 3.1), the end of which is marked by a team meeting with all the major players. This is a key feature (Boehm, 1986) of a risk-management model; at this point progress to date is reviewed (feedback loop) and goals reset (look-ahead) to maximize gains and minimize loss, with the whole project constrained by budget and time.

In this model, theory-based research benefits the development of innovative exhibits and programs, which in turn provide a test bed for research on cognitive development. The outcome should be improved exhibits and programs based on an understanding of cognitive developmental processes; as well, the research on children's reasoning should improve our understanding of experience-based learning. The unique aspect of this model is that the learning experiences (exhibits and associated programs) are both an output of the initial research, and, through the research and evaluation findings, they are also inputs into the next stage of research and development. As a result, the spiral model has the potential to address the ongoing need in the informal science community for the integration of research and practice. Next, we will describe how the model functioned as we try to capture the challenges and opportunities that informed the key decisions that characterized each year of the project.

Applying the Spiral Model: Key Decision Points

Year one goals: The beginning. (See Figure 3.1.) Research questions were used to help frame the original exhibition proposal and, in the end, research was used to determine whether or not the learning goals of the exhibition were met. Rather than detail the ongoing decision-making process that occurred almost on a weekly basis, we will describe those key decision points that led to a radical change in the goals of the exhibition. To reiterate, the project, originally named *Life Changes*, addressed a basic research question: *Can informal museum-based science learning experiences prepare children, aged 5 to 12 years, to grasp the scientific basis of evolutionary change by targeting their intuitive concepts?*

To address this question, we had already established five initial project goals in our NSF proposal: (1) This would be an informal museum-based science learning experience; (2) The target audience would be 5- to 12-year-olds and parents because they represent typical school-age and family visitors, and the research indicated that these age groups are grappling with core ideas relevant to the theme; (3) We would produce a traveling exhibition, to more broadly disseminate the content and the results of our research to a variety of institutions, as few museums have the expertise to mount a research project like this one or the content expertise to produce an exhibition on evolution for this age audience; (4) The cognitive science would focus on children's intuitive biological reasoning and how it varied with age and changed with experience; and (5) The biological science would focus on the basic building blocks for reasoning about evolution: variation, inheritance, selection, time, and adaptation (*VISTA*).

The original *VIST* framework (we added "*A*" for adaptation) can be found on the University of California Berkeley Museum of Paleontology's (evolution. berkeley.edu) website. As a cognitive organizer to help visitors understand evolution, *VIST* had played a key role in the exhibition *Explore Evolution*. We hoped it could play a similar role in the current project, but given the major differences between the two projects, we will first describe how *VIST* was used in *Explore Evolution*. The latter focused on seven current research programs illustrating the evolution of diverse organisms, from the virus to the whale. In the final exhibition, the *VIST* framework was presented as an advance organizer and then repeated at each research station with a more concrete *VIST* description targeting the focal organism. Visitors learned that within a particular population there were genetic differences, or *variations*, which were *inherited*; *selection* was described as the process by which those organisms with traits that were advantageous in a particular environment were more likely to survive and reproduce, and over *time*, this could lead to adaptive changes in the population. Visits to *Explore Evolution* brought about significant changes in adolescent and adult visitors' understanding of evolution, which were attributed, in part, to the targeted repetition of *VIST* (Spiegel et al., 2012; Tare, French, Frazier, Diamond, & Evans, 2011). Thus, this seemed a reasonable starting point for the current project.

Year one: The Big Idea—*what is it?* Based on the initial project goals our first task as a team was to develop *The Big Idea* (Serrell, 1996), which served as the initial project "prototype" (see Figure 3.1). However, our first meetings with the project advisory board members and the core team members produced a series of challenges that made this goal seemingly elusive. The major challenge was that the expectations of the research team and that of the exhibit development team were at odds. This conflict can be summed up as one of opposing worldviews, with the research focusing on decomposing the *VISTA* concepts to be included in the exhibit, each of which could be studied separately, whereas the exhibit team adopted a holistic viewpoint focusing on the big idea that would provide an organizing principle for exhibition development and, eventually, provide a fun and engaging experience.

As just described, we had planned to include as a cognitive organizer five key evolutionary concepts (*VISTA*) that had been used successfully in *Explore Evolution*. However, in that exhibition the target population was adolescents, who might be expected to read the exhibit scripts and who were likely to know something about the content, whereas in the current proposal, the target population was elementary school children in three age groups: 5 to 7 years, 8 to 9 years, and 10 to 12 years. Evans's (2000, 2001) earlier research with children raised in Christian fundamentalist and non-fundamentalist communities indicated that pivotal changes in understanding the relevant biological concepts occurred over this time period, with the youngest and oldest groups representing the endpoints, and the 8 to 9-year-olds in a transitional phase. For example, younger children were more likely to use anthropomorphic reasoning to explain biological change (the animal "wanted" to change), whereas the oldest age groups might use intuitive biological reasoning (the animal changed out of necessity) or informed reasoning (e.g., differential survival). Moreover, a further implication of this research was that for each of the five *VISTA* concepts there would be a different developmental trajectory: three age-related concepts of "time," for example. The consequences of this scope meant that there could be as many as fifteen ideas to address in a small traveling exhibit.

In addition, there was the issue of generalizability; how many exemplars would be needed for children to generalize these ideas to all living kinds? From earlier research (Evans, 2001, 2013) we knew that creationist (God made them) explanations were more likely to be applied to humans and evolutionary explanations to species taxonomically distant from the human, regardless of community beliefs. However, the inclusion of several species as well as the presentation of five *VISTA* concepts to three age groups raised protests from the exhibit development team. This would be near impossible. Was there some way of focusing the task?

This was a major exhibit development problem! How to convey this complexity in a small traveling exhibit of 1,500 square feet or so? In what turned out to be a momentous meeting, the team decided to focus on a compelling exemplar of the animal world, one that was likely to be familiar to children: birds. Several reasons motivated this focus. Birds are easy to observe and moreover they can be seen in flocks; thus, children could easily view variations within a population, rather than single idealized exemplars. Further, although we knew that children would likely be unaware of the evolutionary connection between dinosaurs and modern birds (Evans, 2000), their typically strong interest in dinosaurs complemented their interest in birds as an intriguing entry point to the topic of the exhibition: evolution. As we developed the project, the focus on dinosaur to bird evolution suggested additional foci including geology and macroevolution, in particular the research on Darwin's Galapagos finches by Peter Grant and Rosemary Grant (2014). Moreover, we realized that an added bonus would be the inclusion of living birds as examples of variation in the exhibition itself. (We had hoped to use finches, but it turned out that they are too sensitive for live exhibits, so we used parakeets/budgies instead.)

Year one evaluation: All about birds. Once the initial decision was made to focus on birds, the evaluators Martin Storksdieck and Judy Koke stepped in to help us better understand children's interest in and knowledge of birds. In their front-end evaluation, 5- to 13-year-olds from rural and urban areas were asked, "What birds do you see? What do you like about birds?" Collectively, they mentioned 39 different kinds of birds (everything from robins to crows) and many different activities (flying, nesting, social behavior, feathers, communication, migration), some of which required more than casual observation (Koke & Storksdieck, 2006). Notably, children focused on the notion of birds as families, thus they already saw the connections between several key concepts and the relation to human families. This study strongly confirmed our hunch that children would be able to recognize variation and diversity in bird populations and affirmed our decision to use birds to illustrate the big idea and to serve as the exemplar for natural selection in the exhibition. Midway through year one, the whole team gathered at the University of Michigan's Museum of Natural History (UMMNH) in Ann Arbor to flesh out the *Big Idea* and to tour *Explore Evolution*, on display at the museum, in particular the exhibit on the Galapagos finch research. There was a palpable sense of relief when the idea of focusing on birds was confirmed by the evaluators, which offered the exhibit development team a way of dealing with the problem of generalizability of natural selection and evolutionary origins, from one compelling example to all living things.

Year one research: Framing the **Big Idea.** With one problem solved, another arose. In many free-choice learning experiences, visitors can enter an exhibition from any direction and spend as little or as much time as they like at each individual component. Short of forcing them to visit each component in a pre-specified direction, which is antithetical to many museums' practices (and to the team) and often impractical, there seemed to be no obvious way to convey the *VISTA* concepts in a coherent manner. At this point the researchers stepped in; perhaps a story-line or narrative would work (Avraamidou & Osborne, 2009; Bruner, 1991; Martin & Toon, 2005)?

First, we had to find out more about the child's perspective. Using a semi-structured interview format, Ashley Hazel (a U-M graduate student in evolutionary biology) probed children's understanding of the *VISTA* concepts as they interacted with the bird and dinosaur exhibits at UMMNH, including the Galapagos finch exhibit from *Explore Evolution*. In an in-depth pilot study, thirty 6–12 year-old museum summer campers were asked about bird diversity, the bird–dinosaur connection, and natural selection. The 40–60 minute, two-part, videotaped interviews enabled detailed analyses of children's understanding of *VISTA*. From this research it became clear that while individual exhibits were not capable of conveying the entirety of *VISTA*, a story-telling structure could be used to scaffold children's grasp of natural selection, especially in older children. We gained further insights into the development of children's understanding by coding their mention of differential survival and differential reproduction separately. From this research we obtained clear age differences, with differential reproduction being the more difficult; furthermore, with this naturalistic narrative structure intuitive biological reasoning was relatively rare (see Figure 3.2). Regression analyses indicated that children who knew more about the *VISTA* concepts, irrespective of age, were most likely to benefit from this narrative structure. Conversely, children's ability to name dinosaurs or birds (dinosaur and bird fluency) did not have any predictive value, independently of the effects of age (Legare, Hazel, French, Witt, & Evans, 2007). Overall, this pilot work gave us a more nuanced analysis of the trajectory of children's understanding of the *VISTA* concepts.

A key finding from this work was that young children were able to grasp the basics of natural selection if the information was scaffolded appropriately. For example, in the interviews Ashley introduced children to the story of adaptive change in the Galapagos finches' beaks (Grant & Grant, 2014) found in the *Explore Evolution* interactive display. In this object-based learning experience, children observed the relationship between climate change (rainfall), change in seed availability (size), and the survival of particular finches. Ashley scaffolded the storytelling experience with targeted questions that elicited key concepts, as in the following excerpt (in the video, the interviewer and child were gesturing toward the exhibit):

INTERVIEWER: "What . . . happened to all the other finches that cannot eat those seeds?"

9-YEAR-OLD: ". . . but a lot of birds weren't meant to eat those, so they died." (*Differential Survival*) [these finches' beaks were too small to crack the big tough seeds]

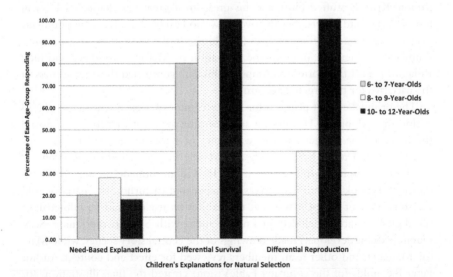

FIGURE 3.2 Children's explanations of the relationship between climate change and beak shape in the Galapagos finch population.

INTERVIEWER: ". . . Except some finches could eat those seeds. And what
                 do you think happened to them?" [these finches' beaks were
                 strong enough to crack the big seeds]
9-YEAR-OLD: "Yeah, so they lived, and they had babies." (*Differential
                 Reproduction*)

In sum, carefully crafted stories proved effective in eliciting key natural selection
concepts, in this case, differential survival and reproduction, at least in individual
children. This finding informed our decision to include narrative as a key component in the development of the exhibition. It seemed to be the only way to convey the idea of change over time; and the only way to clearly connect the *VISTA*
concepts.

Year two: Goals, prototypes, evaluation. (See Figure 3.1.) We were now
faced with the challenge of creating a narrative encompassing the elements of natural selection (*VISTA*) in a traveling exhibit that would occupy a relatively small
exhibit space, with a target audience of groups of visitors (families or children).
Based on the research, the solution seemed to be a storytelling experience. But
although the solution now seemed obvious, its execution was not. The problems
ranged from the nature of the experience, through budget issues, to the kind of
language used in the story.

The development of the narrative involved most of the team. Writer Ellen
Campbell joined Judy Rand to develop a story line that incorporated the *VISTA*
components. This involved the time travel of an older elementary-school child,
Charlie, who was writing a school-report on birds. Along with his favorite com-
panion, Kiwi (a stuffed bird), and his great-great-great grandfather (a Darwin
look-alike), a bird expert, they discover how modern birds evolved, their dinosaur
origins, and the adaptations of birds (e.g., kiwis) to the early New Zealand environment (see Figure 3.3). Prototype evaluation by Martin Storksdieck and Judy
Koke, who read the stories to groups of children, confirmed the effectiveness of
the narrative for the targeted age-groups.

The original exhibit plan was for a storytelling experience with actors placed
within the exhibition. However, it soon became apparent that this was beyond
the scope of the budget and the availability of actors at most, if not all, venues. The design team, Jeff Kennedy and Margie Prager, solved this problem by
developing a digital narrative, which unfolded in an intimate theater on a giant
digital storybook screen, with pages that appeared to turn as the narrator told
the story. Part of the plan was that the exhibition itself would be bilingual, so
the digital narrative included an English audio with Spanish captioning. Sean
Duran (exhibit developer) made drawings of the central story scenes, while Martin, Margaret, and other team members reviewed for effect and content. Author
Peter Reynolds (of the company FableVision) created the final illustrations for
the exhibition (and a subsequent book using the narrative and illustrations in
the exhibition style). The first iterations of the twelve-minute storybook video

FIGURE 3.3 Charlie and Kiwi theater video script: Use of *need* and *want* in two scenes.

a. "Animals can't just grow feathers when they *want* to. They have to inherit them from their parents."

b. "No, but you must understand, Charlie: every bird has what it *needs* for where and how it lives. It's adapted to its environment."

appeared to be effective; evaluation showed that the target audience remained engaged when the story was projected on the screen. The story was the one place in the exhibition where we told a complete narrative of natural selection and the origins of birds.

Year two: Research. The downside of narrative and a major challenge when writing about evolution is the tendency to use anthropomorphic language. The classic example, attributed to Lamarck, is that of the giraffes, whose long necks were considered to be a consequence of their intentional efforts to reach the leaves in tall trees (Quammen, 2006). Moreover, museum-going adults in an earlier study had claimed that the beak changes observed in the Galapagos finches came about because the finches deliberately exercised the relevant muscles (Evans, Spiegel, et al., 2010). There is a long line of research purporting to show that such language contributes to the misunderstanding of evolution (e.g., Bishop & Anderson, 1990; Jungwirth, 1975), and Margaret brought this to the attention of the team members.

The writers and researchers worked closely together as the project unfolded. In fact, Margaret scoured the story script and (later) the exhibit text of anthropomorphic (intentional) concepts, which, it was claimed, could seriously undermine children's understanding. Even the images came under scrutiny; while an anthropomorphized kiwi fit the storyline (it was, after all, a stuffed animal), the birds and dinosaurs observed by Charlie were to be portrayed naturalistically. As an example of this collaboration, early in year two as the writers developed the story line (not yet a full script, with characters), they sent an email with a detailed description of their approach with specific questions to team members:

> "Dear Margaret, This is an experiment to see whether [. . .] a phrase like 'seems custom-made' . . . helps/hinders children . . . " [Examples:] "Each kind of bird seems custom-made for where it lives and the job it does" "Over many generations, kiwis developed adaptations, acting like mammals."

Yet even as this collaboration flourished, the research team realized that there were no definitive data at hand demonstrating that anthropomorphic language (*kiwis don't DO jobs*) was causally implicated in evolutionary misconceptions, while it certainly made the narrative more engaging. Did children (or even adults) understand its metaphoric intent?

This pushback forced the researchers to back up their own claims with further data. In the second year of the project, the researchers (now including Cristine Legare and Jon Lane) ran experimental studies with UMMNH summer campers. The findings were surprising and prompted a more nuanced approach: while anthropomorphic language appeared to hinder understanding, this was most likely to be the case for the youngest children. Need-based reasoning, on the other hand, appeared to be helpful (Legare, Lane, & Evans, 2013). The critical twist to this research was that "need" had to be uncoupled from "want"; while younger children conflated the two, older children did not ("Do you really need that ice-cream, or do you just want it?"). The impetus for this line of research stemmed from a key finding in earlier studies with *Explore Evolution*: for adults and adolescents, natural selection understanding and need-based reasoning (change is necessary for survival) were positively associated, whereas want-based (anthropomorphic) reasoning was negatively correlated or uncorrelated, depending on the measure (Evans, Spiegel, et al., 2010; Spiegel et al., 2012). In the summer of year two (and continuing into year three), the research team assessed the nature of this relationship in eighty-eight 5- to 12-year-olds. In this study, children were told three randomly assigned bird evolution stories, each with different explanatory language: Want-based (the bird wanted or desired change), need-based (the bird needed to change, out of necessity), and natural selection (birds with particular characteristics were more likely to survive and reproduce). Following each narrative, the child retold the story and the researchers analyzed their language using the previous year's coding scheme.

Anthropomorphized stories were least likely to elicit scientific explanations, and this was especially true for the 5- to 7-year-olds, who were more prone to anthropomorphism overall. Moreover, we found that both need-based and selection stories scaffold children's grasp of natural selection, especially among the 8- to 12-year-olds, suggesting that need-based language might bridge anthropomorphic and more scientifically accurate ideas. The following example illustrates this age-difference:

INTERVIEWER: "Tell the story back to me."
6-YEAR-OLD: "The finch *wanted* a bigger beak."
9-YEAR-OLD: "You don't evolve because you *want* to. . . . You evolve because you *need* to."

These findings (Legare et al., 2013) echoed the earlier museum studies and, further, provided evidence for a developmental trajectory from want-based to need-based reasoning to natural selection understanding (Evans, 2013; Evans, Rosengren, Lane, & Price, 2012).

Based on these data, the research team was more confident in its approach and spent time working with the writers to craft a narrative that conveyed an accurate sense of evolution. In addition to excluding intentional language from the theater narrative (and the subsequent book), the team even went further and incorporated need-based reasoning as a stepping-stone from an intuitive biology toward a more complete understanding of evolution. For example:

Charlie (thinking about why the kiwi's ancestors might be flightless in prehistoric New Zealand, where VERY large eagles search for prey): "So . . . maybe birds that don't fly do a little better here. Maybe those birds don't really *need* wings." (See Figure 3.3: Use of "need" versus "want" in the video script.)

Year three goals: Integrating authentic objects—the evidence for evolution. (See Figure 3.1.) The power of authentic objects, Conn argues, derives from their ability to "tell stories" (Conn, 1998, p. 4). Given the nature of the exhibition, which was designed as a traveling exhibition for both natural history museums and for science museums, we clearly needed authentic objects as evidence to support the central narrative and to illustrate the *VISTA* concepts in greater depth. This was both a challenge and an opportunity. In developing the various exhibit components, we faced two hurdles: (1) how to integrate *VISTA* concepts into a comprehensive story that included an explanation of the mechanism of natural selection, which we had solved, in part, with the storybook video; and (2) how to present the evidence for evolution and integrate it into the narrative.

In the earlier year two research with the UMMNH summer museum campers, the research team had also asked children whether various authentic objects provided good evidence for evolution (each child took part in two sessions, one on language, the other on objects). One striking set of findings emerged from children's interpretation of an Archaeopteryx fossil cast. The interviewer asked: "What do you think this is? Scientists use this fossil as evidence that birds and dinosaurs are related. Do you agree with the scientists?" Seventy percent of the campers agreed that it was good evidence, citing the features of dinosaurs and birds that they could see in the fossil; however, 30% disagreed. One 10-year-old said,

> No, not really ... I just don't see how it is possible for a ferocious, meat-eating dinosaur to change into a bird. They aren't the same kind of thing. How could that be possible?

Without an understanding of the evolutionary mechanism or exposure to the evidence, it was impossible for this child to reconcile the apparent disparity in features and behaviors of birds and dinosaurs and reason that they were from the same lineage. This reinforced our sense that while the central narrative was likely to provide a significant entry for children to the concepts of evolution, both common descent (origins) and natural selection, we needed to provide additional entry points.

Year three prototypes, evaluation, and research. Consequently, in our prototype development the exhibit design and development team included the Archaeopteryx fossil in the theater experience and skeletons to illustrate bone homologies as evidence for the dinosaur–bird lineage, while another exhibit included live birds to convey the concept of variation. Standalone puzzles illustrating adaptation and a fossil hunt were interleaved with computer games as well as discovery boxes developed by Sarah Clarke and Margie Marino. This unusual grouping of discovery boxes and exhibit components provided an opportunity for family groups to explore individual elements of natural selection illustrating *VISTA* concepts, which were then augmented and supported by the central narrative. (See Figure 3.4 for exhibit components.)

More specifically, each exhibit component addressed a *VISTA* concept and a key aspect of the evidence for evolution, while simultaneously providing an engaging and memorable activity. The exhibit *Which Is a Bird? Which Is a Dinosaur?* illustrated the homology between several bones (sternum, foot, and limb) of a theropod dinosaur, Bambiraptor; an early bird, Archaeopteryx; and a representative of modern birds, a crow. Visitors could see the fossilized bones that show

FIGURE 3.4 Charlie and Kiwi exhibition components:

a. Meet the budgies

b. Hawaiian finch puzzle

FIGURE 3.4 (Continued)

c. Which is a bird? Which is a dinosaur?

d. Theater entrance

the relationship between dinosaurs, a transitional form, and modern birds (see Figure 3.4). The fossil dig is an activity that was extremely popular with children of all ages. They could dig into a sand and wax matrix to find fossilized bones, just as paleontologists have done in discovering the fossil evidence for evolution over the past 200 or so years. *Natural Selection* and *Dino-to-Bird* were the two computer interactives. The *Natural Selection* interactive is about Darwin's finches in the Galapagos Islands. Though Darwin noted aspects of finches' evolution in his book *On the Origin of Species*, it was evolutionary biologists, Grant and Grant (2014) and their students, who demonstrated conclusively that we can observe evolution in the short term, something Darwin and others had thought impossible. *Dino-to-Bird* is an interactive adapted from one developed by the New Mexico Museum of Natural History, which illustrates, in accelerated time, changes in bone structures, from the theropod dinosaurs to the first birds to modern birds—again illustrating homologies.

Visits to the twelve-minute storybook video experience could occur at any point while visitors were exploring the entire exhibition. In effect, the context provided by the video storybook guided the interpretation, encouraging children to "perceive" authentic objects, such as the Archaeopteryx fossils, differently than if they had seen the objects with no interpretive guide. Remedial evaluation of the prototypes and discovery boxes was carried out in year three, prior to the production of the complete exhibition. In year three, the research team expanded the year two studies, adding more participants and including more authentic objects. This accomplished two goals: the first was the important research goal of having sufficient participants to achieve a publishable study, and the second was an exhibit goal—an increased understanding of children's grasp of the scientific concepts used in the exhibition. Margaret and Martin read the scripts that accompanied the exhibits to check for intentional language and to suggest the most appropriate wording for the science ("traits" rather than "characters," for example). In terms of the risk-management aspect of the spiral model (Boehm, 1986), the changes that could be made at this point were minimal, as change was expensive, both in terms of cost and time. Exhibit text was a relatively low-cost though critically important part of the whole enterprise, while major changes to the story line or to the exhibits were out of the question.

Year three: The title. We vigorously discussed whether we should include the word "evolution" in the title of the exhibit. This had been an ongoing discussion from the inception of the project when the evaluation team had surveyed museum visitors' acceptance of evolution (Stein & Storksdieck, 2005), but at this point a final decision had to be made. Some members felt that using evolution in the title would deter museums who were deciding to rent the exhibition because of controversy surrounding the topic. This had been a concern of museum professionals in our early survey about attitudes within science museums about hosting a traveling exhibition on evolution. Others felt it was a mistake to exclude "evolution" in the title. Clearly both arguments had significant support, and there was no apparent compromise, though it seemed that visitors had a right to know about the content of the exhibition they were about to enter. In fact, the original title, *Life Changes*, gave few obvious hints as to the content, as an earlier evaluation had demonstrated.

The research, so far, was of little help. What swayed the decision was a pivotal experience during the year two prototyping of the narrative at the North Museum of Natural History in Lancaster, Pennsylvania, which was chosen as a partner in part because of the conservative nature of their visitors. While the narrative was being read to a group of children, one of the fathers who was close by rose up shouting: "Stop! Stop! I don't want my children to hear this." He believed, and was raising his children to believe, that the Earth was only 6,000 years old and objected to their hearing the process of evolution taking "millions, and millions of years." He stormed out of the session with his children. One of the narrators went after him to discuss not the issue of Earth's age but his obvious discontent. The father pointed out that he felt fooled, as the sign announcing the session had said nothing about evolution and he would not have brought his children to the session if it had. We changed the sign, which may have reduced the numbers of participants, but we do not think we alienated any other museum visitors. More importantly, this event solidified our feeling that evolution had to be in the exhibition's title, which eventually came to be, in year three: *Charlie and Kiwi's Evolutionary Adventure*.

Year Four: So We Built It; But Did They Learn? Evaluation and Research Perspectives.

Year four: Summative evaluation. (See Figure 3.1.) With the year four opening of the exhibition at the host venue, the New York Hall of Science, final tweaks were made to the exhibit components based on a further remedial evaluation. Following this process summative evaluation was carried out both in New York and (later) at the Miami Museum of Science (Palmquist, Danter, & Yalowitz, 2011). Timing and tracking of the visitors indicated that the fossil dig, Hawaiian finches puzzle, and live birds were the most engaging exhibits, with text panels the least popular; overall, of those visitors who stopped (and were tracked), the most time was spent at the story theater. An unmatched pre- and post-visit 10-minute interview of children's interest and understanding was also carried out with one hundred seventy-three 5- to 12-year olds (82 pre, 91 post) with an additional parent survey.

One of the questions motivating both the evaluation and research projects was whether children grasped the significance of the evidence for evolution. Using the Archaeopteryx as the focal example, there were significant pre- to post-visit differences in participants' identification of salient features of dinosaurs and birds; additionally, on the posttest, 57% of participants provided evolutionary explanations for the origins of birds, a significant improvement over the pretest (29%). In the case of participants' understanding of natural selection, however, there were no pre- to post-visit differences, though there were the predicted age-related differences, with older children doing better. Unlike the findings for children, most parents (65%) were aware of the evolutionary relationship between dinosaurs and birds with no significant differences pre- to post-visit. Overall, these findings indicate that a typical museum visit with families from a range of religious and ethnic backgrounds was successful. The target population of elementary-school aged children found the exhibition highly engaging and were likely to leave with a significantly better grasp of the evidence for evolution; in particular, they were more aware that species can change over time, that there are relationships between dinosaurs and birds, and that these relationships have evolutionary explanations.

Year four: Final research project. (See Figure 3.1.) The fundamental goals of the research project were to address the original research question: *Can informal museum-based science learning experiences prepare children, aged 5- to 12-years, to grasp the scientific basis of evolutionary change by targeting their intuitive concepts?* As summarized above, the goals of the evaluation were necessarily much broader, including families' interest in and engagement with the exhibits as well as the effects of the exhibit on children's understanding of evolution. The methods employed by the evaluation and research teams differed as well. For example, data collection for the evaluation was typically carried out in short bursts of two to three days, including the weekend when visitors were the most frequent; while the number of participants sampled this way was often impressive, there is only so much that can be accomplished in a single 10-minute interview (anything longer would interrupt the visitor experience). Both teams strove to use comparable instruments to measure evolution understanding; however, the research protocol included multi-item measures, while, because of the time constraints, the evaluation protocol called for single-item measures, which are likely to be less sensitive. Moreover, the evaluation team focused on the species included in the exhibit, whereas a goal of the research team was to gauge children's ability to generalize beyond the focal species. These protocol differences yielded somewhat different results, which will be detailed following a description of the research methods.

Research methods. Both research and evaluation teams designed studies that were as ecologically valid as possible. Both studies were carried out in a naturalistic setting in which children enjoyed a relatively unstructured non-didactic learning experience, governed by little other than their own free-choice explorations of the exhibition. While the evaluation team focused on the typical museum visitor experience, the research team focused on the likely experience of school groups rather than family groups. School groups often visit a targeted subset of the exhibitions—those which complement some aspect of the school curriculum. Given the difficulties of recruiting school groups (especially in the summer), the research team recruited summer campers at the New York Hall of Science (NYSci), instead. In comparison with the evaluation, this was a less effective recruitment strategy, as only about 30 campers attended each week-long science camp and consent (obtained via mail) from the parents (many of whom were Spanish speaking) was difficult to obtain; moreover, parents were unlikely to return surveys, even though a weekly family pizza party was added to encourage participation.

Over the course of the summer, eighty-nine 5- to 14-year-old NYSci campers were interviewed in a matched pre- and post-visit experimental randomized controlled trial (RCT) design. NYSci serves a linguistically and socioeconomically diverse population and many students win summer scholarships; thus, 77% of the participants had minority culture backgrounds (according to the camp records), which made this sample more ethnically diverse than the evaluation sample, an advantage. At pretest, one to two days before exhibition attendance, the children's understanding of the *VISTA* concepts was assessed with individual interviews. Children were then randomly assigned to one of two museum exhibitions on different floors of the museum: half to *Charlie and Kiwi's Evolutionary Adventure*, and the other half to a control exhibition—*Marvelous Molecules and Hidden Kingdoms*.

All campers, whether or not they were study participants, visited the exhibitions on Wednesday mornings for about 40–45 minutes in groups of about fifteen. They were given no specific guidance, but the counselors encouraged them to watch the video storybook for *Charlie and Kiwi* or a similarly timed orientation video for *Marvelous Molecules*. As is true of any free-choice experience, children visited those components in any order that appealed to them; indeed, they were just as likely to chat with their friends or wander over into adjacent exhibit spaces (we did not track them). Such exhibit "grazing" is typical of museum visitors, particularly of school groups. One to two days after exhibition attendance, children were interviewed about the evidence for dinosaur–bird evolution and the *VISTA* concepts. The pre- and post-visit interviews each lasted 20–30 minutes and were designed to be fun experiences, consistent with the ethos of the summer camps. With the help of the camp organizers, the whole study was timed to fit into the camp schedule, which typically included visits to the exhibitions, as well as more focused science activities, none of which were on evolution or related topics.

Evidence for evolution. To link to the summative evaluation results, the research team used a between-subjects design to address the first research question: *How does the* Charlie and Kiwi *exhibition affect children's consideration of the evidence for dinosaur–bird evolution?* Children were not told that the Archaeopteryx was a fossil; instead, the researchers just showed the cast (not the skeleton) and asked children to describe what they saw. To provide a more direct comparison with the summative evaluation, this was asked at post-visit only; this also ensured that participants were not sensitized to the evidence by pre-visit exposure to the fossil. The kinds of explanations children gave included the following: "I think it's a fossil of an animal," "A remain of an animal," "I think it's a picture of a dinosaur," "A bird that lived a long time ago," "I think it's the first bird slash dinosaur thing." In addition to these explanations, children who visited *Marvelous Molecules* were significantly more likely to give diverse answers, such as other living kinds or objects from "praying mantis" to "desert map." Significant group differences demonstrating the effects of *Charlie and Kiwi* on children's responses to this open-ended question can be seen in Figure 3.5. On the additional scaled closed-ended questions, younger (5–8 years) and older (9–14 years) children who visited *Charlie and Kiwi* were also

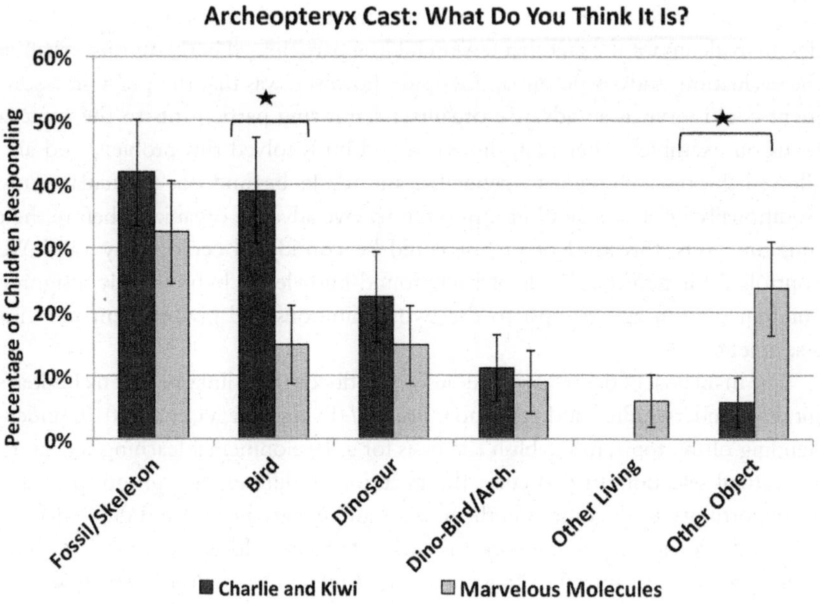

Archeopteryx Cast: What Do You Think It Is?

FIGURE 3.5 Interpreting an Archaeopteryx cast: Differences between children who visited the *Charlie and Kiwi* and *Marvelous Molecules* exhibitions.

significantly more likely to agree that the Archaeopteryx was a bird and a fossil when compared with their peers who visited *Marvelous Molecules*.

After giving their own explanations, children were told that scientists use this fossil as evidence for bird–dinosaur relationships and were asked how much they agreed with the scientists. Younger children who attended *Charlie and Kiwi* were significantly more likely to agree with the scientists (89%) than children who visited *Marvelous Molecules* (53%); however, overall, older children were more likely to agree with the scientists (Evans, Lane, et al., 2010). These findings established that regardless of method and with diverse samples, results from both the evaluation and research studies demonstrated that child visitors to *Charlie and Kiwi* were attentive to the evidence for evolution and with that expertise at hand were better able to interpret the significance of the fossil evidence.

The VISTA concepts: Establishing a learning trajectory. To address the second research question: *How does an exhibition on dinosaur–bird evolution affect children's understanding of evolution*, the research team used a matched pre- and post-visit RCT design. Because the same children participated in the pre- and post-visit assessments, this design is more sensitive to changes in children's understanding than the unmatched pre-post design used in the summative evaluation; moreover, the increased length of the interviews, an advantage of the summer camps, made it possible to ask a broader range of questions in an in-depth analysis of children's grasp of the *VISTA* concepts. Overall, the strengths of this within-subject RCT design made up for the fact that fewer children participated in the research than in the evaluation study. A potential downside, however, was that the pre-visit assessment could serve as an advance organizer sensitizing participants to the topic; a focus on examples other than dinosaurs and birds solved this problem and also allowed the research team to generalize the results beyond this particular study. Additionally, because school groups often receive advance organizers before their museum visits, this kind of pretest could be considered ecologically valid. We controlled for differing levels of background knowledge by randomly assigning children (within age groups) to the two exhibitions and giving them pre-visit assessments.

The main goal of the research studies was to discover the links between children's intuitive understanding and their more *informed* (Evans, Spiegel, et al., 2010) understanding of the topic, to establish the basis for a developmental learning trajectory for natural selection. In particular, the inclusion of different age groups provided an opportunity to document both the age- and experience-related differences in reasoning, providing a framework for such a trajectory. Ideally, informal learning experiences are organized so they encourage children to explore those aspects of the topic they find most intriguing, with the ensuing activity scaffolding children's learning as they transition from an intuitive to a more informed understanding. In this scenario, children's intuitions provide an initial stepping stone from which they can traverse the topic. Of course, this necessitates a thorough knowledge of children's prior reasoning. Details of the trajectory are beyond the scope of this chapter (see Evans, 2013; Evans et al., 2012), but here we focus on two critical changes. From the earlier developmental evidence (Evans, 2000, 2001), we were predicting that while younger children would be more likely to reason anthropomorphically, this should decrease following their visit to *Charlie and Kiwi*. Additionally, the year one pilot study (Figure 3.2) had revealed developmental differences in two components of natural selection understanding, differential survival and reproduction, so we were interested in the effects of *Charlie and Kiwi* on this reasoning. These investigations of both age and experiential changes allowed the research team to assess the similarities and differences between the two measures of change.

Anthropomorphic reasoning: Species origins. Children were asked open-ended questions about the origins of three familiar species not in the exhibition. Responses to the question, "How do you think the very first deer got here on earth?," were coded as *Anthropomorphic/creationist* if they said that someone made them: "Someone made it (deer)," "I think that God made them also," and *Evolutionary* if they mentioned change from a different kind of animal "I think the deer evolved from a stegosaurus," "I think they used to be birds cause a lot of things originated from birds." Before the visit, 5- to 8-year olds often used anthropomorphic reasoning to account for the origin of the three species. At posttest, the younger children who attended the *Charlie and Kiwi* significantly decreased their *anthropomorphic* reasoning, unlike the control group. The 9- to 14-year-olds, in contrast, were much more likely to use *evolutionary* reasoning than their younger counterparts, regardless of which exhibition they visited.

Natural selection reasoning. To assess whether children were generalizing concepts of natural selection, they were told stories about the adaptation of species not in the exhibition (one story was also used in the evaluation). After being told about guppy adaptation, for example, children were asked: "How come there were so many plain colored guppies in the river? How do you think that happened?" The following are some examples of their coded responses:

- Want-based reasoning: "They didn't *want to* get eaten and *they knew* that if they were brightly colored they'll be seen more easily."
- Need-based reasoning: "They *had to* camouflage to the new setting . . ."
- Differential survival: "Because all the bright-colored males were dead and eaten and all that was left was the plain ones."
- Differential survival and differential reproduction: "The colored guppies got eaten by bigger fish and the plain guppies, they were safe and they made more babies and they inherited their mom or dad's color scales."

Consistent with the research team's earlier studies, at pretest, in contrast with younger children, older children more often mentioned need-based reasoning, variation, and differential survival. At posttest, there was a significant increase in mention of these concepts among older children who visited *Charlie and Kiwi*, but not for the control group. Younger children (5–8 years old) were more likely to use and endorse "want-based" reasoning. Thus, even though at post-visit younger children's anthropomorphic explanations of species origins decreased, they still used such concepts to describe evolutionary processes. However, they shifted from stating that someone else (or God) caused the change to stating that the organism itself desired the change in order to adapt to the environment, thus conflating want- with need-based reasoning. In comparison with the control group, children who attended *Charlie and Kiwi* significantly increased their references to the relationship between environmental and species change.

Combining the age- and experience-related differences, we found shifts in reasoning suggesting a developmental learning trajectory from want- to need-based reasoning to variation and differential survival and differential reproduction, though the latter concept was mostly found in the 9- to-14 year olds (Lane, Hetherington, Emerick, Leider, & Evans, 2011). In contrast to the results from the summative evaluation, the final research study demonstrated that the *Charlie and Kiwi* exhibit had positive effects on children's natural selection understanding. The reason for the differences can probably be traced to the multi-item measures and within-subject design of the research study, which gave it greater statistical power. Overall, the strengths of one design often mitigated the weaknesses of the other and allowed the teams to study the effects of the exhibition on museum visitors in family groups as well as on children in loosely supervised peer groups.

With *Charlie and Kiwi's Evolutionary Adventure*, the evaluation and research studies demonstrated that we (collectively) were able to bring about a shift in children's reasoning about evolution. We utilized a compelling narrative along with carefully designed and engaging exhibits that clearly presented the evolutionary content based on children's intuitions about the biological world. This, we argue, provided a solid foundation for children's initial grasp of evolutionary theory (Evans, 2013; Evans & Lane, 2011; Weiss, Evans, Lane, Palmquist, & Yalowitz, 2010, 2011). We witnessed a decrease in anthropomorphic reasoning among the younger children, while older children increased their understanding of key natural selection concepts. All age groups were also sensitized to the evidence for evolution and more likely to articulate evolutionary ideas. Although researchers have demonstrated that narrative is an effective means of conveying natural selection, in those cases the narratives were carefully scaffolded, as in our initial pilot studies, and presented to children individually (Kelemen, Emmons, Seston Schillaci, & Ganea, 2014; Legare et al., 2013). The current studies were naturalistic, demonstrating a broader effect with children visiting an informal non-didactic learning experience in family or peer groups. Thus these results are of relevance to school as well as museum settings.

Collaboration Considerations

In this chapter, we formalized the implementation of a collaborative model of exhibit development that, we claim, yields an evidence-based knowledge generation process. Here we summarize some of the advantages (and some difficulties) of this collaboration.

Language and communication. Researchers, used to communicating theory in the jargon of their own discipline to like-minded individuals, rarely find it easy to communicate outside their discipline. In this case, the problem was exacerbated by the fact that it was not just a matter of communicating basic ideas; the core members of the team had to understand, at a very deep level, the conceptual problems that children and adults face when learning about evolution, so that the problems could be directly addressed in exhibit development and evaluation. The communication problem was overcome only with repeated iterations in which the research concepts were conveyed in different formats over successive meetings with the entire group. The development of the exhibit emerged out of this iterative process, and as the concepts became tied more tightly to the exhibit elements, this made communication easier.

Communication was a two-way problem. What seemed to be a straightforward conceptual issue from the research perspective turned out to be an almost intractable exhibition development issue. As described in years one and two, the research goals were developmental, targeting three different age groups with five major evolutionary concepts. But an exhibition that hit all these targets would be unfocused (and in all likelihood, boring). Where was the main message?

Additionally, as detailed in the year two and three research (see Figure 3.1, lower left quadrant) phases, there were other language issues. From a research perspective, the introduction of anthropomorphic language into the narrative was anathema, as it was likely to elicit fundamental misconceptions about evolutionary processes. From the exhibit development perspective, however, anthropomorphic language arouses interest and supports personal connections. Overall, though, this constant iterative process added clarity and conceptual depth both to the research and the exhibit development process. Inspired by these design issues, for example, new research on the role of anthropomorphic language in visitors' understanding of evolution (Legare et al., 2013) informed label writing in the exhibit scripts and in the language used to convey evolutionary concepts both in the narrative and a subsequent children's book on evolution (Reynolds & NYSCI, 2011).

Timeline. The Institutional Review Board (IRB) requirements for the researchers complicated the time factor as a complete research proposal is required for IRB submission, while the needs of exhibit development may necessitate a shift mid-research; formative evaluation does not have this constraint. Because of the IRB and research requirements, research is less iterative than formative evaluation, making planning and integrating surprising results from research a bit more problematic. This results in an exhibition development process that has to take time into consideration. Most of the compromises were in scheduling as well as in the budget. However, with good rapport, cooperation, understanding, and commitment, this can be a process that results in a very different and nuanced product.

Evaluation and research perspectives. Evaluators and evaluation programs have long been integrated into the exhibit development process and the familiar stages of front-end, formative, remedial, and summative evaluation are likely to be included in most informal learning experiences (see Figure 3.1, lower right quadrant). Additionally, the goals of the evaluation are clear, which are to ascertain the effects of the learning experience on the target population at various well-defined stages of the process; moreover, the results of the evaluation do not have to generalize beyond the particular learning experience (of course, sometimes they do, but it is not a necessity). The major evaluation research questions focused on the effectiveness of the exhibits: Did they function as designed? Did they convey the main ideas? Did they convey content, clearly? Did visitors find them appealing?

The research program, in contrast, had no such well-defined parameters and the researchers had to basically innovate as the exhibit took form. The original purview of the research was to help define or refocus the goals of the exhibit development based on the research team's in-depth investigation of children's understanding of the main ideas and to generalize the results beyond the exhibition. This led to a somewhat ambiguous role for the researchers. But what focused their contribution was a clear research aim: to help develop an exhibit that reflected current knowledge of children's evolution concepts and to help develop a learning experience that functioned, in essence, as a lab for investigating children's newly acquired ideas. The spiral model encapsulated where in the exhibit development process the research team best functioned, which was prior to the goal setting, both at the initiation of the project and in the subsequent yearly iterations (see Figure 3.1, lower left quadrant).

The evaluation and research teams collaborated closely throughout the project, with a constant interchange between the two teams and a cross-referencing of ideas, measures, and results. With the evaluation occurring mostly before the research took shape (see Figure 3.1), this made it easy for the research team to capitalize on the evaluators' findings; in turn, the more in-depth measures developed by the researchers were used by the evaluation team in the subsequent iterations of the spiral as well as in the summative evaluation. As detailed earlier in year four, even though the evaluation and research teams used different methods, reflecting their somewhat different aims, the two approaches complemented one another and this collaboration contributed to a much better outcome for the project as a whole.

Conclusion. Overall, the knowledge generated by this process was transformative in the sense that it offered a new way of approaching exhibition design and research. In the iterative framework, based on Boehm's *spiral model*, feedback from the design team elicited new research, which then informed design. This resulted in a successful exhibition that simultaneously advanced our understanding of conceptual development and of exhibit development. In the original conception of this exhibition, our working assumption was that an exhibition involving (primarily) low-tech, hands-on activities would best suit our target audience of elementary school children. Over the course of research and concept development, it became clear that a narrative approach was required to get the exhibition's interrelated main messages across for this audience. Since evolution is a process, it cannot be communicated as a series of independent elements. A storytelling theater evolved as the primary exhibit experience. A unique and somewhat controversial approach involved the integration of discovery boxes, interactives, and multimedia exhibits in this storybook context. The real difference with this process is that all members of the team asked questions for which there were no answers in the literature, and that makes *Charlie and Kiwi* a different product, for exhibit developers and for researchers.

In the final years of the project (see Figure 3.1) and beyond, *Charlie and Kiwi* was configured as a children's book and the exhibition traveled to the partner museums in Lancaster (PA) and Miami (FL), followed by visits to ten other museums ranging in location from the Carnegie Museum of Natural History in Pittsburgh, PA, to the Dallas Museum of Nature and Science. Currently, it is on permanent display at the New York Hall of Science.

Acknowledgements

Life Changes NSF #0540152: Martin Weiss, Ph.D., PI., Demetrius Lutz, Jasmine Maldonado, Sylvia Perez, *New York Hall of Science*; Margaret Evans, Ph.D., Co-PI, *University of Michigan*; Sean Duran, Co-PI, Carlos Plaza, *Patricia and Philip Frost*

Museum of Science, Miami, FL; Margie Marino, Co-PI, Sarah Clarke, *North Museum of Nature & Science, PA*; Wendy Pollock, *ASTC*; Eileen Campbell, *Farallon Media*; Judy Rand, *Rand and Associates*; Jeff Kennedy, Margie Prager, Sandra Liu, Greg Sprick, *JKA Associates*; Martin Storksdieck, Ph.D., Judy Koke, Sasha Palmquist, Ph.D., Steve Yalowitz, Ph.D., *Institute for Learning Innovation*. Alphonso DiSena, Ph.D., NSF Program Officer.

University of Michigan Research Team. Graduate Students: Ashley Hazel, Jon Lane, Cristine Legare; *Undergraduate:* Jessie Emerick, Jason French, Chelsea Hetherington, Andrea Kiss, Becca Leider.

References

Avraamidou, L., & Osborne, J. (2009). The role of narrative in communicating science. *International Journal of Science Education, 31,* 1683–1707.

Bishop, B.A., & Anderson, C.W. (1990). Student conceptions of natural selection and its role in evolution. *Journal of Research in Science Teaching, 27,* 415–427.

Boehm, B. (1986). A spiral model of software development and enhancement. *ACM SIG-SOFT Software Engineering Notes, 11,* 14–24.

Bruner, J. (1991). The narrative construction of reality. *Critical Inquiry, 18,* 1–21.

Conn, S. (1998). *Museums and American intellectual life, 1876–1926.* Chicago: University of Chicago Press.

Diamond, J., & Evans, E.M. (2007). Museums teach evolution. *Evolution, 61,* 1500–1506.

Evans, E.M. (2000). The emergence of beliefs about the origins of species in school-age children. *Merrill-Palmer Quarterly: A Journal of Developmental Psychology, 46,* 221–254.

Evans, E.M. (2001). Cognitive and contextual factors in the emergence of diverse belief systems: Creation versus evolution. *Cognitive Psychology, 42,* 217–266. doi:10.1006/cogp.2001.0749

Evans, E.M. (2013). Conceptual change and evolutionary biology: Taking a developmental perspective. In S. Vosniadou (Ed.), *International handbook of research on conceptual change* (2nd ed.; pp. 220–239). New York: Routledge.

Evans, E.M., & Lane, J.D. (2011). Contradictory or complementary? Creationist and evolutionist explanations of the origin(s) of species. *Human Development, 54,* 144–159. doi: 10.1159/000329130

Evans, E.M., Lane, J.D., Hetherington, C., & Weiss, M. (2010). Authentic objects and children's understanding of evidence: The case of archaeopteryx. In J. Martin (Chair), *From object to evidence: Rethinking what's real in science museums?* Annual Meeting of the Association of Science and Technology Centers, Honolulu, Hawaii.

Evans, E.M., Mull, M.S., & Poling, D.A. (2002). The authentic object? A child's-eye view. In S.G. Paris (Ed.), *Perspectives on object-centered learning in museums* (pp. 55–77). Mahwah, NJ: Lawrence Erlbaum Associates.

Evans, E.M., Rosengren, K., Lane, J.D., & Price, K.S. (2012). Encountering counterintuitive ideas: Constructing a developmental learning progression for biological evolution. In K.R. Rosengren, S. Brem, E.M. Evans, & G. Sinatra (Eds.), *Evolution challenges: Integrating research and practice in teaching and learning about evolution* (pp. 174–199). New York: Oxford University Press.

Evans, E.M., Spiegel, A., Gram, W., Frazier, B.F., Tare, M., Thompson, S., & Diamond, J. (2010). A conceptual guide to natural history museum visitors' understanding of evolution. *Journal of Research in Science Teaching, 47,* 326–353. doi: 10.1002/tea.20337

Evans, E.M., Weiss, M., Koke, J., Storksdieck, S., & Kennedy, J. (2008). Conversations across disciplines: From theory to practice—The spiral model. Panel presentation at the Annual Meeting of the Visitor Studies Association, Houston, TX.

Grant, P.B., & Grant, B.R. (2014). *40 years of evolution: Darwin's finches on Daphne Major Island.* Princeton, NJ: Princeton University Press.

Kelemen, D., Emmons, N.A., Seston Schillaci, R., & Ganea, P.A. (2014). Young children can be taught basic natural selection using a picture-storybook intervention. *Psychological Science, 25,* 893–902. doi: 10.1177/0956797613516009

Koke, J., & Storksdieck, M. (2006, June 30) *Life changes front end study one: General audience personal connection with birds.* Unpublished Report, Institute for Learning Innovation.

Jungwirth, E. (1975). Preconceived adaptation and inverted evolution: A case of distorted concept formation in high school biology. *Australian Science Teacher's Journal, 21,* 95–100.

Lane, J.D., Hetherington, C.C., Emerick, J.K., Leider, B.M., & Evans, E.M. (2011). Building on children's intuitions: How an informal learning experience changes children's minds about evolution. Presented at the Biennial Meeting of the Society for Research in Child Development, Montreal, Canada.

Legare, C., Hazel, A., French, J., Witt, A., & Evans, E.M. (2007). Children's understanding of evolution: Learning from museum exhibits about natural selection. Poster presented at the 2007 Biennial meeting of the Cognitive Development Society, Santa Fe, NM.

Legare, C.H., Lane, J D., & Evans, E.M. (2013). Anthropomorphizing science: How does it affect the development of evolutionary concepts? [Special issue]. *Merrill-Palmer Quarterly, 29,* 168–197. doi: 10.1353/mpq.2013.0009

Martin, L., & Toon, R. (2005). Narratives in a science center: Forms of interpretation and people's identities as science learners. *Curator: The Museum Journal, 48,* 407–425.

Palmquist, S., Danter, L., & Yalowitz, S. (2011, February). *Life changes summative evaluation.* Unpublished report. Institute for Learning Innovation.

Quammen, D. (2006). *The reluctant Mr. Darwin.* New York: Norton.

Reynolds, P., & New York Hall of Science. (2011). *Charlie and Kiwi: An evolutionary adventure.* New York: Simon & Schuster.

Serrell, B. (1996). *Exhibit labels: An interpretive approach.* Walnut Creek, CA: Alta Mira Press.

Spiegel, A., Evans, E.M., Frazier, B.F., Hazel, A., Tare, M., Gram, W., & Diamond, J. (2012). Changing museum visitors' concepts of evolution. *Evolution: Education and Outreach, 5,* 43–61. doi: 10.1007/s12052-012-0399-9

Stein, J., & Storksdieck, M. (2005, June). *Life changes front end study: Museum visitor survey.* Unpublished report. Institution for Learning Innovation.

Tare, M., French, J., Frazier, B., Diamond, J., & Evans, E.M. (2011). Explanatory parent-child conversation predominates at an evolution exhibit. *Science Education, 95,* 720–744. doi: 10.1002/sce.20433

Weiss, M., Evans, E.M., Lane, J.D., Palmquist, S., & Yalowitz, S. (2010). If we build it will they learn? Presented at the Annual Meeting of the Association of Science and Technology Centers, Honolulu, Hawaii.

Weiss, M., Evans, E.M., Lane, J.D., Palmquist, S., & Yalowitz, S. (2011). If we built it, would they learn? *Informal Learning Review, 107,* 19–21.

4

THE LIVING LABORATORY® MODEL

A Mutual Professional Development Model for Museum-Based Research Partnerships

*Kathleen H. Corriveau, Becki (Rebecca) Kipling,
Samuel Ronfard, Marta C. Biarnes,
Brittany M. Jeye, and Paul L. Harris*

The Team

Kathleen Corriveau is the Peter Paul Assistant Professor in Human Development at Boston University, where she directs the Social Learning Laboratory. Her research focuses on social and cognitive development in childhood, with a specific focus on how children decide what people and what information are trustworthy sources.

Becki Kipling oversees early childhood education initiatives at the Museum of Science in Boston, where she is responsible for creating exhibits and programs that support the development of science, math, and engineering process skills for the youngest visitors. Her work, including co-innovating Living Laboratory in 2005, firmly established the museum's Discovery Center as a regional and national leader in informal science education for early childhood audiences.

Samuel Ronfard is a doctoral student in human development and education at Harvard University in the Graduate School of Education. His research focuses on knowledge acquisition and transmission in childhood. From June 2012 to June 2014, as a National Living Laboratory Research Liaison, he helped develop a toolkit of resources for scientists and museum professionals interested in beginning new partnerships.

Marta Biarnes is a co-founder of Living Laboratory, developed at the Museum of Science in Boston, and has worked at the intersection of informal science education and early childhood education for over a decade. As Co-PI for the National Living Laboratory Initiative, she currently facilitates national and international collaborations between museum professionals and scientists.

Brittany Jeye is a graduate student in the Memory and Perception Laboratory at Boston College, where she studies the functional role of the hippocampus in human memory. She has more than five years of experience as a staff educator in the Discovery Center at the Museum of Science, Boston, where she is actively involved with Living Laboratory. She previously served as educational coordinator for the National Living Laboratory Initiative.

Paul Harris is a developmental psychologist with interests in the development of cognition, emotion, and imagination. For many years, he taught in Europe. In 2001, he moved to Harvard University, where he holds the Victor S. Thomas Professorship in the Graduate School of Education. His latest book is: *Trusting What You're Told: How Children Learn From Others* (Harvard University Press, 2012).

The Museum Setting

The Museum of Science's mission is to play a leading role in transforming the nation's relationship with science and technology. Our Discovery Center is the keystone experience for young children (ages 0–8 years) and their adult caregivers, and home to the flagship Living Laboratory program. This 4,200-square-foot exhibition provides a safe and supportive environment for early learning and exploration. Since its inauguration in 1988, more than four million children and accompanying adults have experienced the center's dynamic activities—including live animal exhibits, discovery boxes, sensory activities, an experiment station, and unique hands-on experiences with the museum's collection. The museum is nationally recognized for its work connecting public audiences with STEM, leading not only the National Living Laboratory Initiative, but also the Nano-Scale Informal Science Education Network (NISENet) and the award-winning Engineering is Elementary® project.

The Living Laboratory at the Museum of Science, Boston (MOS), educates the public about child development by immersing museum visitors in the process of developmental science research. We invite scientists to conduct their studies on the floor of the museum amidst the everyday museum activities. This partnership allows visiting families to participate in ongoing research studies and learn more about developmental science through one-on-few conversations with researchers. One unique feature of the Living Laboratory is the partnership between the MOS and multiple laboratories from universities across the Boston area. Indeed, since its launch in 2005, the MOS Living Laboratory has hosted scientists from Harvard University, Boston University, Boston College, Tufts University, MIT, and other local research institutions. These collaborators have studied a wide range of topics, including mathematical reasoning, language cognition, causal learning, emotion recognition, and social reasoning. Based on the success of the MOS program, a broad implementation project funded by the National Science Foundation[1] began in 2011 to disseminate the Living Laboratory model to other institutions across the United States, and to bring together a community of learners that shares resources associated with successful museum-university collaborations.

We have organized our chapter as follows. We first describe the history of the Living Laboratory model; its benefits for researchers, museum educators, and the general public; and its essential elements. Second, we highlight some of the research findings that have resulted from the museum–researcher partnership. We focus on research from two laboratories: the Early Childhood Laboratory at Harvard University, and the Social Learning Laboratory at Boston University. Third, we describe how we are evaluating the efficacy of the Living Laboratory model. Fourth, we highlight some lessons learned from effective researcher-museum partnerships. We close with our current and future directions: the creation of a national network of museum educators and researchers in developmental psychology.

History: Why Living Laboratory?

Living Laboratory was originally developed to engage adult visitors in MOS's Discovery Center, an early childhood exhibition that serves nearly 300,000 visitors annually. Discovery Center exhibits allow young children and their accompanying adults to explore a variety of real objects and age-appropriate tools, often set in immersive fantasy environments that encourage learning through play. Staff and volunteer interpreters play a crucial role within the exhibition, facilitating activities, experiments, and conversations that aim to help children develop their emerging science and engineering skills.

Despite a long history of success engaging children in science learning in the Discovery Center, in 2004, the staff at the Discovery Center realized that, while in the exhibition, many adult visitors within family groups were not experiencing meaningful learning themselves. Given that one of the missions of the MOS is to promote appreciation of science across the lifespan, the Discovery Center aimed to devise novel approaches to engage with this "lost audience." At the same time, the museum noticed that the science of child development was infrequently represented in science center offerings, even though this topic is highly relevant and interesting to caregivers of young children.

To address both of these concerns, the first collaborations between the MOS and child development researchers (from Harvard University and MIT) were initiated. Our initial meetings aimed to create a shared understanding of our goals for the collaboration, and to discuss the day-to-day logistics of introducing research to the museum setting, including details of the proposed studies, temporal and physical setup within the Discovery Center, and interactions among researchers, museum staff, and visitors to ensure a positive visitor experience. It was also agreed that the graduate students and museum educators working to build the collaboration would have frequent meetings to openly communicate challenges and work together to bridge cultural differences (e.g., incongruence of museum and academic annual calendar cycles, and differences in the complexity of organizational hierarchies for internal approvals among the institutions involved, among others).

By designing a researcher–scientist partnership, we hoped to create a dynamic and interactive program that would 1) provide the museum staff and visitors with direct access to the latest theories, methods, and findings in the field of child development; 2) engage parents and other caregivers by introducing them to the scientific study of children's learning and development; and 3) allow researchers an opportunity to work with parent and child participants in a unique setting. Our goal was to make participating in research studies and speaking with researchers about their ongoing work a seamless part of the free-choice family learning environment found in the Discovery Center.

This initial collaborative work with MIT and Harvard University laid the foundation for what is now called the Living Laboratory. In 2007–2011, with support from the National Science Foundation,[2] the Living Laboratory model expanded to include researchers from additional Boston institutions, including Boston College, Boston University, Boston Children's Hospital, and Tufts University. The program has been extremely popular with museum visitors: as of December 2014, more than 61,000 families visiting the Discovery Center have interacted with research activities, with approximately half serving as formal participants in scientists' ongoing studies, and others learning about scientists' research through informal demonstrations.

Figure 4.1 depicts the Living Laboratory in the Discovery Center as it currently stands in 2015. A few key features warrant attention. First, the researchers and their

FIGURE 4.1 The Living Laboratory physical space, one of eight distinct areas within the Discovery Center. Note that all research happens clearly in view of the public and is seamlessly integrated with other interactive activities available.

research studies are placed "on the floor" of the museum (and, in fact, directly next to a station where young visitors engage in daily hands-on chemistry, physics, and engineering experiments). This is in keeping with the above goal of devising a program in which developmental scientists conduct their research studies in plain view of the public, *within* the dynamic educational environment of the early childhood exhibition. Second, a permanently rotating video screen provides adults with an opportunity to learn more about research studies, even if they choose to have their child not participate in the current study. Third, each ongoing study is associated with a brief (1/3 page) handout. Researchers use this handout to recruit participating families, as well as to provide families with "try this at home" activities. Each of these features will be described in more detail in subsequent sections.

Benefits of Living Laboratory to Research Scientists, Museum Educators, and Museum Visitors

The museum–researcher partnership has highlighted several *essential elements* (see Table 4.1), both from our continued discussion between museum educators and researchers, and from evaluation of the Living Laboratory model, which we describe in more detail in subsequent sections. Table 4.1 highlights what we see as the most important and unique aspects of our model. Inspection of Table 4.1 indicates that at its core, the Living Laboratory brings together three audiences who benefit from participating in the program: child development research scientists, museum educators, and museum visitors. Below, we highlight some of the benefits between research scientists, museum visitors, and museum educators.

TABLE 4.1 The essential elements of the Living Laboratory model. Note that this partnership yields benefits for three communities: research scientists, museum educators, and museum visitors.

Essential Elements of the Living Laboratory Model	
Breaking Down Barriers Between Research Scientists and the Public	1. Visitors contribute to the process of scientific discovery through participation in active studies.
	2. Visitors engage in one-on-few educational interactions with scientists conducting the research.
	3. Visitor education focuses on the process of science, increasing interest in and understanding of research questions and methods, as well as results.
	4. Studies occur in plain view of the public, on the exhibit floor.
	5. Nonparticipant visitors talk with researchers and learn about ongoing studies in ways similar to study participants,
	6. On-site research is an expected and predictable part of the visitor experience.

(*Continued*)

TABLE 4.1 *(Continued)*

Essential Elements of the Living Laboratory Model

Mutual Professional Development for Scientists and Educators	1. Researchers receive training from museum staff in effective museum-style education techniques, improving researchers' communication skills with public audiences.
	2. Museum educators gain direct access to current science that is relevant to their work with the public, improving educators' understanding of science and its potential application to practice.
	3. Museum educators and researchers communicate regularly, collaboratively monitoring the program to ensure scientific and educational goals are met, and that programmatic needs (e.g. logistical, financial) are fulfilled.

New Insights: Benefits from Researcher–Visitor Interactions

Working in a museum setting offers plenty of opportunities for dialogue and observation. Researchers can (and do) discuss their proposals with interested parents. Parents can watch as children go through the research procedure and can ask questions when they are being recruited to participate in the study or once the interview with the child is completed. In fact, if children are old enough, they may ask their own questions about the research they have just been a part of. In one particularly memorable exchange, a curious eight-year-old girl asked whether all children "played the same game" with the experimenter. Her question began a discussion about the difference between an experimental and a control group and the need for such groups to help answer research questions.

Second, discussion with parents quite often leads researchers to think about unexpected areas of research. For example, over a 4-year period, the Social Learning Laboratory at Boston University conducted a series of studies on how children understand that a story can have a real or a make-believe protagonist (Corriveau, Kim, Schwalen, & Harris, 2009; Corriveau & Harris, 2015). The results indicated that by the age of 5, young children are able to correctly categorize these protagonists based on situational cues in the story, notably whether or not the story contained events that were impossible or improbable. For example, if the story portrayed a soldier involved in ordinary, realistic events, children were likely to say that he was a real person, but if the story described his special sword that saved him in every battle, they were likely to say that he was a fictional character. Over the months, many parents asked how children categorize other types of stories—for example, fictional stories in which no causal violations occur or religious stories in which a miracle occurs. This led the researchers to consider the effect of church attendance and schooling on children's judgments of reality and fantasy. Subsequent studies, conducted outside of the museum, found that children who had a religious education (whether at school or in church) were more likely to think of the protagonist in stories involving miracles as a real person (Corriveau, Chen, & Harris, 2015). Were it not for parental questions, the researchers might not have explored this very fruitful area of research.

The dialogue between parent and researcher can also provide parents with a glimpse of the way that psychological research is conducted with children—and not just a sense of how their own child fares in a given study. That dialogue can highlight how the mind of a child is as complicated and as worthy of scientific study as the more traditional targets of research that are typically on display in a museum of science. In particular, the dialogue can illustrate and underline how developmental psychologists are not primarily interested in children as well-adjusted or troubled individuals—that is the purview of the clinician. Rather, they have a broader canvas—they want to understand the development of children's curiosity, their observational skills, their imagination, and their ways of thinking. Such dialogues also highlight the evolving and cumulative nature of the scientific enterprise. Occasionally, parents will ask researchers questions about the anticipated scientific and educational implications of particular studies. Such questions lead to conversations about the limitations of individual studies, the need for follow-up experiments, and the importance of replication. These questions also lead to conversations about the limits of researchers' own expertise. For example, researchers cannot (and should not) give advice about what reading interventions would be most effective for a particular child. These conversations help broaden parents' understanding of psychological research and of the knowledge that individual researchers hold.

This last point is closely linked to a mission that researchers and museum educators can share. A science museum can and should offer its visitors the opportunity to learn about a given domain of science. However, it can also invite visitors to think about and even participate in the way that science is conducted. A museum can go beyond the documentation and display of the known. It can underline the incomplete but evolving nature of the scientific enterprise. Watching data being gathered, and especially watching a familiar child make his or her contribution, is likely to be a memorable illustration of that process.

Mutual Professional Development: Benefits From Researcher–Museum Interactions

Collaborating researchers not only gain access to the diverse and accessible participant pool of museum visitors, but they also work closely with museum educators as they learn to interpret their research questions and methods effectively for the public. Similarly, by conversing with active research scientists, museum staff become engaged in the research process and use that experience to inform their practice. We ensure such *mutual professional development* through a variety of regular interactions.

For example, researchers receive ongoing training in informal education practices through an initial orientation and daily "greetings" by a museum staff member or a museum volunteer. The daily greeting works as follows. At the beginning of every 3-hour research shift, a museum staff member approaches the researcher and asks her to run the study with the staff member acting as a child participant, and then to describe the study with the staff member acting as an adult visitor. The researcher is then asked a series of targeted questions designed to ensure they are being given the support they need in the recruitment process. This daily greeting has two intended purposes. First, although the collaborating laboratories provide extensive training to their research assistants well before they arrive at the museum, the initial greeting helps to place the researcher in the appropriate mindset: for the next 3 hours, s/he will be tailoring the discussion of the research to the museum's many audiences: museum staff, parents, and other visitors, who come from a variety of cultural and educational backgrounds. Second, through the same exchanges, museum educators are given an opportunity to learn about developmental science, including the methods the researchers use to study children's development.

A second example is related to the daily greeting, and comes from how the Discovery Center has approached times of the year when partnering university researchers are less likely to be able to be on-site (for example, during winter break, and summer holidays). Because of the daily greeting, museum educators have become familiar with the researcher studies taking place in the Living Laboratory. Instead of closing the Living Laboratory, the Discovery Center invited their high school and undergraduate interns to choose some of their favorite studies and create hands-on activities inspired by the research. For example, consider the line of research described above exploring children's understanding of fictional and historical narratives (Corriveau et al., 2009; Corriveau & Harris, 2015). In the research study, children were shown a picture of a novel figure and told a short story about her. Based on the story, children were invited to place the picture into a "real" box or a "pretend" box. Museum educators created a very popular storybook that included some of the novel figures used in the research. An adult (a museum educator, a parent) would then read a story to the child and ask her to choose whether the figure was real or pretend. The end of the storybook included a description of the original research study, and the study's findings. Thus, even when researchers are not present, children and adults might have an opportunity to learn about research from the Living Laboratory model.

Finally, the Discovery Center has incorporated, into several exhibits, adult-focused activities that encourage caregivers to observe their children interacting with components in ways similar to how scientists might observe and interact with children during studies. The most robust examples are in the Infant Area (with components and related labels that draw attention to research from MIT's Early Childhood Cognition Lab) and the Ball Maze (which is complemented by a set of activity cards that reference studies conducted in the exhibition by Bascandziev & Harris, 2010, 2011). For both components, the original research methods are presented to adult visitors as strategies for interacting with children that will allow caregivers to observe the same kinds of behaviors in their own children that have been documented in published research studies. Museum educators routinely incorporate similar strategies into casual interactions with caregivers throughout the Discovery Center—daily volunteer briefings frequently train volunteers to engage adult visitors in such conversations. A collective fluency—in study questions, methods, and results—that has resulted from educators' daily interactions with researchers has transformed the way early childhood educators interact with visiting families, putting a spotlight on psychology as a STEM discipline on a par with those traditionally represented in science museums, and helping caregivers observe and consider their own children within the context of a larger body of research.

Between 2005 and 2014, the MOS Living Laboratory partnership has included 31 unique research labs from across nine institutions. Because each of these research laboratories includes postdoctoral fellows, graduate students, undergraduate students, lab managers, and high school interns, in total more than 600 developmental science researchers have been trained in informal science education practices through the MOS Living Laboratory. In turn, hundreds of museum educators and other staff from departments across the institution have interacted with the collaborating researchers, and through these interactions learned about developmental science methods and research.

Examples of Specific Research from the Living Laboratory

In the following section, we review in more detail some of the research studies that have taken place in the Living Laboratory. We do this by highlighting research from two research lab partnerships. Both the Early Childhood Laboratory at Harvard University (PI: Paul Harris) and Social Learning Laboratory at Boston University (PI: Kathleen Corriveau) have conducted research studies in collaboration with the Living Laboratory since 2007 and 2011, respectively.

As mentioned above, because the research studies take place on the main floor, the research projects are competing with many other options. Thus, whether or not the research projects are appealing is an important practical consideration. The best projects are ones that actively engage children and are relatively brief. The issue of engagement might seem obvious: after all, the participants are volunteers, and if the tasks appear to be fun, parents are more likely to volunteer their child (the promise of a sticker is also very helpful). But there is also a benefit for the researchers. Once the family has agreed to participate, having the child actively engaged helps to focus the child toward the task and away from the myriad distractions going on all around the museum.

For example, in a series of studies exploring children's conceptions of fairness, children were asked to divide up some stickers between themselves and another child (Smith, Blake, & Harris, 2013). In another set of studies exploring gravity, children were asked to predict where a ball would land when it was dropped down some tubes (Bascandziev & Harris, 2010, 2011). Finally, to explore children's preference for learning from written information over spoken information, we asked them to listen to the advice from two puppets and then drop a marble down a Y-shaped tube based on which puppet they thought was correct (Corriveau, Einav, Robinson, & Harris, 2014). In all of these cases, we had no difficulty having children complete all of the trials—indeed, many children asked to play the game again after we had finished! As a result of such positive experiences with research in the Living Laboratory, many parents and children often seek out researchers to participate in additional studies on their next visits.

Designing a brief and engaging experiment can be challenging, but this challenge can prompt the development of new means to test complex relationships. Consider the example we discussed above where we were interested in how children learn from written over spoken information. We thought it was likely that children's own reading ability might be related to their preference for learning from text. Yet a 7-minute time window (the approximate length of time we have found children can remain engaged in a study within the Discovery Center) does not allow us to administer many standard reading assessments in addition to our experimental task. We solved this problem by creating a very short test of emerging reading ability in which children were asked to point to a color circle that matched a color word. Thus, even in 7 minutes, we can begin to explore some—but not all—complex relationships.

Indeed, we have found that any experiment requiring that the child attend carefully to a spoken message can be challenging. For example, over many years at the museum, we have explored how children come to decide that a particular person is a trustworthy source of information when learning about the world (Corriveau, Fusaro, & Harris, 2009; Corriveau & Kurkul, 2014; Chen, Corriveau, & Harris, 2013; Fusaro, Corriveau, & Harris, 2011; Harris, 2012). In this research, we often use videos to present children with sets of people who differ in one variable of interest. For example, children might see one person label an object accurately (labeling a shoe as "a shoe") and the other person might label the same object inaccurately (labeling a shoe as "a ball"). We can then ask which person children prefer to turn to when learning novel information—the previously accurate person, or the inaccurate person. By presenting these people on video, we can control for all aspects of the people beyond what they have said. However, in a museum setting, this requires that the child has actually heard what the two people have said above the background noise of the museum. We have solved this problem in several ways. First, we provide headphones for the child (and disinfecting wipes so that parents are not concerned!). Second, we build into our procedure multiple checks to ensure that the child has actually heard the information. Finally, in some cases, we show movies to the children that do not require sound. For example, instead of labeling an object orally, children watch as people point or gesture (Corriveau et al., 2009; Chen et al., 2013; Morgan, Laland, & Harris, 2015). In sum, we have found that procedures that work just fine in educational or university settings may need to be modified to accommodate the unique constraints and challenges of the museum setting.

Before leaving these practical considerations—considerations that weigh heavily in the day-to-day conduct of research even if they are not especially exalted—it is worth underlining a related, cognitive issue of considerable, theoretical interest. As described above, much of our own recent work has examined the degree to which children trust an informant to supply reliable information, especially about matters that children cannot investigate or determine for themselves. We have found that even preschool children are sensitive to a surprisingly large number of informant characteristics. They prefer to learn from familiar, hitherto accurate informants and from those who appear to "belong"—either to the same cultural group as themselves or to a larger consensus. Stated differently, children are not so receptive to dissident voices. In very recent research, we have begun to examine children's sensitivity to expertise. One way that young children might determine that an informant is an expert is by evaluating his or her explanations. We have found that even 3-year-olds are able to evaluate the quality of an informant's explanations—and more impressive, they are able to use that information to make inferences about whom to turn to when learning new information (Corriveau & Kurkul, 2014; see also Mercier, Bernard, & Clément, 2014).

What do young children do when faced with an informant who presents him or herself as an expert—for example, by wearing a white coat? Do children accept what such a person claims and does their acceptance of those claims depend on the nature of the particular claim (Lane & Harris, 2015)? For example, do they trust an animal expert who makes surprising claims about animal behavior but not when he or she makes surprising claims about physical artifacts? Indeed, we have found that children as young as 3 and 4 years old are more trusting of claims made by people who have relevant expertise; and this is true whether they are learning about ordinary or extraordinary phenomena (Lane & Harris, 2015). Lurking behind these questions is a deeper one that we have yet to tackle. At what point do children come to think of particular institutions—schools, churches, hospitals, zoos, and, of course, museums—as places where the adults belonging to the institution speak with special authority, an authority that is closely connected to the larger function of that institution in the transmission of a particular body of knowledge? By the age of five or six, children have begun to realize that their teachers in school have a distinctive type of expertise—different from that of their mothers, for example (Ronfard, Lane, & Harris, 2015). However, what leads to this realization: Their own experience with teachers, the endorsement of teachers by their family and culture, or a combination of both? This same question can be asked about children's perception of researchers and museum educators in museum settings: Do children perceive them as experts, and, if they do, why exactly? It seems plausible that older children will increasingly assume that the museum staff and the researchers that they meet during their visit have a particular type of authority or expertise. This developing understanding of the role played by cultural institutions and the people who work for them may lead children to develop expectations about their interaction with these individuals. As psychologists, we need to think more about whether these expectations impact the way that children perceive experimental tasks. As educators, we need to think more about how these expectations impact how children learn from their interactions with professional staff (e.g., museum educators or teachers) and with museum exhibits. In short, understanding the development of children's thinking about the role of institutions and their members and the inferences that these developments license has important implications for research and practice.

Lessons Learned From Evaluation

This museum–researcher partnership has been highly productive. As of August 2014, the authors were aware of at least 40 scientific articles using data collected in the Discovery Center that have been published in peer-reviewed academic journals. Many more are in preparation or under review. In addition to the numerous publications that highlight the effectiveness of the partnership, the MOS has conducted internal formative evaluation, and commissioned external summative evaluation of the Living Laboratory model. These evaluations are described in more detail in the following sections.

From 2007–2011, the Living Laboratory received generous support from the National Science Foundation[3] to develop and evaluate various mechanisms for communicating the research to museum visitors. The summative evaluation had two main goals: to explore whether Living Laboratory had any effect on adult visitors' understanding of research in developmental science, and to explore the impact of the Living Laboratory on participating MOS educators and research scientists. Below, we outline the evaluation process and highlight some findings of interest.

In 2008 and 2009, an independent evaluator conducted observations of child and adult visitor interactions with Living Laboratory researchers and MOS educators presenting hands-on research activities. The evaluator also observed adult visitors interacting with their children at two exhibits highlighting completed Living Laboratory studies (now permanent components installed in the Discovery Center) and surveyed visitors who interacted with any aspect of Living Laboratory (e.g., as research participants, users of staff-led activities, and/or users of exhibit components) as they exited the Discovery Center. Finally, the evaluator conducted a series of individual interviews and focus groups with researchers, MOS educators, parents whose children participated in the Living Laboratory, and the cohort of non-MOS museum professionals.

The evaluation documented measurable positive outcomes associated with both of the goals. Interaction with the Living Laboratory helped to enhance adult visitors' understanding of developmental science research. For example, of the 127 adult visitors surveyed, about half (49%) felt more informed of the methods used in developmental science research after visiting the Discovery Center.

Moreover, just over one third of the adults (37%) felt that their visit changed how they thought about how children learn. The survey findings were remarkably similar to the findings from individual interviews with adult visitors after their child participated in a Living Laboratory research study. About two thirds (62%) of adults felt that they understood the "process" of the research, and 42% of adults outlined research-related observations they would make while interacting with their child at home (Soren, 2009). Taken together, the Living Laboratory is an effective mechanism for stimulating adults' understanding of the value and process of developmental science research.

In addition to enhancing adult visitors' understanding of research, the Living Laboratory had positive impacts on both research partners and museum educators. To evaluate the impact of the Living Laboratory on researchers' ability to explain their questions and methods to a lay audience, both "novice" (new to the museum) and "expert" (collaborating with the Living Laboratory for many years) researchers were observed. These researchers also participated in focus groups. After a semester of regular interactions with museum educators and visitors, qualitative differences emerged in how researchers spoke with adult visitors. Living Laboratory researchers improve in their ability to use lay language to describe their research questions, to explain the method they use to conduct the research, and to highlight the practical implications of their work. In turn, museum volunteers and staff have expressed increased comfort in talking with visitors about child development, have changed their own approaches to teaching in the exhibit, and have noticed changes in the way parents interact with their children since the introduction of the Living Laboratory (Soren, 2009). By drawing on the strengths of both research scientists and museum educators and encouraging ongoing interactions between our teams, our emphasis on both the *process of science* and the *process of communicating science to the public* has resulted in a more effective educational program for museum visitors.

Lessons Learned Through Researcher–Museum Collaboration

We now turn to consider the intellectual gains from conducting research in a museum setting. Some of these are less obvious than others. At the Museum of Science in Boston, considerable effort has been invested in training researchers—training them to approach and talk to potential volunteer families and to convey the nub of a given experiment in a simple and accessible fashion. With some exceptions, researchers, especially at earlier stages in their career, tend to have a particular audience in mind when they think about their research: their mentor, their immediate colleagues, and readers of the journals in their field where they hope to publish their findings. When these young researchers make an oral presentation, it is typically in the context of a scientific conference or job talk. In those contexts, certain assumptions can be made about what notions will be shared between speaker and audience, what might be novel for the audience, and what will provoke discussion or probing questions. In that sense, then, conducting research in a museum setting has an educational impact on researchers. Describing a research project to museum staff or parents calls for different skills from those needed in narrower, professional settings. Some of those skills are obvious—an ability to avoid jargon and to provide a clear, concrete description of the procedure. Some, however, are less obvious. For example, museum educators would often like to get a sense of the larger agenda that guides a particular experiment, but researchers may take that larger agenda so much for granted that they do not think to articulate it. In addition, having watched their child answer an experimenter's questions, parents may want to know how their child compares to others. An explanation that the questions are not pass–fail but meant to illuminate children's thinking—especially the way of thinking that characterizes a given age group—can be reassuring for parents. In other words, researchers working in a museum have to present and explain what they are doing. They are prompted to set their study in a less narrowly scientific context—to think about how a nonspecialist audience will gauge its value and to give consideration to the personalities and families of the individual children who pass through a given study.

One of the most valuable parts of researchers' training at the museum consists of, with assistance from museum staff members, writing short and accessible descriptions of the studies that are conducted in the museum. These abstracts are meant to provide background information about the study, to introduce the research questions, to describe the experimental procedure, and to outline possible results and their implications. They are used to recruit and debrief parents and help to facilitate conversations between researchers and museum visitors. Writing these educational pamphlets requires several rounds of revisions to ensure that they are appropriate for museum visitors. In addition, annually, researchers present their findings to a diverse group of museum volunteers and staff, ranging from high-school students to scientists with advanced degrees. Following these presentations, attendees can ask questions of the researchers, allowing audience members the opportunity to learn from the presentation and from one another's questions, and providing an opportunity for researchers to hone their skills in addressing a diverse audience.

In summary, we believe there have been many benefits to such collaborations between academic researchers and museum educators. The most important aspect of the Living Laboratory is the ongoing communication and collaboration between the many stakeholders. It is only through sharing the strengths and challenges with the model that we have developed a viable and sustainable program.

Future Directions: The National Living Laboratory Project

Taken together, the Living Laboratory model has been highly productive for researchers, museum educators, and museum visitors. Because of the model's success, we were interested in extending our reach beyond the Boston area. The

National Living Laboratory[4] (NLL) project was designed to connect a growing community of museum and research professionals who are interested in bringing current research in child development to science centers, children's museums, and other informal education institutions.

Three additional sites were first approached: Maryland Science Center (Johns Hopkins University), Madison Children's Museum (University of Wisconsin–Madison), and Oregon Museum of Science and Industry (Lewis and Clark College). Each of these sites has adapted and implemented the Living Laboratory model in their own early childhood exhibitions. These three sites and the MOS work together as the NLL project team and now serve as *hub sites* for disseminating resources about the model to other museums and academic institutions (see Table 4.2 for a list of current museum–researcher partnerships). As the NLL

TABLE 4.2 Active Living Laboratory sites, March 2015. More than 230 informal learning and research institutions are represented by members of the NLL community (see www.livinglab.org/directory).

Current Living Laboratory Sites

Informal Education Institution	Research Institution(s)	Location
Museum of Science, Boston—HUB	Harvard University Boston University Boston College MIT Tufts University Boston Children's Hospital	Boston, MA
Stepping Stones Museum for Children	Yale University	Norwalk, CT
Connecticut Science Center	Wesleyan University	Hartford, CT
Sciencenter	Cornell University	Ithaca, NY
Explore and More Children's Museum	SUNY Buffalo	Buffalo, NY
Please Touch Museum	Monell Chemical Senses Center	Philadelphia, PA
Phipps Conservatory and Botanical Gardens	Carnegie Mellon University	Pittsburgh, PA
Da Vinci Science Center	Lehigh University	Allentown, PA
Maryland Science Center—HUB	Johns Hopkins University	Baltimore, MD
Delaware Children's Museum	Penn State Brandywine	Wilmington, DE
Children's Museum of Richmond	Virginia Commonwealth University	Richmond, VA
Madison Children's Museum—HUB	University of Wisconsin–Madison	Madison, WI

(Continued)

TABLE 4.2 (*Continued*)

Current Living Laboratory Sites

Informal Education Institution	Research Institution(s)	Location
Ann Arbor Hands-On Museum	University of Michigan	Ann Arbor, MI
Museum of Natural History at University of Michigan	University of Michigan	Ann Arbor, MI
Fort Worth Museum of Science and History	University of Texas	Fort Worth, TX
Children's Museum of Southern Minnesota	Gustavus Adolphus College	Mankato, MN
Children's Museum of Fond du Lac	Marian University, Wisconsin	Fond du Lac, WI
Oregon Museum of Science and Industry—HUB	Lewis and Clark College	Portland, OR
Science World	University of British Columbia	Vancouver, BC (Canada)
Children's Museum of Denver	University of Colorado Boulder	Denver, CO
KidsQuest Children's Museum	University of Washington	Bellevue, WA
Reuben H Fleet Science Center	University of California, San Diego	San Diego, CA
Science Factory Children's Museum and Exploration Dome	University of Oregon	Eugene, OR
Bay Area Discovery Museum	University of California, Berkeley	San Francisco, CA

project team has scaled up the Living Laboratory model at these and additional sites, a focus has been on how each site achieves their intended goals. In particular, we are learning about the ways that different institutions adapt the model based on their varying mission, organizational structure, community dynamics, and scale.

Evaluation has been a key tool to determine how the model can be implemented in different informal settings, with collaborating laboratories focused on a wide range of child development topics. At each site, it is important to maintain a high-quality visitor experience as well as an effective mutual professional development program for museum educators and researchers. While the nature of each museum–academic collaboration differs, formative evaluation during year one of the Living Laboratory's nation-wide implementation indicated that each of the three new sites adopted the model with a high degree of fidelity (Lussenhop, Cahill, & Lindgren-Streicher, 2013). Partnership logistics and mutual professional development programs at each site were iteratively improved throughout implementation, with a focus on ensuring effective interpretation of the research for visitors by both scientists and museum educators.

Summative evaluation of the national implementation (conducted by Evergreene Research and Evaluation, LLC) has three phases. Phase one (2012–2014) examined the short-term impacts of the Living Laboratory's mutual professional development program on the two professional audiences at each of the NLL hub sites (Beaumont, 2015). Phase two (2014–2015) examines the spread of the model from hub sites to new adopter sites—documenting the transition from "Potential Adopter" to "Partial Adopter," and from "Partial Adopter" to "Full Adopter" of the Living Laboratory model at informal learning institutions across the United States. Phase three (2015–2016) will examine broad national implementation of the Living Laboratory by drawing on Coburn's (2003) theory of scaling up to consider depth of change, shift in ownership, spread, and sustainability of the model across a variety of Living Laboratory partnerships (e.g., those at science centers, children's museums, and other informal learning settings; those collaborating with large research universities, small liberals arts colleges, or independent research institutions). The summative evaluation uses a mixed-methods approach, which includes direct observation of interactions among the three audiences, as well as surveys, interviews, and focus groups with researchers, museum educators, and adult visitors across sites.

The NLL project[5] also works to connect with museum and research professionals who have worked successfully in other collaborative models (for examples, see Callanan, 2012). Such a community has the potential to serve as the initial infrastructure for a national network of professionals interested in studying and promoting early learning across museum, lab, and home contexts. This community bridges academic research and educational practice and aims to develop and document best practices in scientist–museum collaborations across a variety of settings. By working together through common challenges and identifying opportunities, we hope to support the sustainability of Living Laboratory sites as well as other academic–museum collaborative projects that benefit scientists, museum professionals, and the general public.

Notes

1 *Broad Implementation: Creating Communities of Learners for Informal Cognitive Science Education* (PI: Kipling; NSF Award #1113648)
2 *A Participatory Model for Integrating Cognitive Research into Exhibits for Children* (PI: Kirshner; NSF Award #0714706)
3 *A Participatory Model for Integrating Cognitive Research into Exhibits for Children* (PI: Kirshner; NSF Award #0714706)
4 *Broad Implementation: Creating Communities of Learners for Informal Cognitive Science Education* (PI: Kipling; NSF Award #1113648)
5 For more information about the national initiative and to connect with the community, see www.livinglab.org

References

Bascandziev, I., & Harris, P.L. (2010). The role of testimony in young children's solution of a gravity-driven invisible displacement task. *Cognitive Development, 25*, 233–246.

Bascandziev, I., & Harris, P.L. (2011). Gravity is not the only ruler for falling events: Young children do not commit the gravity error if given rich perceptual information about the tubes mechanism. *Journal of Experimental Child Psychology, 109*, 468–477.

Beaumont, L. (2015). National Living Laboratory broad implementation—Year 2 and year 3 summative evaluation of *Creating Communities of Learners for Informal Cognitive Science Education* (NSF grant #1113648). Manuscript in preparation.

Callanan, M.A. (2012). Conducting cognitive development research in museums: Theoretical issues and practical applications. *Journal of Cognition and Development, 13*(2), 137–151.

Chen, E.E., Corriveau, K.H., & Harris, P.L. (2013). Children trust a consensus composed of outgroup members—But do not retain that trust. *Child Development, 84*, 269–282.

Coburn, C.E. (2003). Rethinking scale: Moving beyond numbers to deep and lasting change. *Educational Researcher, 32*(6), 3–12.

Corriveau, K.H., Chen, E.E., & Harris, P.L. (2015). Judgments about fact and fiction by children from religious and non-religious backgrounds. *Cognitive Science, 39*, 353-328.

Corriveau, K.H., Einav, S., Robinson, E.J., & Harris, P.L. (2014). To the letter: Early readers trust print-based over oral instructions to guide their actions. *British Journal of Developmental Psychology, 32*, 345–358.

Corriveau, K.H., Fusaro, M., & Harris, P.L. (2009). Going with the flow: Preschoolers prefer non-dissenters as informants. *Psychological Science, 20*, 372–377.

Corriveau, K.H., & Harris, P.L. (2015). Children's developing realization that some stories are true: Links to the understanding of beliefs and signs. *Cognitive Development, 34*, 76-87.

Corriveau, K.H., Kim, A.L., Schwalen, C., & Harris, P.L. (2009). Abraham Lincoln and Harry Potter: Children's differentiation between historical and fantasy characters. *Cognition, 112*, 213–225.

Corriveau, K.H., & Kurkul, K. (2014). "Why does rain fall?": Children prefer to learn from an informant who uses non-circular explanations. *Child Development, 85*, 1827–1835.

Fusaro, M., Corriveau, K.H., & Harris, P.L. (2011). The good, the strong, and the accurate: Preschoolers' evaluations of informant attributes. *Journal of Experimental Child Psychology, 110*, 561–574.

Harris, P.L. (2012). *Trusting what you're told: How children learn from others*. Cambridge, MA: Belknap Press/Harvard University Press.

Lane, J.D., & Harris, P.L. (2015). The roles of intuition and informants' expertise in children's epistemic trust. *Child Development, 86*, 919–926.

Lussenhop, C., Cahill, C., & Lindgren-Streicher, A. (2013). National Living Lab broad implementation—Year 1 formative evaluation of *Creating Communities of Learners for Informal Cognitive Science Education* (NSF grant #1113648). http://informalscience.org/images/evaluation/NLL%20HUb%20Site%20Implementation-Y1%20Formative%20Evaluation.pdf

Mercier, H., Bernard, S., & Clément, F. (2014). Early sensitivity to arguments: How preschoolers weight circular arguments. *Journal of Experimental Child Psychology, 125*, 102–109.

Morgan, T.J.H., Laland, K.N., & Harris, P.L. (2015). The development of adaptive conformity in young children: Effects of uncertainty and consensus. *Developmental Science, 18*, 511–514.

Ronfard, S., Lane, J.D., & Harris, P.L. (2015). Teaching and children's conception of teachers and mothers as sources of information. Manuscript submitted for publication.

Smith, C.E., Blake, P.R., & Harris, P.L. (2013). I should but I won't: Why young children endorse norms of fair sharing but do not follow them. *PLoS One, 8*(3), e5910.

Soren, B.J. (2009). Summative evaluation of *A Participatory Model for Integrating Cognitive Research into Exhibits for Children* (NSF grant #0714706). http://informalscience.org/images/evaluation/MOS_DC_Final_Summative_Evaluation_Report.pdf

5

BUILDING LEARNING

Narrating Experiences in a Children's Museum

Catherine A. Haden, Tsivia Cohen, David H. Uttal, and Maria Marcus

The Team

Catherine A. Haden is a professor in the Department of Psychology at Loyola University Chicago. She directs the Children's Memory and Learning Lab (www.luc.edu/childrensmemory/index.shtml). Her research centers on the ways children's conversational and narrative interactions with their caregivers can influence developmental changes in remembering, and learning about science and engineering.

Tsivia Cohen is associate vice president of Play and Learning Initiatives at Chicago Children's Museum. She was the PI of the National Science Foundation project, *Partnership for Playful Learners*, which led to the collaborations described in this chapter. Cohen's work includes the development of two opportunities for visitors to record reflective narratives about their museum experiences: the *Skyscraper Challenge* multimedia exhibit and *Story Hub*. In addition to coordinating research efforts at the museum, Cohen leads a team that designs and facilitates playful learning experiences for visitors.

David H. Uttal is a professor of psychology and education at Northwestern University. His research focuses on the development of spatial and symbolic thinking (see http://groups.psych.northwestern.edu/uttal/). He is president-elect of the Cognitive Development Society.

Maria (Mia) Marcus is a doctoral student in the developmental psychology graduate program at Loyola University Chicago. Her research examines linkages between parent–child conversations and children's STEM learning.

The Museum Setting
The mission of Chicago Children's Museum (CCM) is to improve children's lives by creating a community where play and learning connect. With 57,000 square feet of space, the museum features interactive exhibitions and public programming with engaging educational content focusing on literacy, science, math, visual and performing arts, and health. The museum includes novel, sensory, hands-on experiences and is on the vanguard of exploring approaches to making informal learning visible to the visitors it serves. In addition to a new tinkering workshop and a multifaceted construction exhibit, the museum includes immersive environments, water exploration, a dinosaur dig, and a fully equipped art studio. CCM is a popular destination for Chicago families and tourists, and attracts an audience from diverse backgrounds.

Memories stored as stories
are learning depositories.
Narratives
illuminate,
communicate.
They annotate.[1]

The poem provides a nice epigraph for this chapter in which we describe some of the fruits of our collaborative partnership that began about 10 years ago. It started when Tsivia Cohen (the author of the poem) and Chicago Children's Museum (CCM) were moving forward with several research initiatives in CCM's National Science Foundation (NSF) supported project, *Partnership for Playful Learners* (NSF grant #0452550). One important goal was to forge new connections between CCM and university researchers. Dr. Suzanne Gaskins of Northeastern Illinois University—already a CCM research partner—and Cohen reached out to a number of Chicago-area researchers, including Dr. Catherine Haden. Haden's research on parent–child conversations and memory development linked nicely with Cohen's focus on enhancing collaborative learning through narrative reflection (and Gaskin's research on individual and cultural variations in learning). We sowed the seeds of our partnership from these common interests. Over the years the partnership has grown to include Dr. David Uttal, and has gained additional NSF funding (NSF collaborative grant #1123411/1122712, *Engineering Learning*) to study how parent–child conversations during hands-on activities help children remember what they have learned and apply their learning to new situations. A number of Haden's and Uttal's graduate and undergraduate students and research assistants have been involved in the work over the years, including doctoral student, Maria Marcus.

TABLE 5.1 Levels of university researcher–museum partnerships at Chicago Children's Museum.

Partnership	Alignment	Relationship	Methods	Support (Amenities)
Collaborative	• Answers CCM's questions • Demonstrates impact • Informs practice	• Long-term faculty connection • Joint planning • Funded and/or symbiotic	• Primarily or exclusively in exhibits • May include: intervention video recording interviews/ surveys observation	• Museum staff member acts as liaison • Use of exhibits, research platform, equipment
Supported	• Addresses issues in fields of informal learning and/or child development	• Faculty led • Single study/ short-term	• In exhibits or in separate room • May include: intervention/ experi- mentation video recording interviews/ surveys	• Staff member as point-of-contact • Use of exhibits • Equipment, if funded
Cooperative	• Concerns issues and/ or interests consistent with the museum's philosophy and basic positions	• Student-led (with faculty advisor) • Short-term/ single study	• Observation only • Little to no interruption of visitor experience	• Staff member as point-of-contact

Defining Partnership

As illustrated in Table 5.1, the kinds of research that has been conducted at CCM can be characterized in terms of three levels of partnership. Because CCM was reaching out to, and being approached by, a number of researchers, the museum needed a system for thinking about and responding to different kinds of requests. Table 5.1 summarizes the system CCM developed. As shown in Table 5.1, with each type of partnership, the museum considers the costs and potential benefits of the research. For example, to what degree might the research provide answers or insights that inform practice within CCM, and to what degree might the research interfere with the visitors' museum experience? The level of partnership is determined by the degree of alignment between the research and the museum's interests and needs. The different levels are also associated with different kinds of relationships forged between the researchers and CCM, the research methods that are used, and the commitment of CCM staff time and amenities. With all levels of partnership, the museum works to ensure that anyone collecting data on the museum floor behaves in ways consistent with the museum's philosophy and practices. Depending on the research methodology, and especially the length of the study and the number of research assistants participating in data collection, the research team may receive face-to-face training sessions in addition to written materials delineating rules of conduct and museum policies.

This chapter focuses on some of the work that has been done through the *collaborative partnership* between Cohen, Haden, and Uttal. Other partnerships with CCM have included a recent *supported partnership* with Gentner, Levine, and colleagues (Gentner et al., 2015). Characteristic of work at the supported partnership level, Gentner et al.'s was a single, short-term study about children's spatial learning. In this case, it involved cordoning off a portion of an exhibit so that only the visitors participating in the research could access that space during data collection. Aspects of the findings from this study are interesting from the perspective of exhibit design (e.g., creating more opportunities to make comparisons across exhibit objects). But as is typical with this level of partnership, the potential for a connection between research and practice was not central to Gentner et al.'s work.

Other partnerships at the cooperative level have included thesis and dissertation projects by students from the many area universities. These projects have been brief both in terms of the amount of time the researchers were working at the museum, and time involvement by visitors. The studies typically entailed naturalistic observations in exhibits or during staff-facilitated programs.

We turn now to a description of some of the research we have done at CCM. We select these studies because they illustrate an important aspect of our collaborative partnership to date: understanding how narrative reflection can provide a tool for supporting learning and for understanding learning processes and outcomes. We begin with the theoretical and conceptual underpinnings for this focus on reflective narratives, and then describe several sets of findings from our analysis of narrative reflections recorded during families' visits to CCM and afterward.

Supporting Family Learning Through Narrative Reflection

Narrative reflection is the telling and sharing of experiences through conversations with others. In a museum setting, narrative reflection can support learning when visitors are given an opportunity to step back to think, consider, deliberate, ponder, and remember their museum-based experiences. CCM's interest in reflective narratives led to the development of exhibits and programs to support this practice, while concurrently motivating the museum to expand its research partnerships. Not only did the museum want to know more about how narrative reflection could enhance learning, but the staff and researchers saw the data-rich reflective narratives families were telling as a source of information about visitors' learning process and outcomes.

Our partnership has involved readings and discussions about the role reflective narratives can play in supporting learning. As we see it, reflective narratives are important in moving beyond reporting what happened, beyond information about actions, objects, and people involved in the event. Reflective narratives also include inferences, evaluations, reactions, explanations, and so forth, conveying why an experience was interesting, emotional, and meaningful (Fivush & Haden, 1997; Nelson & Fivush, 2004). Narrative reflection can continue for hours, days, and even years after an experience. Indeed, narrative reflection can be an integral part of the learning process, providing possibilities for *extended encoding* (i.e., additions to learning) beyond the duration of the activity itself (Haden, 2010; 2014). Importantly, for young children, the construction of reflective narratives is a social activity, one that is guided to a considerable extent by adult conversational partners who can play a critical role in helping children to talk about, organize, and represent their experiences in a narrative form.

CCM's emphasis on narrative reflection as a tool for family learning is well grounded in theory and research in psychology, education, learning sciences, and related areas. For example, sociocultural theory proposes that language allows for fundamentally new forms of thought (Vygotsky, 1978), such that as children talk with adults about experiences, it can change how children understand their experiences (Haden, 2010). Research on narrative in the memory development literature demonstrates long-term impacts of parent–child narratives about past events on children's abilities to think about and remember their experiences (see Fivush, Haden, & Reese, 2006, for a review). Narrative reflection is something many families naturally do following museum-based experiences. Indeed, studies that have tracked families longitudinally make clear that it can be very common for parents and children to tell narratives about their museum visit in the days and weeks afterward (e.g., Anderson, Storksdieck, & Spock, 2007; Rennie & Johnson, 2007; Stevenson, 1991).

Why might narrative reflection be especially important for learning from a visit to a children's museum? Consider that many museum exhibits are designed to encourage active, hands-on engagement with concrete objects to enhance early learning (Borun, 2002; Paris & Hapgood, 2002). But a critical requirement for learning is that children be able to use what they learn through object manipulation in new and different contexts (e.g., from museum to home and/or school). Narratives can help to meet this challenge of constructing understandings of experiences that are portable and relatable across contexts and time (Jant, Haden, Uttal, & Babcock, 2014). This is because narratives can make physical engagement with objects the topic of conscious reflection, and ultimately of long-term retention and generalization. Narrative reflection can facilitate the process of what Sigel (1993) called *distancing* and what Goldstone and Sakamoto (2003) called *concreteness fading*—learning to focus less on the specific objects and more on the general knowledge and concepts that can be learned from object manipulation (see also Uttal, Liu, & DeLoache, 2006). Narrative reflection can help make individual object-manipulation experiences part of a more integrated and cohesive cognitive representation. Opportunities for narrative reflection can add layers of understanding of events beyond what is available from direct hands-on engagement alone (Bruner, 1991; Fivush & Haden, 1997; Nelson &

Fivush, 2004). Our collaborative partnership has provided the opportunity to explore how these ideas about the ways narrative reflection can influence learning in a children's museum.

We have also found that narrative reflection can be an important tool for making learning visible to families, museum educators, and researchers. For families, reflective narratives can help caregivers recognize learning, which in turn, might put them in a better position to help their children make connections to new experiences after leaving the museum. For educators and researchers, reflective narratives can provide an organic method of viewing the learning process and learning outcomes during and after a museum visit. We turn now to describe how narratives have served as a tool for understanding learning processes and outcomes in our research at CCM.

Narrating Museum Experiences

We begin this section by describing the exhibit setting for the studies, and particularly, an exhibit component that CCM developed to provide families with the opportunity to engage in narrative reflection.

Skyline exhibit: A platform for research. The research we describe in this chapter took place in CCM's 2,500-square-foot permanent exhibition called *Skyline*. The exhibit features two building areas with construction systems that are analogous to one another in the way visitors connect pieces (e.g., righty tighty) and stabilize structures (triangles/diagonal bracing are the conceptual basis for both construction systems). As shown in Figure 5.1, in the *large-scale building area*, visitors can build with wood strut pieces of various lengths, triangular braces, real hardware, and tools (e.g., bolts, washers, nut drivers, goggles). As shown in Figures 5.2a and 5.2b, in the *small-scale building area*, visitors are invited to build the tallest and most stable building possible within a time limit—in what is called the *Skyscraper Challenge*—also using materials that include nuts, bolts, and triangular braces.

The *Skyline* exhibit allows observation of how children engage in the exhibit with their families, and ways they can learn simple but fundamental principles of engineering, including both specific concepts (e.g., cross-bracing, structural integrity) and general approaches to problem-solving. The exhibit is especially conductive to research examining family learning because of its built-in *research platform*. The research platform consists of multiple cameras and microphones that are integrated into both the large and small-scale building areas. The positioning of the recording equipment allows for less obtrusive observations of research participants (with their consent) than is possible using hand-held equipment. A control room adjacent to the exhibit provides a space where researchers can observe the interactions on the exhibit floor, and make adjustments to the equipment in the exhibit to improve the quality of the audio and video recordings. The large-scale area also features an accordion wall to close off one part of the exhibit

FIGURE 5.1 Large-scale building area.

for research projects that involve special presentations of materials or information to participants.

In the small-scale building area, the research platform includes the *Skyscraper Challenge*, a multimedia component (Figures 5.2a, 5.2b). The *Skyscraper Challenge* combines hands-on building and the creation of a *photo-narrative* record of the experience. As families build in the small-scale building area (see Figure 5.2a), a camera (see Figure 5.2b) snaps time-lapsed photos of them. When they finish building, families are prompted (in English or Spanish) to sit at a computer kiosk and choose six of the photos and tell personal reflective narratives about their experiences building (see Figure 5.2b). To facilitate the telling of the narratives, the computer can be programmed to ask six questions, one for each photo. The questions families are asked can be changed for research or other purposes. The different choices of prompts available for selection were developed in consultation with researchers who planned to use the space for their work.

Visitors' photo-narratives are audio recorded and can be accessed via CCM's website (https://qs1565.pair.com/chchmuse/), if families choose to review them at home.

Creating a built-in research platform, including the programmable photo-narrative component, is a tangible manifestation of CCM's commitment to research on ways to support family learning through narrative reflection. We turn now to describe three ways we have studied families' narrative reflections in the *Skyline* exhibit. We begin with a study that was conducted before the research platform and photo-narrative component were added to *Skyline*.

Reunion narratives. The first study we describe here was conducted in the large-scale building area in *Skyline*, pictured in Figure 5.1 (Benjamin, Haden, & Wilkerson, 2010). It involved several measures of learning and remembering, including one form of narrative reflection that we called *reunion narratives*. We wanted to design a semi-naturalistic measure of children's learning for the museum setting. We drew inspiration from what some families do naturally in

FIGURE 5.2 Skyscraper challenge (*a*) building area and (*b*) photo-narrative component.

FIGURE 5.2 (Continued)

museums: split up for a period of time, and then get back together and talk about what they have experienced while apart. The reunion narratives involved children telling about what they had done and learned in the exhibit to an adult from their visitor group who had not been present during building. Consequently, our sample in this study was limited in a particular way: We only recruited children who arrived to the museum with two adults in their visitor group, one adult with whom they built with and one adult to whom they told the reunion narrative with. Also, to meet requirements for our informed consent procedures, one of these adults needed to be a parent or guardian. Nevertheless, whereas some of the visitor groups included two parents, others included a parent and a grandparent, a parent and an aunt or uncle, or a parent and an adult friend.

We recruited the 121 visitors groups from CCM's general admission line. We simply extended invitations to visitors with a child in our target age range of 4 to 8 years old (the sample was on average six and a half years old). If they agreed to participate, we let the children choose which adult they wanted to build with in the exhibit. The other adult was given a pager and told we would ring when we wanted him/her to meet us at the exhibit.

The reunion narratives provided a lens on the children's learning. One question we had was whether the content of the learning evidenced in the reunion narratives would vary as a function of information the children and adults received prior to building together. More specifically, before visiting the exhibit, each child and his or her adult building partner were led to a multipurpose space adjacent to the museum entrance. There, the adults and children received building information (*Build—Only*), conversation information (*Talk—Only*), building and conversation information (*Build + Talk*), or neither (*Control*). The *building information* focused on how triangular cross-bracing makes structures strong. Parents and children engaged in a hands-on test of this engineering concept by adding cross-braces to two different wobbly structures made of materials from the exhibit. The *conversation information* focused on two conversational techniques: (1) *open-ended Wh-questions* such as *Who, What, Where, Why*, and *How* (e.g., *What is this called?; What is this used for?*); and (2) *associations* connecting the exhibit experience with what the child might already know (e.g., *Skyscrapers have lots of floors.*) or have experienced in the past (e.g., *This looks like what we saw at the Hancock Tower* [skyscraper in Chicago with triangle cross-bracing visible on the exterior of the building].). Dyads practiced these by generating several examples of each type of talk about a hard hat (e.g., *What is this? What does a workman use a hard hat for?*). Adults and children who received both sets of information received the conversation information immediately after the building information. The *control* group heard no information about building or conversation prior to visiting the exhibit (see Benjamin et al., 2010, for further details).

Once in the large-scale building area in the exhibit, all participants were told they could build whatever they wanted for as long as they wished. Across groups, the average time spent building was 27 minutes, although the Talk—Only information group did elect to build for longer than the other groups. We expected that dyads who received the building information would build sturdier buildings with more cross-braces in the exhibit. We further expected that dyads who received the conversation information would ask more *Wh*-questions and make more associations to prior experiences while building in the exhibit. Both of these hypotheses were confirmed. Additionally, even though they were not specifically prompted to do so, parents and children who received building information talked more about engineering (e.g., *"What should we do to make this stronger?"*; *"Why do you think this is wobbling?"*; *"We need to brace it."*) compared with families that did not receive building information. Also, children in both groups that received conversation information answered a greater percentage of their caregivers' questions (e.g., caregiver asks *"Why do you think this is wobbling?"* and child responds *"Because it needs more triangles."*) than did children in the other groups.

The reunion narratives occurred immediately after dyads finished building. The second adult from each visitor group met up with the child and together they looked at the structure the child had built. The adult was asked to pose *What*, *Why*, and *How* questions to elicit as much information as they could from the child about what the child had done and learned. These reunion narratives were short, about two and one-half minutes on average, but tended to be longest—up to 7 minutes—for children who had received both the building and conversation information. Across groups, the children received roughly the same number of adult prompts, about seven *Wh*-questions, on average. The children provided similar amounts of information in response to the adult's probes, about 11 pieces of information on average. When we looked at the content of what the children reported, we found that children in the Build + Talk group spoke more about engineering during the reunion narratives than did the Control group. This result suggested combined benefits of building and conversation information for what children learned and were able to report about their building experience. Also, compared with their peers, children in the Build + Talk information group tended to provide the most information *spontaneously*. In other words, the children who received building and conversation instructions were highest in reporting information that was not in direct response to an adult's questions. Overall, the combination of engineering and conversation information, and the conversations it engendered during the building activity, led children in the Build + Talk group to demonstrate greater understanding and learning from the experience in their reunion narratives.

Memory narratives. In the study just described, we also invited our participants to take home audio recorders to use to record two memory narratives about their museum visit (Benjamin et al., 2010). These reflective narratives provided an opportunity to observe what children and adults remembered and how they may have elaborated their understanding of their museum experience days and weeks afterward (see Haden, 2014, for discussion).

Of the families in the museum-based portion of the study, 35 (29%) made recordings 1 day and 2 weeks after the museum visit. Interestingly, children in the Build + Talk group recalled significantly more information in memory narratives 2 weeks following the museum visit than they had after a 1-day delay. Put another way, children in the combined engineering and conversation information group demonstrated *hypermnesia*, or an increase in reporting over time. The children in the Build + Talk group went from spontaneously reporting about 10 unique pieces of information about their experiences 1 day after the visit to reporting more than 13 unique pieces of information spontaneously after a 2-week delay. As with the reunion narratives, again it seemed that the engineering information combined with the conversation information helped children understand the building experience in a way that made it more available for retrieval and reporting over time (see Jant et al., 2014, for similar results).

Different activities and interaction patterns at home might help explain the increases we observed in children's memory narratives over time. We aim in future work to understand how the information we provide to families in the museum may be important in beginning a chain of interactions that fostered substantial learning and generalization across contexts and over time. Despite the difficulties with obtaining the memory narrative data in particular, we believe they can provide important insights into what is retained about a museum visit, and the conditions that foster memory and the extension of learning beyond the museums' walls (see also Jant et al., 2014; and Marcus, Haden, & Uttal, 2015; for further illustration of this point).

Photo-narratives. We have also used the *Skyscraper Challenge* multimedia component in CCM's construction exhibit (described previously) to study families' narratives about their building activities (Haden et al., 2014). In one of these studies, the participants were 130 families with children averaging six and one-half years old. They were recruited at the entrance to the *Skyline* exhibit. Before building, some families were engaged in a specially-designed facilitated education program that was conducted in the exhibit. The program was modeled after the kinds of on-the-exhibit-floor educational activities staff conduct daily at museums to personalize and enhance visitors' learning experiences.

There were two program groups, both of which interacted with "Inspector Sturdy"—a research assistant dressed in a white lab coat and carrying a triangle-shaped magnifying glass, who played the role of a building inspector. As illustrated in Figure 5.3, the *Build-Only* program involved Inspector Sturdy asking families to test out the sturdiness of two model skyscrapers built of exhibit materials, one that was sturdy and one that was wobbly. Inspector Sturdy pointed out how differences in the ways that triangles were used in these buildings either did or did not serve to brace the structures. Inspector Sturdy summarized the building information with a sign with photos of the two model structures and in writing, "Triangles make strong buildings." that was left in plain view while the families built. Families in the Inspector Sturdy Build + Talk program experienced the same program as the Build—Only group. In addition, Inspector Sturdy encouraged Build + Talk families to ask *What?*, *Where?*, and *How?* questions. Inspector Sturdy showed families in this program group a second sign with example *What* ("What could we do to make this stronger?"), *Why* ("Why do you think this is wobbling?"), *Where* ("Where could we put a triangle piece?"), and *How* ("How can we make this stand up?") questions, indicating that families who had asked each other questions like these had built stronger buildings. This sign was placed alongside the "Triangles make strong buildings." sign while the families in the Build + Talk program built.

As expected, families who received the Inspector Sturdy program built the strongest buildings with the highest ratio of pieces that braced the structure to total pieces. Parents who received the Inspector Sturdy Build + Talk program asked double the number of *Wh*-questions compared with parents who did not receive this program. Moreover, during the building activity, without explicit instruction to do so, parents who received the Build + Talk program demonstrated the most talk about the scientific method (*"First we need to plan, then we can start to test our ideas."*), technology (*"How can we use the nuts to hold the bolts in place?"*), engineering (*"Remember, righty tighty, lefty loosey."*), and math (*"We need 4 pieces to start."*). Similar to the study described earlier (Benjamin et al., 2010), just receiving information about building from Inspector Sturdy was not enough to increase the amount of talk about science, technology, engineering, and math (STEM) while building. Rather, it was the prompts to ask more questions that also increased the amount of talk about STEM.

Examining the photo-narratives families told about their building experiences also revealed learning from the Inspector Sturdy program (Haden et al., 2014). We scored what the families said in response to the six narrative prompts provided

FIGURE 5.3 Inspector Sturdy building information.

to them (one prompt for each photo taken while building). We awarded points for mentions of one of five categories of STEM talk. Children who received the building information, with or without the conversation information, discussed a greater range of STEM-related content in the photo-narratives. Adults in the Inspector Sturdy Build + Talk group also tended to mention the most categories of STEM in their contributions to the photo-narratives. Overall, the photo-narratives prove to be a valuable way to assess some of what children took away from their building interactions with their parents in a manner that was a part-and-parcel of the museum exhibit experience. Also, from our perspective, these reflective narratives may have helped families make their experiences more understandable and meaningful as well, thus serving to enhance learning in the exhibit. It would be interesting to know if the experience of telling a photo-narrative predicts later retention and use of learned information in different contexts over time. This is among the future plans for extensions of our collaborative partnership, which we discuss in the next section.

Mutual Benefits and the Future of Connecting Research and Practice

Reflecting on mutual benefits. Our examination of narrative reflection has yielded information about learning processes and outcomes that has implications for research and practice at CCM and beyond. The work also illustrates the value of "front loading" caregivers with critical information when prior knowledge or experience is lacking. The research findings are leading CCM to consider how programs and exhibit components might be put in place that enable caregivers to be more successful in guiding interactions and otherwise supporting their children's learning and narrative reflection. As we appreciate what these research findings can tell us, we also recognize some limits we have faced in making connections between research and practice. For example, one study (Benjamin et al., 2010) involved providing families with information outside of the target exhibit, which is out of character for an open-ended, flexible children's museum. In contrast, the Inspector-Sturdy-facilitated program (Haden et al., 2014) was designed to convey information to visitors once they were in the exhibit and do so in a playful way that made it more like natural interactions facilitators already have with visitors in the museum. Since the completion of the study, the museum has developed a drop-in program based on the Inspector Sturdy intervention. Although museum staff are sometimes provided scripts or sample language when receiving training on new programs, facilitators are not expected to memorize or even mimic these texts. The closely followed scripts the researchers used have given way to more spontaneous exchanges between families and museum staff when this program is used in practice. Other elements of the *Skyline* exhibit today connect with outcomes of the research, including newer signage illustrating

Wh-questions and associations. *Skyline* also has a demonstration station (see Figure 5.4) that mirrors the type of activities families in the building information group participated in in the Benjamin et al. study.

These contributions notwithstanding, as we reflect on the *mutual* benefits to our collaborative partnership, they are not principally connected to individual research findings. For example, research is increasingly part of the culture at

FIGURE 5.4 Demonstration station in the *Skyline* exhibit.

CCM, referenced in conversation and used in decision-making. The partnership has raised capacity within the museum to access and understand relevant research and the nature of empirical evidence. It has also permitted detailed conversational analyses and tracking of visitors that simply would not be possible without the research. This work puts CCM in the position to talk about mechanisms by which learning occurs through parent–child conversations, and to demonstrate long-term impacts of a museum visit. The research is helping us understand conditions (e.g., design components, information, conversation patterns) that can set in motion a learning process that extends beyond the duration of an activity in an exhibit. Also, CCM attracts a large and varied visitorship, and families participating in our research have closely matched the diverse demographics of the families CCM serves. This has meant that the research at CCM has involved participants than might not ordinarily visit the researchers' university laboratories, including, for example, more people of color and more fathers. But even more important, by involving families from diverse backgrounds in our research, we are building a knowledge base for the practice of informal education that can be broadly applied.

Other benefits of our work together come from the meetings and day-to-day exchanges that occur between museum professionals and researchers. It is exciting for the graduate and undergraduate students who are assisting in the research at the museum to discover the real-world utility of their work. They also learn that research with children and families in natural settings can be very different (and messier!) than in the laboratory. Several students have commented on how they have gotten better at communicating about research in an accessible way as a function of their interactions with families and museum staff at CCM. The short distances between our two universities and CCM allows face-to-face meetings between Cohen, Haden, and Uttal, in addition to regular email contacts, which in turn, facilitate our partnership. Although sometimes a challenge to schedule, these meetings are time well-spent, often serving as the launch point for ideas for new projects and even collaborative grant proposals.

We also see benefits from our joint engagement in dissemination activities. When we have learned something we think families can use, it is posted to the museum's website and/or through social media. We also share information that has resulted from our discussions, readings, and research findings at periodic workshops for educators and staff at CCM, and at twice-yearly meetings with individuals from more than a dozen Chicago-area informal learning institutions and universities (the Chicago Cultural Organizations Research Network). These and other dissemination activities (e.g., professional conference presentations, journal articles) mean that we communicate what we are learning together with others through academic and nonacademic venues. Overall, we can count the benefits of our collaborative partnership in many ways. We believe ultimately our union will benefit hundreds of thousands of annual visitors to CCM, and informal learning research and practice broadly.

Future directions. Our collaboration to date has inspired a range of new ideas, and provides a strong foundation for us to move forward together. Central to our approach to future activities will be the use of *design-based research* (Collins, Joseph, & Bielaczyc, 2004; Sandoval & Bell, 2004) that can directly inform practice. Design-based research is well suited to studying informal learning in museums because it allows us to iteratively test how design plays out in practice and understand what is happening in the richness of family interactions. Design-based research will enable us to identify and study practices that museum educators and designers at CCM feel will foster family conversations and children's learning. We will combine this research approach with so-called *blitz* coding (Callanan, 2012). Detailed conversational analysis takes time, but we will supplement this effort with faster, live, simplified scoring of families' hands-on and conversational behaviors. This will allow us to provide more immediate feedback to the team about how variations in practice affect learning to inform design planning.

One specific area of future work extends our focus on the importance of reflective narratives for learning. Given the success of the photo-narrative component, CCM is creating a new opportunity for narrative reflection in the museum. This new multimedia component, *Story Hub: The Mini Movie Memory Maker*, is being developed with funding from the Institute of Museum and Library Services. *Story Hub* will allow visitors to create and share reflective narratives about their choice of the museum's current exhibits. In conjunction with the design process, we have been working together to think about how this component will be used in research that can inform practice (something that was also true with the development of the photo-narrative component). The flexibility of this component creates opportunities for us to understand what exhibits families choose to talk about and how they elect to report about different exhibit experiences. For example, we can examine questions the team has about how these narratives vary in content (e.g., science, math, collaboration/teamwork) and structure (e.g., collaboratively constructed, told mostly by the caregiver or by the child) by exhibit and across different families, and what implications this has for learning.

We will also continue our efforts to understand the kinds of engagement with materials and conversations in the museum that can support exhibit experiences that live beyond the museums' walls. Like the photo-narratives in the *Skyscraper Challenge*, the narratives constructed in the *Story Hub* can be reviewed via the CCM website before and after visitors leave the museum. We plan to work together to examine what happens when families access these narratives at home, and if retrieving and reviewing these narratives engenders further discussion and elaboration of the museum-based experience days and weeks after the event. This will potentially lead to new ways of understanding how learning transcends a single museum visit.

In conclusion, when we think about what has made our collaborative partnership work, several things standout. First and foremost is having one dedicated, even passionate person on each end of the partnership who can make the time to find common ground. At the museum, there needs to be someone with a vision for the benefits of connecting research and practice who can also create a social milieu among museum professionals to recognize the potential for mutual gains. On the researcher side, there has to be a commitment to research that is use-inspired (e.g. Newcombe et al., 2009) that is conducted in a way that can really lend itself to implementation in museum practice. There also has to be a mutual willingness to set aside time to meet together. Big *ah-hah* moments can happen when we get together, such as when we discuss closely held, conflicting assumptions (e.g., that children learn best when left to explore on their own vs. the benefits of guided play), or share findings from research and practice and explore how they line up. Our partnership has worked better when there has been early shared planning for activities with the right people around the table, so that our work is focused on questions that everyone wants and needs answered, and best leverages our collective expertise. Impacting what is happening in a museum setting requires practitioners and researchers who are willing to discuss and determine together interventions and methodology that can advance research and practice.

Fortunately, the few practical challenges we have faced in communication, time, and setting priorities have been outweighed by the mutual benefits. We look forward to continuing to iterate our collaborative partnership. As we refine our approach, we aim to better understand and improve conditions for young children's informal learning, and to draw still closer reciprocal relations between research and practice.

Acknowledgements

The preparation of this chapter was supported in part by the NSF under collaborative grant #1123411/1122712. Some of the work presented was funded under NSF grant #0452550 to the Chicago Children's Museum. We are grateful to Dr. Suzanne Gaskins for initiating our partnership, and Rick Garmon for keeping the partnership humming on a day-to-day basis.

Note

1 Poem by Tsivia Cohen, presented to CCM's Board of Directors and staff, 2014.

References

Anderson, D., Storksdieck, M., & Spock, M. (2007). Understanding the long-term impacts of museum experiences. In J.H. Falk, L.D. Dierking, & S. Foutz (Eds.), *In principle, in practice: Museums as learning institutions* (pp. 197–215). Lanham, MD: AltaMira Press.

Benjamin, N., Haden, C.A., & Wilkerson, E. (2010). Enhancing building, conversation, and learning through caregiver-child interactions in a children's museum. *Developmental Psychology, 46*(2), 502–515. doi: 10.1037/a0017822

Borun, M. (2002). Object-based learning and family groups. In S.G. Paris (Ed.), *Perspectives on object-centered learning in museums* (pp. 245–260). Mahwah, NJ: Lawrence Erlbaum Associates.

Bruner, J. (1991). The narrative construction of reality. *Critical Inquiry, 18*(1), 1–21.

Callanan, M.A. (2012). Conducting cognitive developmental research in museums: Theoretical issues and practical considerations. *Journal of Cognition and Development, 13*(2), 137–151. doi: 10.1080/15248372.2012.666730

Collins, A., Joseph, D., & Bielaczyc, K. (2004). Design research: Theoretical and methodological issues. *Journal of the Learning Sciences, 13*(1), 15–42. doi: 10.1207/s15327809jls1301_2

Fivush, R., & Haden, C. (1997). Narrating and representing experience: Preschoolers' developing autobiographical recounts. In P. van den Broek, P.A. Bauer, & T. Bourg (Eds.), *Developmental spans in event comprehension and representation: Bridging fictional and actual events* (pp. 169–198). Hillsdale, NJ: Erlbaum.

Fivush, R., Haden, C.A., & Reese, E. (2006). Elaborating on elaborations: Role of maternal reminiscing style in cognitive and socioemotional development. *Child Development, 77*(6), 1568–1588. doi: 10.1111/j.1467–8624.2006.00960.x

Gentner, D., Levine, S., Ping, R., Isaia, A., Dhillon, S., Bradley, C., & Honke, G. (2015). Rapid learning in a children's museum via analogical comparison. *Cognitive Science, 7*(2), 1–17. doi: 10.1111/cogs.12248

Goldstone, R.L., & Sakamoto, Y. (2003). The transfer of abstract principles governing complex adaptive systems. *Cognitive Psychology, 46*(4), 414–466. doi: 10.1016/S0010–0285(02)00519–4

Haden, C.A. (2010). Developmental science in children's museums. *Child Development Perspectives, 4*(1), 62–67. doi: 10.1111/j.1750–8606.2009.00119.x

Haden, C.A. (2014). Interactions of knowledge and memory in the development of skilled remembering. In P. Bauer, & R. Fivush (Eds.), *Wiley-Blackwell handbook on children's memory, vol. 2.* (pp. 809–835). New York: Wiley-Blackwell.

Haden, C.A., Jant, E.A., Hoffman, P.C., Marcus, M., Geddes, J.R., & Gaskins, S. (2014). Supporting family conversations and children's STEM learning in a children's museum. *Early Childhood Research Quarterly, 29*(3), 333–344. doi:10.1016/j.ecresq.2014.04.004

Jant, E.A., Haden, C.A., Uttal, D.H., & Babcock, E. (2014). Conversation and object manipulation influence children's learning in a museum. *Child Development, 85*(5), 2029–2045. doi: 10.1111/cdev.12252

Marcus, M., Haden, C.A., & Uttal, D.H. (2015). *STEM learning and transfer in a children's museum and beyond its walls.* Manuscript under review.

Nelson, K., & Fivush, R. (2004). The emergence of autobiographical memory: A social cultural developmental theory. *Psychological Review, 111*(2), 486–511. doi:10.1037/0033–295X.111.2.486

Newcombe, N.S., Ambady, N., Eccles, J., Gomez, L., Klahr, D., Linn, M., Miller, K., & Mix, K. (2009). Psychology's role in mathematics and science education. *American Psychologist, 64*(6), 538.

Paris, S.G., & Hapgood, S.E. (2002). Children learning with objects in informal learning environments. In S.G. Paris (Ed.), *Perspectives on object-centered learning in museums* (pp. 37–54). Mahwah, NJ: Lawrence Erlbaum.

Rennie, L.J., & Johnson, D.J. (2007). Understanding the long-term impacts of museum experiences. In J.H. Falk, L.D. Dierking, & S. Foutz (Eds.), *In principle, in practice: Museums as learning institutions* (pp. 197–215). Lanham, MD: AltaMira Press.

Sandoval, A., & Bell, P. (2004). Design-based research methods for studying learning in context: Introduction. *Educational Psychologist, 39*(4), 199–201. doi: 10.1207/s15326985ep3904_1

Building Learning **103**

Sigel, I.E. (1993). The centrality of a distancing model for the development of representational competence. In R.R. Cocking, & K.A. Rennigner (Eds.), *The development and meaning of psychological distance* (pp. 141–158). Hillsdale, NJ: Erlbaum.

Stevenson, J. (1991). The long-term impact of interactive exhibits. *International Journal of Science Education, 13*(5), 521–531. doi: 10.1080/0950069910130503

Uttal, D.H., Liu, L.L., & DeLoache, J.S. (2006). Concreteness and symbolic development. In L. Balter, & C.S. Tamis-LeMonda (Eds.), *Child psychology: A handbook of contemporary issues* (2nd ed.; pp. 167–184). Philadelphia, PA: Psychology Press.

Vygotsky, L.S. (1978). *Mind in society: The development of higher psychological processes.* Cambridge, MA: Harvard University Press.

6

LEARNING ABOUT SCIENCE AND SELF

A Partnership Between the Children's Museum of Manhattan and the Psychology Department at New York University

Marjorie Rhodes and Leslie Bushara

The Team

Marjorie Rhodes is an associate professor of psychology in the Psychology Department at New York University. Rhodes directs the Conceptual Development and Social Cognition Lab at NYU. Her research seeks to reveal how children build the basic conceptual frameworks that they use to make sense of the social and biological worlds.

Leslie Bushara is the Children's Museum of Manhattan's (CMOM) deputy director for education and guest services. She oversees the development, management, and evaluation of educational programs at CMOM and its community partners. Bushara served as project director for two Institute of Museum and Library Services-funded projects, including CMOM's national health initiative and the development and testing of a new health education professional development program for childcare providers in NYC. She has extensive experience in curriculum and manual development and was the lead developer for CMOM's early childhood education curriculum *Working with Young Children*, and the *EatPlayGrow* curriculum developed with the National Institutes of Health.

The Museum Setting

CMOM has been serving families across New York City for over 40 years and is a nationally recognized leader in the field of informal education. Over 350,000 people visit CMOM every year, with 50,000 free visits per year for low-income families. CMOM is at the forefront of improving early learning for children and families in New York City and beyond. Through its interactive exhibitions and educational outreach programs at the museum and in the community, CMOM combines early childhood education, health education, arts and science education, and cultural awareness to stimulate children's learning from an early age, providing a foundation to support formal education. It serves as a trusted resource to parents, educators, and caregivers, and as a key collaborator for public and private initiatives.

Children's museums provide powerful contexts for children to learn about the world around them. Museums excel at creating places where children can learn about physics, biology, literacy, art, and math through their own creative actions. By providing spaces where parents and children come together to learn, museums also create opportunities for children to learn about themselves and their families. For example, by spending an afternoon with their parents at the museum, children might learn that their parents value science—or find art exciting—and therefore that these are activities that they should value as well. Through a research partnership between New York University and CMOM, we have been developing new approaches to support the potential of children's museums to provide experiences that leave children not only with new understanding, but also with increased enthusiasm for learning and stronger beliefs in their own capacities to succeed.

CMOM—A Long History of Commitment to Research

CMOM, located on the upper west side of Manhattan, is at the forefront of improving early learning for children and families in New York City and beyond. In its efforts to develop new, creative programming to support early learning, CMOM has built strong partnerships with New York University (NYU), Barnard College, Hunter College School of Public Health, and the National Institutes of Health. These partnerships have enabled CMOM to develop exhibits and programming based on the latest research on how children learn. To illustrate, *PlayWorks* is one of CMOM's major exhibit spaces for young children (ages 0–5) and is designed to facilitate the development of children's physical, social, math, art, science, literacy, and problem-solving abilities via play. *PlayWorks* was developed with leading experts in child development, including Kathy Hirsch-Pasek (Temple University), Dorothy Singer (Yale University), and Lois Bloom (Columbia University). Key goals of *PlayWorks* are to provide experiences that allow parents and children to engage together in learning, to make visible to parents and caregivers how children learn through play, to motivate parents and caregivers to seek and find everyday opportunities that nurture play and a love of learning, and to create an environment that supports the skills needed for school readiness. By working with research partners, CMOM designed *PlayWorks* to meet these goals in an effective, evidence-based manner.

As further illustration of CMOM's commitment to research, as part of its three year, *EatSleepPlay Health Initiative*, CMOM partnered with the National Institutes of Health and a national advisory board of medical and health experts to develop and test *EatPlayGrow*—the first ever federally approved early childhood health curriculum for use with children five years and younger. As part of this initiative, CMOM also worked with its advisory board to translate the latest research on health and early childhood obesity into family-friendly activities and educational experiences as part of a new health exhibit at the museum: *EatSleepPlay: Building Health Every Day!*

As an organization dedicated to improving early childhood learning and health, CMOM also provides a vital link between leading researchers and families most in need. It has become a sought-after partner for researchers and academic institutions looking to study children and families in informal learning settings. As a result, CMOM is in a unique position to bring the pressing needs and challenges facing families today to the attention of researchers through its on-the-ground "feedback loop" with community partners, to develop new programs and resources that directly respond to these needs, and to bring the latest research affecting children and families directly to the community.

Although CMOM has a long history of involvement with research, CMOM's commitment to research took on a more central and visible role within the daily life of the museum in 2010, when CMOM partnered with Dr. Marjorie Rhodes, associate professor of psychology at New York University, to establish an active child development research laboratory within the museum. This laboratory is located in classroom space adjacent to the *PlayWorks* exhibit and provides families visiting the museum with an opportunity to take part in and learn about current research on early cognitive and social development.

The laboratory is open four days per week at CMOM. During these times, undergraduate and graduate student researchers from Rhodes's lab approach families within the *PlayWorks* exhibit and invite them to participate in research. Interested families are brought to the private testing space and are given detailed information about the research so that they can decide whether or not to participate. To date, over 5,000 families have participated in research via this onsite laboratory. Due to CMOM's extensive outreach activities, and because CMOM serves a diverse audience daily, the sample of participating families reflects the diversity of New York City. Opening this lab at CMOM had two immediate positive consequences for the research process—it increased the efficiency of research and allowed researchers to include a more diverse sample of families than would otherwise visit a laboratory at a research university. Studies conducted via this lab at CMOM have composed the basis of 15 academic publications, two grants from the National Science Foundation, and over 25 conference and colloquia presentations. In this chapter, we will discuss several of the key findings from this research program that have been particularly important to growing the NYU–CMOM partnership.

Another key benefit of the research lab at CMOM is that it provides training for student researchers in communicating with parents and the broader community. Students are trained to treat each research session as an opportunity to provide educational outreach to families. Student researchers explain the purpose of the study that the family participated in and its implications for child development, and also answer parents' questions about related areas of cognitive and social development. Students also provide a newsletter detailing other recent research findings and their implications. Thus, another key benefit of conducting basic research within CMOM is the potential for rapid dissemination of important research findings to the public.

Research Overview

The research conducted via the lab at CMOM examines basic questions in early cognitive and social development. Consistent with CMOM's educational approach, Rhodes's research takes the perspective that children are active explorers of their environments who build *theories* to try to make sense of the world around them. Children's theories are not as detailed or elaborate as scientific theories, but their beliefs are theory-like in that they provide children with a conceptual framework for understanding and predicting events in their daily lives. A major goal of much cognitive development research is to determine how children construct these theories, how theories change across development, and the implications of children's theories for their beliefs and behavior. In turn, CMOM is interested in designing environments that optimally support the development of children's theories.

Much of the research in the lab at CMOM integrates theories and methods from developmental, cognitive, and social psychology to examine how children develop theories of the **social world** (e.g., Rhodes, 2013). Young children have the task of making sense of a rich and complicated social environment. During the early childhood years, children's conceptual and social development is focused on trying to understand questions such as: "What kinds of people are there in the world?," "What kind of person am I?," "What sorts of behaviors do people 'like me' do?," and "What are we good at?" How children answer these questions has broad implications for their development—including for their tendencies to engage in social stereotyping, for their interests and persistence in various subjects at school, and for their friendships and pro-social behaviors. Thus, an important goal of Rhodes's research has been to examine how these beliefs—or theories—about the social world develop. In particular, we test how children's intuitive conceptual biases (Rhodes, 2012; Rhodes, Gelman, & Karuza, 2014) interact with cultural input (Chalik & Rhodes, 2014; Diesendruck, Goldfein-Elbaz, Rhodes, Gelman, & Neumark, 2013) to shape the development of their understanding of the social world (Rhodes, 2013).

Our recent research has revealed that subtle features of the language that children hear powerfully shape children's understandings of the social world. Through Rhodes's conversations with Bushara and other educators at CMOM, we have discovered that these findings have clear implications for educational practice. Thus, a major focus of our current partnership is developing and testing new applications based on this research. We will next describe our research framework, questions, and findings in some detail, before moving on to describe current and future plans to build on this research to develop and evaluate new educational practices.

Rhodes's previous research has focused on *psychological essentialism*—a pervasive conceptual bias to construe some categories (e.g., *tigers*, *girls*, *scientists*) as reflecting highly coherent and distinct kinds whose members are fundamentally similar to each other and different from nonmembers (Medin & Ortony, 1989). Psychological essentialism entails thinking that membership in these categories is determined by a stable, intrinsic property, which causally constrains observable behaviors. For example, essentialist beliefs about *tigers* entail thinking that whether an animal is a tiger is determined by birth and stable, that tigers are fundamentally similar to each other and different from non-tigers, and that an animal—once born a tiger—will inevitably grow up to be ferocious (Gelman, 2003). In this way, category membership is viewed as a natural and unchangeable part of an individual's identity that fundamentally shapes who they are and what they can grow up to be.

In the case of animal categories—like tigers—psychological essentialism may facilitate conceptual development and knowledge acquisition by allowing children to overlook superficial differences (e.g., between orange and white tigers) and focus on the properties that category members share. Yet essentialism reflects a biased, inaccurate picture of the world; most categories—even biological species—have no real essences (Leslie, 2013), species change over time in ways that essentialist thinking does not allow (Gelman & Rhodes, 2012; Shtulman & Schulz, 2008), and category members often vary more widely from each other than essentialism implies. Indeed, essentialist thought—particularly its emphasis on within-category homogeneity and stability over time—interferes with people's understanding of the mechanisms that drive evolutionary change (Shtulman & Schulz, 2008) as well as with normative reasoning regarding how properties are distributed across categories (Rhodes & Brickman, 2010).

Psychological essentialism underlies children's understanding not only of the biological world of animals and plants, but of certain components of the social world as well. For example, by age 4 years, essentialist biases shape how children understand gender categories. Thus, they expect girls to be fundamentally similar to each other and different from boys, and that being born a girl, for example, means that a baby will inevitably grow up to prefer tea sets to toy trucks (Taylor, Rhodes, & Gelman, 2009). In this way, essentialism leads children to overlook the role of culture and experience in contributing to gender differences and can contribute to social stereotyping. Further, as essentialism begins to shape how children understand social groupings—including those based on gender, race, ethnicity, or religion—essentialism can lead to the development of prejudice and discrimination (Allport, 1954). Finally, by shaping how children understand their own category memberships, essentialism influences children's beliefs about their own interests and capabilities (Dweck, 2006).

As Rhodes discussed research on essentialism with Bushara and other educators at CMOM, we began to consider that essentialism might shape not only how children understand animal species and social categories based on gender or race, but might also be relevant to how children and parents think about categories like *scientists, mathematicians,* or *artists.* For example, essentialist beliefs about scientists would entail thinking that scientists are deeply different from nonscientists, that scientists are born—not made, and that whether one is a scientist or not is stable across development. In our conversations, we thought that these types of beliefs might be quite prevalent among young children and their parents, as we informally observed that families often discuss these categories in essentialist terms—terms that imply that some children are scientists and others are artists, for example, and that imply that a child's true nature is something to discover (rather than something that develops over time).

We became very interested in the possibility that essentialism might shape how children understand achievement-relevant categories in particular, such as scientists or mathematicians, because it is easy to see how such beliefs could be problematic and maladaptive. Such essentialist beliefs imply that one's ability to succeed in science, for example, is determined not by the effort that one puts in, but by whether one is born with some necessary quality (e.g., something like innate talent). Further, these beliefs could lead children to interpret any setbacks—an inevitable part of science, in particular—as evidence that they are in the "nonscientist" group, leading to disengagement. Finally, such beliefs could be particularly problematic for girls, as these beliefs could combine with gender-stereotypes to yield the conclusion that *only boys are capable scientists* (e.g., Dweck, 2006; Leslie, Cimpian, Meyer, & Freeland, 2015). An essentialist conception of scientists can be contrasted with one in which scientists are viewed as being just like anyone else, but have chosen to put time and effort into the study of science.

We decided to study these issues directly in our child development research laboratory at CMOM. In particular, we wanted to address (a) whether children hold essentialist beliefs about science, (b) if such beliefs interfere with achievement-relevant behaviors, and (c) what might cause (or prevent) the development of these beliefs. We planned a series of studies to address these questions, with the goal of taking what we learned, along with other related work in the field (Dweck, 2006; Gelman & Heyman, 1999; Cimpian & Markman, 2011), to develop new educational strategies that might prevent the development of essentialist beliefs about science and increase children's achievement-relevant behaviors.

To begin to address these questions, we drew on Rhodes's and others' previous research examining the features that lead children to adopt essentialist beliefs about particular categories (Gelman, Ware, & Kleinberg, 2010; Rhodes, Leslie, & Tworek, 2012). Although psychological essentialism is a pervasive conceptual bias, children do not construe all categories in an essentialist manner. For example, children have more essentialist beliefs about animals (e.g., *dogs*) than artifacts (e.g., *tables*; Rhodes & Gelman, 2009a, 2009b; Rhodes et al., 2014) and they hold

more essentialist beliefs about certain social categories (e.g., *gender*) than others (*sports teams*; Diesendruck et al., 2013; Rhodes & Gelman, 2009a). Rhodes's
previous research at CMOM discovered that cultural input—in the form of
language—guides **how children map** general essentialist beliefs onto particular
categories they encounter in their environment.

In particular, Rhodes' research at CMOM indicated that *generic
language*—language that refers to abstract kinds (e.g., "tigers have stripes")—guides
children to apply essentialist beliefs to particular categories (Rhodes et al., 2012;
also Gelman et al., 2010). On this account, generic language does not *create* essentialist thought. Essentialist beliefs reflect basic conceptual biases, and go far beyond
the content of generic language itself. For example, there is no explicit content
in the sentence "tigers have stripes" that communicates that being a tiger is a
matter of innate and immutable category membership. Yet children conclude that
new categories have those features after fairly limited exposure to such generics,
as described below. Thus, children seem to have abstract expectations that *certain*
categories in their environment reflect essential kinds and then rely on linguistic
cues to determine *which* categories have this structure. Because generic language
communicates regularities regarding abstract kinds, children assume that categories described with generic language are the kinds of categories that are coherent
and causally powerful enough to support such generalizations (Cimpian & Markman, 2011; Gelman et al., 2010; Gelman & Heyman, 1999; Leslie, 2008; Rhodes
et al., 2012).

To illustrate how we came to these conclusions—which provided the direction
for our current work on how children think about achievement categories—we
will briefly describe the methods and findings of Rhodes et al., 2012. In that
project, we introduced children to an entirely new, arbitrary grouping of people
called "Zarpies." First, an experimenter read an illustrated book that presented the
novel category via 16 individual pictures of Zarpies, one per page, each displaying a unique property. The 16 Zarpies were diverse with respect to race, sex, and
age, so that children could not map the category onto any group for which they
might already hold essentialist beliefs. By condition, children heard the property
on each page described either with generic language (e.g., "Look at this Zarpie!
Zarpies climb fences") or nongeneric language (e.g., "Look at this Zarpie! This
Zarpie climbs fences"). None of the properties involved any negative qualities.
The experimenter read the book two times to the child and then assessed children's essentialist beliefs about Zarpies.

Rhodes et al. (2012) found that, in the nongeneric condition, children did not
hold essentialist beliefs about Zarpies after exposure to the book. That is, although
they learned the category "Zarpie," they did not expect Zarpie properties to
be determined by birth, they did not expect individuals to do certain behaviors *because* they are Zarpies, and they did not expect all Zarpies to share either
the properties mentioned in the book or other new properties. In contrast, the
generic condition significantly increased the likelihood of these essentialist beliefs

among preschool-age children. This study thus revealed that a small amount of generic language led children to apply essentialist beliefs to a new category, when they would not otherwise do so, confirming that subtle linguistic cues have powerful consequences on conceptual development.

Current Research Direction: Essentialist Beliefs about Scientists

Building on this previous research, as well as Rhodes's and Bushara's conversations, we considered that hearing certain forms of language about scientists, such as "Let's be scientists!," "Scientists explore the world!," "Scientists conduct experiments"—language that our informal observations suggested was quite common in input to children—might elicit maladaptive essentialist beliefs about science (and likewise, "Mathematicians solve problems" would elicit essentialist beliefs about math, for example). For example, during a review of museum messaging, CMOM discovered it was communicating to the public using generic language, and that museum staff routinely used generics when speaking to children and families. For example, CMOM offered programs titled "Little Scientists" or "Little Artists," which, as described above, inadvertently implies to children that there are categories of scientists and nonscientists or artists and nonartists. These informal observations are also consistent with the findings of more formal child development research, which has revealed that parents and educators often use generics when communicating with young children (Gelman, Coley, Rosengren, Hartman, & Pappas, 1998; Gelman, Goetz, Sarnecka, & Flukes, 2008; Gelman, Taylor, & Nguyen, 2004; Pappas & Gelman, 1998).

Whereas Rhodes's previous research, observations within the museum, and conversations between NYU researchers and CMOM educators all supported these hypotheses, no study had specifically tested whether hearing generic language about scientists elicits essentialist beliefs about science or undermines children's achievement behavior. Thus, to test if this is the case, we conducted a new study in our laboratory at CMOM. This new study was inspired directly by our observation that generics about science are commonly used in early childhood education programs—an observation that resulted from our research taking place onsite at CMOM. If Rhodes had been conducting the research on generic language only via an on-campus laboratory at NYU, the possibility of examining essentialist beliefs about categories such as "scientist," "artist," or "mathematician"—or the role of generic language in the development of these beliefs—would not have come up as an important research direction. Further, the design of the study and the research protocol were inspired by discussions with CMOM educators about how generic language might be used—or avoided—in actual science lessons with children and their caregivers.

To test whether generic language about science elicits essentialist beliefs and interferes with children's achievement behaviors, we conducted a study to examine children's responses to generic vs. nongeneric language about science. First, children (ages 4–5) were randomly assigned to hear one of two introductions to science. One introduction began, "Today we are going to *be scientists* and play a science game!" and continued with language such as "Scientists explore the world and discover new things!" The other introduction began, "Today we are going to *do science* and play a science game!" and continued with language such as, "Doing science means exploring the world and discovering new things." The content of the two introductions was identical; what varied was the type of language used to describe science.

After hearing one of the two introductions, children were asked to complete a science game. For this game, children were asked to sniff covered cups and predict the contents from a range of alternatives. Children completed two easy trials that presented obvious smells and only two possible answer choices. For example, children would smell a covered cup that contained an orange slice, and were asked to guess whether the cup contained an orange or some chocolate. Children then completed two challenging trials intended to elicit incorrect guesses, so that children would experience setbacks. This part of the design was very important because it is particularly upon the receipt of negative feedback that essentialist beliefs become problematic (see Bryan, Master, & Walton, 2014; Cimpian, Arce, Markman, & Dweck, 2007). It is straightforward to see why this is the case—if children have the essentialist perspective that people either are scientists or nonscientists, then they may happily believe they are in the scientist group (perhaps even receiving a boost in motivation from seeing the world this way; Bryan et al., 2014) until they encounter a setback. A setback, however, provides some evidence that they may not be in the scientist group after all (Cimpian et al., 2007; Cimpian & Markman, 2011), a possibility that is particularly problematic if one holds essentialist beliefs, as essentialism implies that whether one is a scientist or not is fixed—not something that can be changed by effort. In contrast, if one does not hold essentialist beliefs about scientists, but instead views science as involving activities and skills that one can build over time, then setbacks are not nearly as threatening. Thus, it is after setbacks—an inevitable part of learning to do science or developing any new skill—that we would expect essentialist beliefs to become problematic.

For this reason, we presented children with two cups to make guesses about for which the smells were misleading. For example, children sniffed a cup that contained a sponge that had been soaked in lemon juice, and were asked to guess whether it contained a lemon, a sponge, or one of three other possible options. For each trial, the experimenter marked whether the child's guess was right or wrong with either a green check or a red "x"—to make the fact that a setback had occurred clear to children. After these four trials, children were asked if they wanted to keep playing the science game or if they wanted to do something else. If children chose to continue, they were given a new cup to smell and asked to make a guess, and then once again, they were asked if they would like to continue playing or do something else. Children could choose to complete up to 10 additional rounds of the science game. How many rounds the children chose to complete serves as a measure of their persistence. After they finished the science game, children were asked to complete a measure of their essentialist beliefs about science, a measure assessing their beliefs about their own performance during the "science game," and a measure of their more general attitudes about science. These questions were completed via a standardized interview with an experimenter.

We found that the generic language increased essentialist beliefs about science among both boys and girls. For example, children in this condition were more likely to say that someone who is good at science has always been good at science and will always be good at science, and less likely to say that someone who has difficulty with science can improve their abilities. Yet, these essentialist beliefs undermined only girls' (not boys') persistence, self-evaluations, and attitudes toward science. Girls in the "be a scientist" condition chose to complete fewer subsequent rounds of the science game (showing less persistence) than girls in the "do science" condition. They also evaluated their own performance more negatively and reported relatively more negative attitudes toward science. The language condition did not interfere with boys' performance or attitudes. Thus, we found that small and subtle differences in language can interfere with female students' achievement in science.

Building on This Research to Develop New Educational Approaches

We believe that our research on the role of generic language in shaping the development of essentialist beliefs about scientists has the potential to address a critical social problem. The persistent underrepresentation of girls and women in science limits their opportunities for cognitive development as well as for economic attainment (Beede et al., 2011). Prior work has extensively documented that girls' beliefs about their own capacity for success in science critically contribute to this problem (Dweck, 2006; Eccles & Wigfield, 2002). For example, girls who view success as determined by stable, innate talent are more likely to withdraw following setbacks and refrain from taking on challenging problems (Cain & Dweck, 1995; Smiley & Dweck, 1994). These beliefs are often better predictors of children's success than their own actual preparation or ability level. For example, across the transition to junior high school, as coursework becomes more challenging, girls who believe that success depends on effort do better in math than those with similar previous grades who view success as dependent on talent (Blackwell, Trzesniewski, & Dweck, 2007). Similar effects have been found at the college-level; controlling for SAT scores, female students who view success as dependent on innate ability begin to underperform relative to their male peers in challenging classes, yet female students who view success as dependent on effort do not (Dweck, 2006).

Further, recent work suggests that gender gaps at the Ph.D. level are predicted by the extent to which a discipline is perceived as requiring raw, innate talent, with women attaining a smaller percentage of Ph.D.s in such fields—many of which are in STEM (Leslie, Cimpian, Meyer, & Freeland, 2015). Notably, these effects emerge already in early elementary school-aged girls (6- and 7-year-olds): when a new activity was described as being "for hardworking kids," girls and boys showed an equal level of interest in it, however, when it was described as being "for smart kids," girls showed significantly less interest in it than boys (Leslie, Cimpian, & Meyer, 2013). Thus, beliefs that success in some disciplines requires innate talent—and assumptions that such disciplines are "for boys"—emerge in early childhood and persist to the Ph.D. level, and perhaps beyond. Considerable stability has been found in children's beliefs about the role of talent in determining success beginning in early childhood (Cain & Dweck, 1995; Eccles, Wigfield, Harold, & Blumenfeld, 1993; Smiley & Dweck, 1994; Wigfield et al., 1997; Wigfield & Eccles, 2002); given the pernicious consequences of these beliefs, it is important to identify the processes that lead to their formation.

With our research, we have identified an underlying conceptual bias—psychological essentialism—that gives rise to the belief that talent determines success. Suppose that one believes that scientists form a highly distinctive category of person, such that their common outward properties are grounded in their shared, inherent natures. Since scientists as a category are marked by their common ability to do science, it makes sense (from an essentialist perspective) to suppose that this ability must be grounded in something underlying, stable, and inherent—in something like *innate, unchangeable talent*. Viewed from this perspective, the belief that science (or math, etc.) requires a special innate gift is a natural corollary of psychological essentialism. Even more importantly, we have identified a modifiable feature of cultural input—generic vs. nongeneric language—that shapes whether children develop these beliefs.

Building on the basic research described above, as well as other related research in the field (Cimpian et al., 2007; Cimpian & Markman, 2011; Dweck, 2006; Gelman et al., 2010; Leslie et al., 2015), NYU and CMOM are currently working together to launch a national project—*The Language Effect*—to test whether training educators to avoid generic language can increase children's—and especially girls'—engagement and achievement in science. The goal of this project is to translate the latest research on the power of language to support the development of more adaptive beliefs during early childhood into practical applications for museums. To do this, we plan to adapt selected existing science lessons to include strategies for communicating more effectively with children and families in museum settings. For this new project, CMOM builds on a strong track record of success adapting existing curricula to new audiences and for new purposes. For example, CMOM adapted the National Institutes of Health's (NIH) *We Can!* obesity prevention curriculum (originally designed for children ages 8 and older) for use with children ages 5 and younger. Through five studies with low-income families in New York and New Orleans, CMOM evaluated and confirmed the efficacy of this *EatPlayGrow* curriculum, and the NIH recently approved it as an obesity prevention curriculum for use with young children. Additionally, CMOM established a network of federal agencies and community-based organizations to disseminate its curricula, including the NIH, *Let's Move!*, Association of Children's Museums, First Book, Family Place Libraries, National Head Start Association, and New York City Department of Health, all of whom are now distributing *EatPlayGrow* at no cost.

Building on these previous experiences, we plan to create *The Language Effect Resource Manual*, which will combine STEM lessons with a comprehensive research report and training materials. We plan to evaluate and refine the manual through a series of pilot programs that will engage educators in specialized training and test for the effectiveness of this training on educational practices—and ultimately on child engagement and achievement. Through these evaluations, we will test whether the manual's materials are successful in training museum educators in how to use language to support child development effectively. After this pilot and evaluation research, we hope to disseminate the manual to museums and libraries across the country through our national network of dissemination partners.

A key component of the *Language Effect Resource Manual* will include ten STEM lessons that have been modified to avoid generic language about science or math. Each lesson will begin with an introduction for educators, which reminds them about the importance of avoiding generic language. For a sample introduction, see Table 6.1.

TABLE 6.1 Sample introduction for educators.

Often, early science programming makes use of generic language, such as "Let's be scientists!," "Scientists discover things about the world!," "Let's be good scientists and make guesses about what we might find!" This language is intended to foster excitement about learning, yet recent research suggests that it has the opposite effect. Children interpret these examples of *generic language* as meaning that there is a group of people who are scientists, but also a group of people who are *not* scientists. This way of thinking about science—that some people do it and some people do not—is threatening because it suggests that whether someone is good at science or not is dependent on inherent abilities. Generic language makes children less willing to persist and try new things, out of concern that they might discover that they are in fact in the "nonscientist" category. Instead of using this kind of generic language, the following lesson uses *effort-focused* language. This *effort-focused* language describes science as something that everyone can learn to do, instead of as an identity-category in which some people are members. This *effort-focused* language is integrated into each component of the lessons and is intended to lead children to view doing science as something they can learn through practice and effort.

Additionally, for each activity in the lesson, there will be educator prompts alerting them to the subtleties of effort-based language and avoiding generic language. For an excerpt from a sample lesson, which is based on similar activities as we used in the scientist experiment described above, see Table 6.2.

To evaluate *The Language Effect Resource Manual*, we plan to conduct a series of studies with museum educators. Through these evaluations, we will test whether providing training in using effort-based—instead of generic—language effectively leads to changes in educators' language use, whether educators are able to

TABLE 6.2 Excerpt from the sample lesson, *The Nose Knows*.

In this lesson, *The Nose Knows*, children (ages 3–5) will learn about the sense of smell while engaging with the practices and vocabulary of science, most specifically: observe, predict, check, and discourse. This lesson will provide children with opportunities to use new vocabulary and engage with new science practices throughout the science activity, read aloud, and art extension.

Observe

Introduce the word "observe" to the children, ask the children if they know what the word means. Accept all answers, and then explain that to observe means to use the senses to get information about an object. Tell the children that they have five senses, ask them if they can name any of the senses, (sight, hearing, smell, taste, and touch). Tell the children that today they are going to observe using their noses, their sense of smell.

Generic language (not recommended)	Effort-focused language (recommended)
Today we are going to be scientists! Scientists explore the world and discover new things.	*Today we are going to do science. Doing science means exploring the world and discovering new things.*
An important part of being a scientist is observing what's around you. Do you know what observe means?	*An important part of doing science is observing what's around you. Do you know what observe means?*
Observing means using your senses to learn what's around you! What are the five senses?	*Observing means using your senses to learn what's around you! What are the five senses?*
Scientists can use their five senses to learn about the world. They can use their eyes to see; their ears to hear; their noses to smell; their mouths to taste; and their hands to touch!	*When people are doing science, they can use their five senses to learn about the world. They can use their eyes to see; their ears to hear; their noses to smell; their mouths to taste; and their hands to touch!*
Today we are going to be scientists by using our noses to smell what's around us.	*Today we are going to do science by using our noses to smell what's around us.*

Tell the children to breathe in through their nose and notice any smells in the room. Ask the children, "What do you smell when breathing in the air in the room?" (Accept all answers. Most children will note smelling the scent of the air freshener.) Point to where the air freshener is across the activity area and ask the children, "How were we able to smell something so far away?" (Accept all answers). Explain to the children that the scent from the air freshener traveled through the air and into their nose, the smelly item does not have to be right in front of us in order for our nose to smell it.

implement the lessons with the intended language, and whether these changes influence child engagement during the target lessons. To answer these questions, we plan to use multiple research methodologies, including surveys, observations, coding of natural language samples, and interviews. We are also developing ways to provide education for parents on language use via these new science lessons that will be offered through the *PlayWorks* exhibit, as well as through the development of new signage throughout the museum.

Long-Term Benefits of the CMOM–NYU Partnership

Research conducted by NYU in the lab at CMOM revealed that remarkably subtle features of language powerfully shape children's beliefs about the social world (Rhodes et al., 2012). Conducting this research within the museum inspired a new research direction, in which we discovered that these subtle linguistic cues also shape how children think about themselves and their own capacities for success in science. After four years of conducting lab-based studies on these research questions, we are now ready to translate our findings into practice by training educators on effective language use and evaluating our approach. We hope that this will provide a powerful new approach for addressing gender gaps in science achievement and interest, and that it will also provide a strong test of the power of language to shape child development outside of laboratory environments. What began as a partnership built on a shared goal—the goal of understanding how child development happens and how we can best support it—has turned into a research collaboration that is poised to advance both the fields of developmental psychology and informal education. Further, we hope that our approach will serve as a model for future collaborations between researchers and museums, and will be an important step toward bridging the gap between the latest research and direct implementation with children and families.

References

Allport, G. (1954). *The nature of prejudice.* Oxford: Addison-Wesley.

Beede, D., Julian, T., Langdon, D., McKittrick, G., Khan, B., & Doms, M. (2011). Women in STEM: A gender gap to innovation (ESA issue brief # 04–11). Washington, DC: US Department of Commerce.

Blackwell, L.S., Trzesniewski, K.H., & Dweck, C.S. (2007). Implicit theories of intelligence predict achievement across an adolescent transition: A longitudinal study and an intervention. *Child Development, 78,* 246–263.

Bryan, C., Master, A., & Walton, G. (2014). "Helping" versus "being a helper": Invoking the self to increase helping in young children. *Child Development. 85*(5), 1836–1842.

Cain, K.M., & Dweck, C.S. (1995). The relation between motivational patterns and achievement cognitions through the elementary school years. *Merrill-Palmer Quarterly, 41,* 25–52.

Chalik, L., & Rhodes, M. (2014). The communication of naïve theories of the social world in parent-child conversation. *Journal of Cognition and Development.* doi: 10.1080/15248372.2014.949722

Cimpian, A., Arce, H.C., Markman, E.M., & Dweck, C.S. (2007). Subtle linguistic cues affect children's motivation. *Psychological Science, 18,* 314–316.

Cimpian, A., & Markman, E. (2011). The generic/non-generic distinction influences how children interpret new information about social others. *Child Development, 82,* 471–492.

Diesendruck, G., Goldfein-Elbaz, R., Rhodes, M., Gelman, S., & Neumark, N. (2013). Cross-cultural differences in children's beliefs about the objectivity of social categories. *Child Development, 84,* 1906–1917. PMCID: PMC3714352

Dweck, C.S. (2006). Is math a gift? Beliefs that put females at risk. In S.J. Ceci & W. Williams (Eds.), *Why aren't more women in science* (pp. 47–55). Washington, DC: American Psychological Association.

Eccles, J.S., & Wigfield, A. (2002). Motivational beliefs, values, and goals. *Annual Review of Psychology, 53,* 109–132.

Eccles, J., Wigfield, A., Harold, R.D., & Blumenfeld, P. (1993). Age and gender differences in children's self-and task perceptions during elementary school. *Child Development, 64,* 830–847.

Gelman, S.A. (2003). *The essential child: Origins of essentialism in everyday thought.* New York: Oxford University Press.

Gelman, S.A., Coley, J.D., Rosengren, K.S., Hartman, E., & Pappas, A. (1998). Beyond labeling: The role of maternal input in the acquisition of richly structured categories. *Monographs of the Society for Research in Child Development, 63,* 1–148.

Gelman, S.A., Goetz, P.J., Sarnecka, B.W., & Flukes, J. (2008). Generic language in parent-child conversations. *Language Learning and Development, 4,* 1–31.

Gelman, S.A., & Heyman, G.D. (1999). Carrot-eaters and creature-believers: The effects of lexicalization on children's inferences about social categories. *Psychological Science, 10,* 489–493.

Gelman, S.A., & Rhodes, M. (2012). "Two-thousand years of stasis": How psychological essentialism impedes evolutionary understanding. In K.S. Rosengren, S.K. Brem, E.M. Evans, & G.M. Sinatra (Eds.), *Evolution challenges: Integrating research and practice in teaching and learning about evolution* (pp. 3–21). New York: Oxford University Press.

Gelman, S.A., Taylor, M.G., & Nguyen, S.P. (2004). Mother-child conversations about gender: Understanding the acquisition of essentialist beliefs. *Monographs of the Society for Research in Child Development, 69,* 1–142.

Gelman, S.A., Ware, E.A., & Kleinberg, F. (2010). Effects of generic language on category content and structure. *Cognitive Psychology, 61,* 273–301.

Leslie, S.J. (2008). Generics: Cognition and acquisition. *Philosophical Review, 117,* 1–47.

Leslie, S.J. (2013). Essence and natural kinds: When science meets preschooler intuition. *Oxford Studies in Epistemology, 4,* 108–166.

Leslie, S.J., Cimpian, A., & Meyer, M. (2013). Gender gaps and conceptions of ability. Symposium conducted at the Biennial Meeting of the Society for Research in Child Development, Seattle, WA.

Leslie, S.J., Cimpian, A., Meyer, M., & Freeland, E. (2015). Expectations of brilliance underlie women's representation across academic disciplines. *Science, 347,* 262–265.

Medin, D., & Ortony, A. (1989). Psychological essentialism. In S. Vosniado & A. Ortony (Eds.), *Similarity and analogical reasoning* (pp. 179–195). New York: Cambridge University Press.

Pappas, A., & Gelman, S.A. (1998). Generic noun phrases in mother-child conversations. *Journal of Child Language, 25,* 19–33.

Rhodes, M. (2012). Naïve theories of social groups. *Child Development, 83,* 1900–1916.

Rhodes, M. (2013). How two intuitive theories shape the development of social categorization. *Child Development Perspectives, 7,* 12–16.

Rhodes, M., & Brickman, D. (2010). The role of within-category variability in category-based induction: A developmental study. *Cognitive Science, 34,* 1561–1573.

Rhodes, M., & Gelman, S.A. (2009a). A developmental examination of the conceptual structure of animal, artifact, and human social categories across two cultural contexts. *Cognitive Psychology, 59,* 244–274. PMCID: PMC2770000

Rhodes, M., & Gelman, S.A. (2009b). Five-year-olds' beliefs about the discreteness of category boundaries for animals and artifacts. *Psychonomic Bulletin & Review, 16,* 920–924. PMCID: PMC2829667

Rhodes, M., Gelman, S.A., & Karuza, J.C. (2014). Preschool ontology: The role of beliefs about category boundaries in early categorization. *Journal of Cognition and Development, 15,* 78–93. PMCID: PMC3940442

Rhodes, M., Leslie, S.J., & Tworek, C. (2012). Cultural transmission of social essentialism. *Proceedings of the National Academy of Sciences, 109,* 13526–13531.

Shtulman, A., & Schulz, L. (2008). The relation between essentialist beliefs and evolutionary reasoning. *Cognitive Science, 32,* 1049–1062.

Smiley, P.A., & Dweck, C.S. (1994). Individual differences in achievement goals among young children. *Child Development, 65,* 1723–1743.

Taylor, M.G., Rhodes, M., & Gelman, S.A. (2009). Boys will be boys; cows will be cows: Children's essentialist reasoning about gender categories and animal species. *Child Development, 80,* 461–481. PMCID: PMC2837505

Wigfield, A., & Eccles, J.S. (2002). The development of competence beliefs, expectancies for success, and achievement values from childhood through adolescence. In A. Wigfield & J. Eccles (Eds.), *Development of achievement motivation* (pp. 91–120). New York: Academic Press.

Wigfield, A., Eccles, J.S., Yoon, K.S., Harold, R.D., Arbreton, A.J., Freedman-Doan, C., & Blumenfeld, P.C. (1997). Change in children's competence beliefs and subjective task values across the elementary school years: A 3-year study. *Journal of Educational Psychology, 89,* 451–469.

7

DEVELOPING MIND LAB

A University–Museum Partnership to Explore the Process of Learning

David M. Sobel, Susan Letourneau, and Robin Meisner

The Team

David M. Sobel is a professor in the Cognitive, Linguistic, and Psychological Sciences Department at Brown University. His research focuses on how children engage in causal reasoning, how children learn from others, and how children understand concepts in social cognition like pretending and intentionality.

Susan Letourneau holds a collaborative research position, working with the exhibits team at Providence Children's Museum and the Causality and Mind Lab at Brown University. She conducts research and evaluation in the museum on children's thinking and learning, and contributes to the development of exhibit materials and resources that make learning through play more visible.

Robin Meisner is the exhibits director at Providence Children's Museum. She oversees the design, creation, assessment, and operation of the museum's play and learning environments. Her work at the museum also includes managing exhibit-based research and evaluation efforts and partnerships with outside researchers in cognitive development.

The Museum Setting

The mission of Providence Children's Museum is to inspire and celebrate learning through active play and exploration. The museum creates and presents interactive exhibits and programs designed to serve the needs of children, ages 1 to 11, and the adults who care for them. The museum is committed to being accessible and responsive to all families—culturally, physically, and economically. Nationally recognized, the museum is a leading advocate for the importance of self-directed play in children's healthy development. The museum welcomes parents as active participants in their children's learning, and works to increase awareness of the ways in which children and families learn.

In this chapter, we describe the collaboration between the Causality and Mind Lab (CML) at Brown University and Providence Children's Museum (PCM). As institutions with distinct missions—one to advance the understanding of cognitive development, and the other to inspire and celebrate learning through active play and exploration—the dynamics of the partnership have evolved over the past 10 years toward meeting the unique interests and needs of both partners.

As Callanan (2012) outlined, collaborations between cognitive development researchers and museums can take a variety of forms, and the partnership between CML and PCM has looked different both over time and based on the goals of a given project. CML and PCM began considering a collaboration in 2003 when the museum approached Sobel about the possibility of evaluating an after-school program that brought children from community centers servicing low SES families in Providence to the museum to foster engagement in the learning process. Practitioners at PCM were interested in knowing more about the efficacy of the program. Upon observing the program, Sobel realized that he did not have the expertise to design procedures that would definitively assess children's conceptions of learning and whether those conceptions changed through participation in the program. Nevertheless, this question lingered for Sobel and inspired a line of research on children's conceptions of learning as a mental state in CML.

Fast-forward to late 2007 when researchers from CML approached the museum to start collecting data for lab-based studies at PCM by recruiting visitors from the exhibits. This initial arrangement was informal. A researcher (and eventually a small research team) would be stationed at a table in a corner of an exhibit or in an open activity room, recruiting families to participate in controlled experiments. There was no signage indicating the researchers' presence, nor was there any regular interaction between the researchers and museum staff.

Wishing to formalize the interaction and learning from colleagues at the Museum of Science, Boston (see Corriveau et al., this volume), PCM branded the partnership as *Mind Lab* in 2010 in order to provide more structure to the research happening at the museum and increase its educational impact. Researchers from CML were given regular shifts to recruit families to participate in or simply observe ongoing studies driven by the researchers' interests and to answer questions about the purpose and implications of the work. Researchers also discussed their research and engaged in professional development with museum staff and volunteers at annual meetings and informal brown bag sessions. With space at a premium, Mind Lab researchers floated among different locations in the museum, some more conducive to research than others, and none able to support permanent communication with visitors about the work. The partners found certain mutual benefits to this level of collaboration: Hosting research from cognitive development laboratories helped PCM share information with staff and visitors about children's learning and development, and how scientists study these processes; being at the museum helped CML find willing research participants and disseminate its work to the general public.

Inspired by the depth of collaboration between University of California, Santa Cruz and Children's Discovery Museum of San Jose (see Callanan et al., this volume), partners at CML and PCM began thinking about where their individual interests and needs might overlap. When considering why they should further the partnership, CML was interested in expanding the broader impacts of their work—not only to disseminate current research findings and the importance of developmental science to the general public, but also to apply ideas that emerged from cognitive development investigations to informal learning settings. The museum's interest centered on an existing effort to make the learning that happens through children's play and exploration more noticed and appreciated by caregivers, staff, volunteers, and children themselves. Besides sharing information about CML research with staff and families, PCM also wanted to move toward working with research partners to study the types of learning experiences that happen naturally in the museum, rather than in controlled experimental situations.

Through conversation and the process of applying for funding, a certain synergy emerged around understanding and supporting children's developing metacognition. A project proposal to the National Science Foundation (NSF) included the specific aim of strengthening the partnership between CML and PCM by incorporating two parallel lines of work: CML-led studies were designed to investigate children's developing metacognitive and scientific reasoning abilities, with the goal of understanding how young children begin to conceptualize the process of learning. And museum-led studies explored children's learning and behavior at the exhibit space and caregivers' understandings of how children think and learn through play at the museum, with the ultimate goal of developing tools and techniques to support children and caregivers in reflecting on the learning that occurs at the museum.

CML was awarded funding for this project (*The Emergence of Diagnostic Reasoning and Scientific Thinking*, NSF #1223777) in 2012. This funding allowed CML and PCM to deepen their partnership in concrete ways: It created a shared researcher position between the two institutions, allowing research studies in Mind Lab and cycles of research (led by museum-based researchers), evaluation, and development in museum exhibits to take place around a common topic. The funding also allowed for the creation of a permanent and dedicated space for the Mind Lab program, which has increased the ongoing research presence at the museum in several ways. First, it provides a more visible site for research at the museum, allowing families to learn about and participate in active research studies. Second, it contains exhibit labels (aimed primarily at caregivers) that describe research topics in child development, allowing caregivers to learn about research on children's learning and its importance in their lives. Finally, it houses a hands-on activity that relates to CML's research on causal learning (designed in collaboration between CML and PCM), which provides opportunities for children to learn by exploring and experimenting and encourages caregivers to reflect on their children's learning.

Research at the museum now exists more visibly, and includes CML and other university-led studies in Mind Lab, PCM-led research taking place in museum exhibits about children's learning and families' experiences, and iterative cycles of development and evaluation of activities and labels based on shared research findings. CML and PCM are still developing the partnership—to this end, we (the authors of this chapter, representing the research team currently involved in the collaboration) think of much of the work we do as cooperative, or "parallel play"—simultaneous ongoing investigations conducted by both groups with some overlap in structure and personnel, finding common ground in our interests and goals, and exploring research questions within this space.

In this chapter, we articulate some of the research done by CML on children's understanding of learning, conducted primarily in Mind Lab. This work examined the factors children use to make judgments about whether learning has taken place in others, what children know about the process of learning, and when they begin to reflect on their own learning. We next describe museum-led observations of children's play at the exhibit space, which examined how children demonstrate and reflect on their own thinking as they play. We then present interviews with caregivers, which examined how they notice, describe, and interpret children's play and learning within the museum. In the final section, we explore some of the ways in which the lines of work have been influenced by the partnership, what we have learned from working with each other, and our goals for sustaining and building the collaboration.

CML Research on Children's Understanding of Learning

What do children know about whether learning has occurred in others? Early research in theory of mind focused on a number of topics related to learning, but not learning directly. For instance, by age 3, young children incorporate the word *know* into their spontaneous conversations (Bartsch & Wellman, 1995; Shatz, Wellman, & Silber, 1983), and at this age, children recognize when someone knows something (as opposed to not, e.g., Pillow, 1989; Pratt & Bryant, 1990). Between the ages of 3–5, children show significant changes in their understanding of beliefs. They begin to understand the distinction between ignorance and knowledge (Hogrefe, Wimmer & Perner, 1986), they recognize that beliefs represent one's ideas about the world and can be false (e.g., Perner, 1991; Perner, Leekam, & Wimmer, 1987; Wimmer & Perner, 1983), and recognize when their own knowledge has changed (Gopnik & Astington, 1988).

None of these lines of work, however, explicitly address children's understanding of learning itself as a mental state. Children's developing knowledge of belief does have some importance for their understanding of learning. Sobel (2015) found that children's developing understanding of false belief predicted their ability to recognize that a person could claim to have learned something when they actually have not learned it. These data are consistent with a more general hypothesis: Children construct a concept of learning based on their understanding of other mental states, like knowledge and ignorance. Because learning involves changes to knowledge states (e.g., replacing ignorance with knowledge), children's understanding of knowledge, ignorance, and how beliefs change all influence their concepts of learning.

On this view, children come to recognize that certain mental states are more directly related to learning than others, through appreciating that some mental states lead to others. For example, in most learning environments, perceiving or paying attention to information should be more directly related to learning than the desire to learn. If an opaque container is opened, one learns its contents by looking inside, regardless of whether one has the desire to learn this information or whether the container was opened intentionally or accidentally. In contrast, if one does not see what is inside, simply wanting to know will not result in any learning.

Based on the hypothesis that children believe learning is related to other mental states, Sobel, Li, and Corriveau (2007) investigated how children made judgments about characters whose desire, attention, and intention to learn varied. Four- and 6-year-olds were introduced to characters who were all in a similar learning situation (e.g., a teacher was teaching them to sing a song at school). Children were told about two of the characters' mental states, which were potentially in conflict with the learning goals. For example, children were asked about characters who wanted to learn, but failed to attend to (and hear) the teacher, or characters who heard, but did not want to learn. When asked whether each character learned, 4-year-olds mostly responded based on the character's desires (saying that characters who wanted to learn would do so); they did not recognize that some mental states were more important for learning than others. Six-year-olds, in contrast, were much more likely to recognize the role of perceptual access and intentionality when making these judgments (stating that characters would learn only if they paid attention to and heard the teacher).

What is learning to the developing child? CML's initial research goal was to understand how children made judgments about whether others learned when faced with specific situations—for example, when particular mental states were pitted against one another, as in the study described above. However, these scripted scenarios may not relate to children's personal experiences, or reveal children's own conceptions of learning or their beliefs about themselves as learners. To address this issue, the CML team used a more exploratory method to investigate children's understanding of and reflection on their own learning. This line of inquiry is one example of the ways that the NSF funding, which allowed a project researcher (the second author) to work at both CML and PCM, influenced the ways that CML approached its research questions, making connections to children's own experiences and using methods that were adapted to less controlled museum settings.

Sobel and Letourneau (2015) used a structured interview to allow children to articulate their understanding of learning in their own words. Researchers asked 4- to 10-year-olds to describe what and how they learned in any way they chose, using examples that were meaningful to them. Interviews began with an open-ended question: "What do you think 'learning' means?" Children's answers were coded as identity responses (in which children simply defined learning as learning), or as being about *content* or *process*. Content responses involved the child defining learning as a subject or topic (e.g., "like reading and math"). Process responses involved the child defining learning as either a source (e.g., "when your teacher tells you something") or a strategy (e.g., "when you practice again and again until you know it") that would result in knowledge change. Figure 7.1 shows the distribution of responses to this question. There were clear relations with age: 4- and 5-year-olds mostly did not respond to the question or defined learning in terms of content. Process-based responses increased with age: 8- to 10-year-olds generated process-based responses ~95% of the time, significantly more often than 6- and 7-year-olds (66%), who were significantly more likely to do so than the 4- and 5-year-olds (42%).

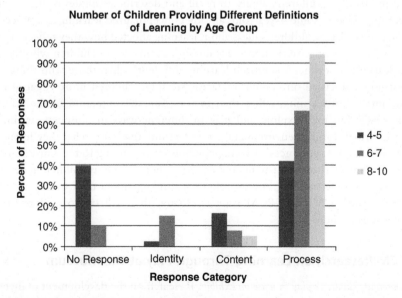

FIGURE 7.1 Distribution of children's responses to the "What do you think learning means?" question in Sobel and Letourneau (2015).

Children's definitions of learning also influenced the ways that they recalled and described their own learning. After this first question, children were asked to give examples of content ("Can you think of something that you have learned?") and process ("How did you learn that?"). Children who generated a process-based definition of learning were more likely to mention learning a skill (e.g., "How to tie my shoes") or a fact (e.g., "Ants have six legs") than children who did not. Moreover, children who generated a process-based definition of learning were more likely to respond to the question about how they learned something by describing a source or a strategy through which they acquired their knowledge (e.g., "My teacher told me," "I watched my friend and then I did it"). Finally, children were asked to talk about other ways they could learn (e.g., "How else could you learn?"). Again, children who had given process-based definitions were more likely to be able to describe different strategies for learning (e.g., "Someone could show you," "You can just try it yourself," "You can read a book"). Importantly, all of these differences held controlling for children's age and a gross measure of their language capacities.

These data suggest two conclusions. First, children's ability to define learning as a process develops between the ages of 4–10 years old, and is related to the kinds of examples they offer of their own learning and to their descriptions of how they have learned in the past. This suggests that children's appreciation of their own learning is developing into the elementary school years.

Second, even though children's definitions of learning changed between ages 4–10, an understanding of learning as a process (rather than age) was the critical predictor of children's ability to recall and describe examples of their own learning. That is, some 4-year-olds already conceptualized learning as a process, and across all ages, children's ideas about learning affected how they reflected on their own learning. Some important questions remain: Do children who think of learning as a process approach learning differently than those who think of learning as focused on content or facts? Are these children more engaged by the process of learning, rather than focusing on the outcomes or the "right answers"? Do they explore and play in different ways in museums or similar informal learning environments, or reflect differently on what they learned through these experiences? If young children are beginning to recognize learning as a process, how can parents and educators better support children in developing this understanding, and scaffold their thinking about their own learning? Future work CML and PCM want to do together will try to explore such questions in more depth.

PCM Research on Learning Through Play at the Museum

Observing children's play in museum exhibits. Research on the development of meta-cognitive awareness in childhood is closely related to PCM's goal of making learning visible within its walls—a goal it shares with many other museums and educators in general. As part of the NSF project described above, the museum's project team (which includes Meisner and Letourneau) used research and evaluation in PCM exhibits to explore existing and new ways of making children's learning more noticed and appreciated by caregivers and by children themselves.

The research findings described in the previous section suggest that museum practices can make learning more visible to children by helping them see learning as a process, rather than as being focused on content or outcomes, or by helping them actively reflect on their own learning. However, research studies on children's metacognitive abilities have often required children to be able to articulate descriptions of their own learning or participate in structured laboratory tasks, making it challenging to apply the results to museum settings. A question that PCM had in this project was how children begin to demonstrate and reflect on their own thought processes during everyday play at the museum. Further, PCM questioned whether there were observable behaviors in children's play that educators (and caregivers) might use as cues to notice and support children's developing awareness of their own thinking. Given that the PCM serves children ages 1–11 (with an average age of 4) and their caregivers, the museum also wanted to relate research to educational practices that are appropriate for young children, not just those who already possess an explicit understanding of learning.

Early in the project, the research team agreed that museum experiences might contribute to young children's general awareness of their own thinking as well as their view of themselves as learners, perhaps scaffolding earlier forms of cognitive self-regulation that feed into metacognitive development. Relevant self-regulatory processes include planning, monitoring, strategizing, and reflecting on the outcomes of one's actions (see Kuhn & Dean, 2004; Schneider, 2008, for reviews and links to educational practice). The foundations of these cognitive skills begin to emerge in early childhood, and with cumulative experience and support from peers and adults, children gradually develop a more explicit understanding of their own learning (Bronson, 2000; Schunk & Zimmerman, 1994, 1998; Whitebread et al., 2010).

Observational studies suggest that children do monitor, regulate, or describe their own thinking in a variety of ways: by working from a plan or with a purpose in mind, self-commentating and describing their ideas, concentrating and resisting distraction, correcting errors, systematically trying different strategies, and reflecting on their accomplishments. Some of these findings are based on observations conducted in school settings (Dermitzaki, 2005; Dermitzaki, Leondari, & Goudas, 2009; Whitebread et al., 2009). However, researchers in informal learning have observed similar behaviors in museums—for example, explaining ideas or noticing and correcting errors while engaging with exhibits (Borun, Chambers, & Cleghorn, 1996; Puchner, Rapoport, & Gaskins, 2001).

To understand what these cognitive processes might look like specifically in children's play at PCM, the research team asked for the input of staff and volunteers at the museum. In group discussions, PCM educators (and later, educators at the Museum of Science, Boston) were asked: "Have you ever seen children planning, monitoring their thinking in the moment, strategizing, or reflecting on what they're doing? How do you know? What shows you that this is happening?" These discussions generated many examples of instances when children noticed or controlled their own thinking—for example, by pausing to look at their work from different angles, by trying different strategies to complete a challenge they had set for themselves, and describing what they figured out to others.

Following these discussions, the research team used the behaviors that educators had mentioned as important for children's learning to structure a set of observations in PCM exhibits. This approach shared some characteristics with action research, in which practitioners guide and contribute to the research process in order to inform their own practices.

The team observed children between the ages of 3–11 in three exhibits and recorded behaviors as running records. The team identified instances of each of the behaviors defined in the group discussions and supported by the research literature and examined whether aspects of the environment or children's interactions with others contributed to their occurrence. Children often showed intense concentration when they could create something of their own design, or when exhibits provided sensory experiences that children could repeat, observe, and make subtle variations on. Children often thought out loud or described their ideas when they collaborated or shared materials with one another, or when they engaged in activities that involved creative construction (e.g., creating patterns with geometric pieces, building with blocks) or that offered visual examples of finished products (e.g., pictures of various patterns that could be made or structures that could be built with the materials available). Children who announced their plans at the beginning of an activity were also more likely to reflect on what happened later.

This study made connections with museum practices on many levels. The observational data provided a rich source of information on the ways that children make their thinking visible in their play and the ways that museum experiences can support them in reflecting on their own learning. Educators' input was critical in the development of observational methods used in the research, and the results of the research were directly applicable to exhibit design and educational practices (e.g., supporting facilitators who engage children in exhibits). More broadly, having observational research at the museum has contributed to a culture of observation and reflective practice among museum staff and volunteers.

Making learning through play visible to caregivers. In addition to examining children's thinking and learning through observable behaviors, the museum's research team also considered the ways that caregivers might support children's learning by noticing and reflecting on their play. Making learning through play visible to caregivers in this way is a longstanding educational goal of PCM because child development experts generally agree that valuable learning occurs through play (see Ginsburg, 2007; Fisher, Hirsh-Pasek, Golinkoff, & Gryfe, 2008), and the museum is committed to advocating for child-directed play as an essential element of children's learning and development. PCM's research team was interested in evaluating its existing exhibit materials and developing new ones that would help caregivers observe children's play, notice thinking and learning in children's behavior, and recognize moments when they might support children in reflecting on their own learning.

Previous research has examined parents' perceptions of children's play in general, and the learning they associate with different kinds of play activities (e.g., Brooker, 2003; Fisher et al., 2008; Göncü & Gaskins, 2006; Rothlein & Brett, 1987; Singer, Singer, Agostino, & Delong, 2009; Tamis-LeMonda, Damast, & Bornstein, 1994). This work has found that caregivers hold generally positive views about the overall importance of play for their children, but vary in their beliefs about what "play" entails and the relative value of different types of play activities for children's learning. A small number of research studies and evaluation reports have examined parents' perceptions of play in children's museums (Downey, Krantz, & Skidmore, 2010; Haas, 1997; Randi Korn & Associates, 2010; Swartz & Crowley, 2004), often focusing on the roles caregivers play in facilitating their children's learning within particular exhibit spaces. To better understand caregivers' perceptions of their children's play and learning specifically at PCM, which places a particularly strong emphasis on child-directed play, the research team conducted several sets of open-ended interviews. One set of interviews focused on what caregivers observed about their children's play at the museum, and the thought processes that they associated with their children's behavior. In these interviews, the experimenter asked parents: What do you notice your children doing while they play at the museum? What are you thinking about as you watch them play here? What do you think *they're* thinking about? What behaviors show you that your children are thinking or learning?

When asked what they noticed children doing, caregivers reported observing where children spent a long time playing and what interested them. Beyond this, many caregivers made specific observations about their children's play: noticing how their children had changed over their development, wondering what they were working on, or thinking about their children's particular strengths, personalities, or interests. Parents also associated many different kinds of thought processes with their children's behavior. When asked what they thought their children might be thinking about as they played, some caregivers focused on children's activity levels or enjoyment: 25% of caregivers replied that children were thinking about having fun, and 23% said that children were mostly being hyper or physically active. However, many caregivers mentioned some kind of cognitive process: 33% described children trying to "figure something out" or "accomplish something" (often refusing help), and 30% described children thinking about exploring and "seeing what happens." When asked if anything showed them that their children were thinking or learning as they played, caregivers often described intense concentration, persistence, independence, or children learning from their mistakes or telling others about what they did. These interviews showed that, with prompting, caregivers did intuitively recognize many aspects of children's thinking in their play, but that this was not necessarily at the top of their minds as they watched their children.

In a second set of interviews, researchers asked another set of caregivers, which included parents, grandparents, and other childcare providers, to describe the kinds of learning that they thought might happen through play at the museum. The goal of this study was to understand whether some types of learning might be more visible or salient to caregivers than others so that the team could begin to develop exhibit materials and activities to communicate more effectively with caregivers about children's learning.

Figure 7.2 shows the results of these interviews. All caregivers stated that their children learn though play in general, but they varied in how they described the learning that might happen through play at the museum. Seventy-two percent of those interviewed described children learning how a particular exhibit component worked (e.g., "How to build a ramp," "How to make the gears turn"), and 41% described content or facts that children might learn in particular exhibit spaces (e.g., "about history," "about water"). Fewer caregivers (27%) described transferable cognitive skills that children might be using when they played at the museum

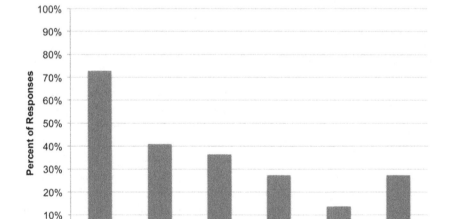

FIGURE 7.2 Distribution of caregivers' responses when asked to describe the kinds of learning that they thought might happen through play at the museum.

(e.g., "experimenting," "problem-solving"). On the other hand, 36% of caregivers said that children might learn social skills, like sharing and cooperating. Less frequent responses included sensory experiences (e.g., "What things feel like"; 18%), and academic topics (e.g., "reading," "counting"; 14%). In light of the interviews, the research team conducted with children about their own learning, these findings suggest that there may be opportunities for the museum to support more process-based ideas about learning in both children and their caregivers, expanding their ideas about what "counts" as learning during their museum visits.

It is important to note that caregivers' views of learning were influenced in part by different expectations and values that they had when visiting the museum. Caregivers who said that they visited the museum mainly so that their children could play independently or with other children were also likely to say that their children learned social skills at the museum. Caregivers who specifically stated that they valued the museum as a learning experience for their children often mentioned topics or facts that children might learn from particular exhibit areas. In other cases, however, caregivers' ideas about learning conflicted with their goals for their visits. For example, caregivers who primarily valued the quality time that they could spend with their children at the museum did not mention these social experiences as a part of their children's learning. They sometimes described "learning" as disrupting their quality time together. Those who valued the novel, hands-on experiences that children could have at the museum often focused on the facts or content within particular exhibits (and questioned whether children retained this information), rather than the overarching skills or general knowledge that children might gain through their direct experiences with the world. In addition, 27% of caregivers openly acknowledged that they were not sure what or how children were learning as they played at the museum, or felt that they lacked the vocabulary to describe it. They felt confident that their children were thinking and learning, but this belief seemed to be based on the common messages that "play is important" and "children learn through play."

To summarize these findings, the majority of caregivers noticed specific details about their children's play and had something to say about the kinds of learning that might happen at the museum. But the results also suggest that without additional prompting, many of the open-ended experiences that children encounter at PCM may not be recognized by caregivers as "learning" in the moment. Although caregivers generally believe that hands-on, open-ended experiences are important for their children, many caregivers find it challenging to describe how learning happens through these experiences. They may fall back on descriptions of topics or facts presented in particular exhibits because they feel they lack the vocabulary to describe how play relates to broader cognitive skills (including the metacognitive skills that were the focus of this project). That said, it is not the case that caregivers fail to notice what children are thinking about or doing as they play. Instead, caregivers come to the museum with different agendas and goals for their visits that shape the way they participate in and interpret their children's play in the moment (see, e.g., Beaumont, 2010; Downey et al., 2010; Gaskins, 2008; Swartz & Crowley, 2004; Wood & Wolf, 2010).

Based on these findings, PCM is currently developing exhibit labels and resources for caregivers to communicate the variety of ways that children can learn through play and the ways that they can help children reflect on their thinking as they play. For example, the exhibit text developed for the Mind Lab space provides multiple concrete examples, based on current research and educational theory, and summarizes research on various relevant topics (e.g., how children learn from sensory experiences, from their peers, and from adults). The aim of these materials is to communicate more effectively that learning is not limited to topics or content, but also includes open-ended cognitive, social, emotional, and physical experiences. The goal is not to negate the value of content-based learning, but rather to broaden visitors' perspectives about other kinds of learning that happen naturally through play. Evaluation of the labels and research synopses has shown that caregivers report learning something novel about children's learning and seeing the relevance of the research findings in their own lives.

Other resources aimed to communicate that caregivers can use their own observations to recognize their children's learning and use what they notice to judge when and how to be involved in their children's play. Prototypes of observation activities for caregivers included a list of behaviors that relate to children's developing cognitive and metacognitive skills, along with brief explanations of their importance for children's learning and development. Caregivers who participated in the activity reported watching their children's play in a more focused way and seeing more meaning and purpose in what their children were doing. In addition, the observation activities validated behaviors that caregivers occasionally viewed as negative or unproductive (e.g., repeating something over and over) and helped caregivers see their children's play in a new light.

Benefits and Challenges of the Collaboration

The collaboration between CML and PCM has grown in many respects since it first began, and has had both planned and unanticipated benefits (and challenges) for researchers, museum staff and volunteers, and museum visitors. Because the benefits outweigh the challenges, we present the challenges first.

Partnership challenges. Developing and sustaining the collaboration across such different institutions has not been without difficulties, many of which are not unique to the CML–PCM collaboration and are represented in several chapters of this volume. Such challenges include negotiating schedules, finding appropriate space within the museum, ensuring that the length of experiments does not detract from the overall visitor experience at the museum, and committing to training new researchers. Communication—another common struggle—is an ongoing issue, as we strive to address challenges as they arise and keep each other more informed about the needs and research activities at the two institutions. Regular monthly meetings and having a shared project researcher working in both settings have been essential to the many successes of the work (see details following).

Perhaps the most salient challenge is appreciating the different goals of the two institutions. The synergistic aspects of the collaboration are exciting to both partners, but each also has individual concerns beyond the partnership. A major motivator for PCM is to understand *how children learn through play within the museum*, and ultimately to use the findings both to better design exhibits and to advocate more effectively for child-directed play, while CML seeks to gain *generalizable knowledge about child development*. The agendas of the two institutions are therefore complementary but work toward different ends. This requires parallel lines of inquiry with different research or evaluation approaches to take place within the larger project, and making connections between them is both an exciting opportunity and an ongoing challenge. In addition, as a children's museum with broad interests, PCM presents hands-on experiences that explore the arts, culture, history, and STEM, and foster children's cognitive, emotional, social, and physical development. CML is specifically focused on children's STEM learning, and as such, the two institutions have to negotiate mutually relevant lines of work. Some research ideas of great interest to CML have little bearing on PCM's mission, and, likewise, some lines of research of relevance to the museum are outside the scope of CML's research goals and expertise. None of the challenges are insurmountable, but they all require increased communication to find common ground.

Partnership benefits. One intended mutual benefit of this project is the presence of the project researcher, whose position is shared between CML and PCM. More so than anything else, the position has increased the capacity for collaboration between the two institutions. By moving between academic and museum cultures, the shared researcher bridges the interests and needs of the two institutions and helps establish a common language to facilitate communications between the partners. She also allows for multiple related projects to take place simultaneously around a common topic, using different approaches that meet the needs of both institutions. Information about ongoing work at each site is shared between partners more quickly and accessibly, and as a result, we have been able to inform and influence one another's work in new ways. For CML, studies on children's developing understanding of learning have been expanded not only to include more open-ended research approaches, but also to address children's perceptions of play and learning through play. These projects were not part of the original NSF proposal's scope of work, but have emerged from the collaboration. For PCM, research findings about children's developing understanding of learning as a process have provided new perspectives about ways that the museum and caregivers can support children in actively reflecting on their own learning.

A second intended mutual benefit of this project is the new Mind Lab space, which is the permanent home at the museum for learning about learning. By allocating space, the museum has elevated the value it places on research partnerships and the potential outcomes they offer for both research and practice. For CML, the new space and deeper partnership not only serve to include researchers as a greater part of the museum community, but also help undergraduate and graduate students learn more about communicating research to the public in order to make their studies accessible and relevant to the caregivers and children who participate.

As alluded to earlier, because of the discussion between the CML and PCM staffs, new research ideas are able to bloom and resonate. Most of the CML-led studies described in this chapter would not have been conducted without discussion between the two institutions, and a clear benefit to CML is thinking through the process of translating between applied ideas and basic science. The development of the Mind Lab space offers an interesting case of research informing practice and vice versa: Based on CML research, PCM developed a tabletop activity to encourage scientific thinking and metacognition in children, as a way of illustrating these research topics for museum visitors. The activity includes a set of circuit blocks (wooden blocks with batteries, motors, buttons, and lights that can be connected in various configurations, similar to those that exist in other museums and maker spaces), along with accompanying information for caregivers about the ways that children learn by exploring and experimenting with the blocks and suggested prompts that caregivers can use to support their children's thinking and learning as they play together. The activity itself may now become the subject of further study by CML researchers in Mind Lab. In this way, the collaboration might allow CML researchers to form novel research projects by building upon a museum experience. Such a project is in its infancy, but will hopefully be of interest not only to other researchers, but to other practitioners as well.

Beyond this, from PCM's perspective, a clear benefit of the collaboration has been to develop the museum's research activities more formally, which sets the stage for the museum to consider a broader research agenda. Having a stronger research presence at the museum (both in Mind Lab and in the exhibits) has also contributed to PCM's efforts to communicate information about the ways that children learn, and about how scientists gather evidence about children's learning. Moreover, research happening in the museum (especially observational research of children's play) has led to many educational interactions with adult visitors—in particular, the presence of an observer often arouses caregivers' interest in their own children's behavior. That is, when caregivers see that researchers from both CML and PCM consider their children's activity to be important and noteworthy enough to study, they seem to focus their attention more closely on their children's behavior.

Future Directions

CML and PCM are motivated by the work that has come out of the recent shared project and the new lines of inquiry that have emerged from the research. A second project funded by NSF, which began in 2015, is allowing the partners to continue to explore the intersections between cognitive development research and museum practices by extending CML research into museum exhibits. In this project, CML and PCM are collaborating with research teams from University of California, Santa Cruz/Children's Discovery Museum in San Jose and University of Texas at Austin/The Thinkery in order to investigate how open-ended exploration and parents' explanations affect children's causal learning in each of the three museums. In addition, the teams will examine how museum exhibit design and facilitation might influence parent–child interactions, as well as children's exploration and learning. In this way, CML and PCM are deepening their collaboration both with one another and with colleagues from other universities and museums by working together to answer research questions that directly relate to families' play and learning within museum environments. The work is exciting to both partners because it meets many of the individual institutions' goals and interests, and acknowledges the unique expertise of both researchers and museum practitioners. With each new project, CML and PCM hope to work incrementally to close the gap between the cultures and practices of the two institutions, learning from one another's perspectives and from the challenges we have worked through as a team.

Acknowledgements

The work described herein was supported by the National Science Foundation (grant #1223777), and the authors were supported by this grant when writing this chapter. We thank Chris Erb, Valerie Haggerty-Silva, Eva Lai, Deanna Macris, Jessica Neuwirth, Janice O'Donnell, Chris Sanborn, and Tiffany Tassin for helpful discussion and assistance in the creation of Mind Lab and Charlotte Crider, Rose DeRenzio, Jenna Eldridge, Julia Franckh, Isobel Heck, Michelle Sullivan, and Andrea Wister for assistance with data collection and analysis for the studies presented here.

References

Bartsch, K., & Wellman, H. (1995). *Children talk about the mind*. New York: Oxford University Press.

Beaumont, L. (2010). *Developing the adult child interaction inventory: A methodological study*. Unpublished manuscript. Boston Children's Museum.

Borun, M., Chambers, M., & Cleghorn, A. (1996). Families are learning in science museums. *Curator: The Museum Journal, 39*(2), 123–138.

Bronson, M. (2000). *Self-regulation in early childhood: Nature and nurture*. New York: Guilford Press.

Brooker, L. (2003). Learning how to learn: Parental ethnotheories and young children's preparation for school. *International Journal of Early Years Education, 11*(2), 117–128.

Callanan, M.A. (2012). Conducting cognitive developmental research in museums: Theoretical issues and practical considerations. *Journal of Cognition and Development, 13*(2), 137–151.

Dermitzaki, I. (2005). Preliminary investigation of relations between young students' self-regulatory strategies and their metacognitive experiences. *Psychological Reports, 97*(3), 759–768.

Dermitzaki, I., Leondari, A., & Goudas, M. (2009). Relations between young students' strategic behaviours, domain-specific self-concept, and performance in a problem-solving situation. *Learning and Instruction, 19*(2), 144–157.

Downey, S., Krantz, A., & Skidmore, E. (2010). The parental role in children's museums. *Museums and Social Issues, 5*(1), 15–34.

Fisher, K.R., Hirsh-Pasek, K., Golinkoff, R.M., & Gryfe, S.G. (2008). Conceptual split? Parents' and experts' perceptions of play in the 21st century. *Journal of Applied Developmental Psychology, 29*(4), 305–316.

Gaskins, S. (2008, Spring). Designing exhibitions to support families' cultural understandings. *Exhibitionist*, 11–19.

Ginsburg, K.R. (2007). The importance of play in promoting healthy child development and maintaining strong parent-child bonds. *Pediatrics, 119*(1), 182–191.

Göncü, A., & Gaskins, S. (2006). *Play and development: Evolutionary, sociocultural and functional perspectives.* Mahwah, NJ: Erlbaum.

Gopnik, A., & Astington, J.W. (1988). Children's understanding of representational change and its relation to the understanding of false belief and the appearance-reality distinction. *Child Development, 59*(1), 26–37.

Haas, N.T. (1997). Project explore: How children are really learning in children's museums. *Visitor Studies Association, 9*, 63–69.

Hogrefe, G.J., Wimmer, H., & Perner, J. (1986). Ignorance versus false belief: A developmental lag in attribution of epistemic states. *Child Development, 57*(3), 567–582.

Kuhn, D., & Dean, D. (2004). Metacognition: A bridge between cognitive psychology and educational practice. *Theory into Practice, 43*(4), 268–273.

Perner, J. (1991). *Understanding the representational mind.* Cambridge, MA: MIT Press.

Perner, J., Leekam, S.R., & Wimmer, H. (1987). Three-year-olds' difficulty with false belief: The case for a conceptual deficit. *British Journal of Developmental Psychology, 5*(2), 125–137.

Pillow, B.H. (1989). Early understanding of perception as a source of knowledge. *Journal of Experimental Child Psychology, 47*(1), 116–129.

Pratt, C., & Bryant, P. (1990). Young children understand that looking leads to knowing (so long as they are looking into a single barrel). *Child Development, 61*(4), 973–982.

Puchner, L., Rapoport, R., & Gaskins, S. (2001). Learning in children's museums: Is it really happening? *Curator: The Museum Journal, 44*(3), 237–259.

Randi Korn & Associates (2010). *Audience research: Understanding visitors and their experiences at Please Touch Museum at Memorial Hall (Vol. 1: Report).* http://informalscience.org/images/evaluation/2010_RKA_PleaseTouchMuseum_AudRsch_Report_Final.pdf

Rothlein, L., & Brett, A. (1987). Children's, teachers' and parents' perceptions of play. *Early Childhood Research Quarterly, 2*(1), 45–53.

Schneider, W. (2008). The development of metacognitive knowledge in children and adolescents: Major trends and implications for education. *Mind, Brain, and Education, 2*(3), 114–121.

Schunk, D.H., & Zimmerman, B.J. (Eds.). (1994). *Self-regulation of learning and performance: Issues and educational applications*. Hillsdale, NJ: Erlbaum.

Schunk, D.H., & Zimmerman, B.J. (1998). *Self-regulated learning: From teaching to self-reflective practice*. New York: Guilford Press.

Shatz, M., Wellman, H.M., & Silber, S. (1983). The acquisition of mental verbs: A systematic investigation of the first reference to mental state. *Cognition, 14*(3), 301–321.

Singer, D.G., Singer, J.L., Agostino, H.D., & Delong, R. (2009). Children's pastimes and play in sixteen nations: Is free-play declining? *American Journal of Play, 1*(3), 283–312.

Sobel, D.M. (2015). Can you do it?: How preschoolers judge others have learned. *Journal of Cognition and Development*, 16, 492–508.

Sobel, D.M., & Letourneau, S. (2015). Children's developing understanding of what and how they've learned. *Journal of Experimental Child Psychology, 132*, 221–229.

Sobel, D.M., Li, J., & Corriveau, K.H. (2007). "They danced around in my head and I learned them": Children's developing conceptions of learning. *Journal of Cognition and Development, 8*(3), 345–369.

Swartz, M.I., & Crowley, K. (2004). Parent beliefs about teaching and learning in a children's museum. *Visitor Studies Today, VII*(II), 4–16.

Tamis-LeMonda, C.S., Damast, A.M., & Bornstein, M.H. (1994). What do mothers know about the developmental nature of play? *Infant Behavior and Development, 17*(3), 341–345.

Whitebread, D., Almeqdad, Q., Bryce, D., Demetriou, D., Grau, V., & Sangster, C. (2010). Metacognition in young children: Current methodological and theoretical developments. In A. Efklides & P. Misailidi (Eds.), *Trends and prospects in metacognition research* (pp. 233–258). New York: Springer.

Whitebread, D., Coltman, P., Pasternak, D.P., Sangster, C., Grau, V., Bingham, S., . . . Demetriou, D. (2009). The development of two observational tools for assessing metacognition and self-regulated learning in young children. *Metacognition and Learning, 4*(1), 63–85.

Wimmer, H., & Perner, J. (1983). Beliefs about beliefs: Representation and constraining function of wrong beliefs in young children's understanding of deception. *Cognition, 13*(1), 103–128.

Wood, E., & Wolf, B. (2010). When parents stand back is family learning still possible? *Museums and Social Issues, 5*(1), 35–50.

8

EXAMINING THE DEVELOPMENT OF SCIENTIFIC REASONING IN CONTEXT

A Museum and Laboratory Partnership

Cristine H. Legare, Robin Gose, and Cybil Guess

The Team

Cristine Legare is an associate professor in the Department of Psychology at the University of Texas at Austin and the director of the Cognition, Culture, and Development Laboratory. She studies cognitive development from an interdisciplinary perspective, using mixed methods to examine how children learn across cultures.

Robin Gose is the director of education at the Thinkery, where she oversees educational programs and exhibit development. She provides leadership in the Thinkery's development of authentic learning experiences that make science fun and meaningful for young learners.

Cybil Guess is the director of experience at the Thinkery. She directs the museum's customer service, volunteerism, teen programming, admissions, reservations, and all direct service staffing functions, aligning internal operations and user experiences with the museum's mission and strategic goals. She provides leadership in the development and implementation of the Thinkery's approach to people-focused facilitation.

The Museum Setting

The educational mission of the Thinkery (formerly the Austin Children's Museum) is to create innovative learning experiences for children and families to equip and inspire the next generation of creative problem solvers. The Thinkery is a foundry for learning and exploration. Galleries such as *Innovators' Workshop* and *Kitchen Lab* emphasize skill development and creative problem solving, while also bringing "STEAM" subjects (science, technology, engineering, art, and math) to life for visitors. The emphasis of all educational programming at the Thinkery is on facilitation and inquiry-based learning. The Thinkery is committed to ensuring that each visit includes a meaningful interaction with educators and staff. This commitment has established the Thinkery as an authority on family education throughout Central Texas.

In this chapter, we describe the collaboration between the Cognition, Culture, and Development Lab (CCD Lab) at the University of Texas at Austin and the Thinkery in Austin, TX. As institutions with distinct missions—one to engage in empirical research with the goal of advancing our understanding of the development of scientific reasoning, and the other to create an inclusive and innovative learning environment where children and their families can play while engaging with science—the collaboration between these two institutions has been a dynamic process that has grown and evolved over the last 5 years. First, we will describe the history of the partnership between the CCD Lab and the Thinkery. Next, we will describe the research that has resulted from this collaboration. Finally, we will discuss the goals of the partnership between the CCD Lab and the Thinkery, provide researcher and practitioner perspectives on the partnership, and discuss mutual benefits and challenges.

History of the Partnership Between the CCD Lab and the Thinkery

The late Becky Jones, director of education at the Austin Children's Museum (ACM) for nearly 30 years, had a passion for educational research and for building university–museum partnerships. Cristine Legare and Becky Jones began working together in 2009 to increase the involvement of the ACM in educational research on children's learning. The partnership began with researchers from the CCD Lab engaging museum visitors as participants in research on the development of children's causal explanations and exploratory behavior. Children's museums provide a venue for collecting data, which contribute to our understanding of early science learning with the added benefit of allowing researchers to sample from a population that is larger and potentially more diverse than the population typically attracted to the university lab setting. This fruitful partnership allowed for the collection of data, which has resulted in more than 10 empirical papers published in top-tier cognitive and developmental journals, including *Child Development, Child Development Perspectives, Cognition,* and *The Journal of Experimental Child Psychology.* The collaboration with the Thinkery has been instrumental to the production of this line of empirical research on early science learning. This partnership has also recently resulted in a collaborative grant funded by the National Science Foundation to Maureen Callanan at UCSC, Cristine Legare at UT Austin, David Sobel at Brown University, and museum partners at the San Jose Children's Museum, the

Thinkery, and the Providence Children's Museum to examine cultural diversity in parent–child explanation and exploration.

Research Conducted at the Thinkery to Date

Curiosity is characteristic of early childhood; there is evidence that both infants (Stahl & Feigenson, 2015) and young children (Legare, Gelman, & Wellman, 2010; Legare & Gelman, 2014) are more motivated to explain unexpected outcomes and engage in causal learning through exploration (Schulz & Bonawitz, 2007). Our collaborative research at the Thinkery is based on research demonstrating that explaining and exploring work in tandem to drive the scientific reasoning process in early childhood. Our long-term objective is to apply our understanding of early scientific reasoning to improve early science education (Gelman, Brenneman, Macdonald, & Roman, 2010).

There is growing evidence from research in developmental psychology that children's explanations and exploration benefits learning (Amsterlaw & Wellman, 2006; Crowley & Siegler, 1999; Nicolopoulou, 2010; Rittle-Johnson, Saylor, & Swygert, 2008; Siegler, 1995; Singer, Golinkoff, & Hirsh-Pasek, 2006). Experimental evidence indicates that generating explanations benefits both causal learning and the capacity to engage in generalization (Lombrozo, 2006; Wellman, 2011). Children's exploratory behavior has also been linked to positive learning outcomes (Baldwin, Markman, & Melartin, 1993; Bonawitz, van Schijndel, Friel, & Schulz, 2012). For example, there is evidence that even young children can disambiguate causal variables by exploring relevant evidence (Cook, Goodman, & Schulz, 2011; Schulz, Bonawitz, & Griffiths, 2007). Research examining the kinds of outcomes children are most motivated to explain and explore has demonstrated that explaining inconsistent outcomes may be especially useful to guiding and directing exploratory behavior in the service of learning (Legare, 2012).

Much of the research conducted by the CCD Lab at the Thinkery has examined the relations between explanation, exploration, and scientific reasoning. One of our research projects has examined how self-explanation may uniquely and selectively benefit causal learning. Although there is some evidence that explanation may benefit learning more than comparison activities in older children (McEldoon, Durkin, & Rittle-Johnson, 2013; Rittle-Johnson et al., 2008), little is known about the process underlying these effects in early childhood. There are a number of ways that explanation may benefit learning. For example, explanation may selectively focus children on identifying unobserved causes, internal mechanisms, causal functions, and causal mechanisms (Keil, 2006; Legare, 2012; Legare, Wellman, & Gelman, 2009; Walker, Lombrozo, Legare, & Gopnik, 2014), and on making generalizations (Walker, Williams, Lombrozo, & Gopnik, 2012; Williams & Lombrozo, 2010).

One series of studies conducted at the Thinkery (Legare & Lombrozo, 2014) examined how and why explanation influences learning in young children. In these studies we examined the unique and selective effects of explanation compared to other tasks that require equivalent cognitive engagement. In two studies, we compared children's performance on measures of causal and noncausal learning based on whether they were asked to explain or observe (Study 1) and explain or describe (Study 2).

First, we gave 3- to 6-year old children a novel mechanical toy with visible interlocking gears. When the gears are connected in the correct way, a crank operates the machine and makes a fan turn. The three middle gears have peripheral pieces attached to them that are used to differentially assess children's memory versus their understanding of the functional mechanism underlying the machine. Children participate in one of two conditions: an observation condition in which children attend to the machine but do not explain or explore (*observe condition*), and an explanation condition in which children were asked to explain how the machine works without exploring it (*explain condition*).

Following the experimental manipulation, children participated in three additional tasks. Two of the tasks are learning measures (presented first) followed by one procedural knowledge measure in which children are asked to reconstruct the machine. In each of the learning tasks, the intact machine is presented to the child with one gear missing. In the *memory learning task*, another five candidate parts are presented to the child to assess the child's memory for the exact missing piece. All five pieces are the correct size and shape, but only one is the same color as the missing piece. In the *mechanism learning task*, five candidate parts are presented to the child, none of which are identical to the missing part. The choices are: a part of the correct size and shape but different color, a part of the correct shape but incorrect size, a part of the correct size but incorrect shape, a peripheral part they have seen before but which is not the correct shape, and a distracter part. In each task the child is asked to select the part that will make the machine work. After completion of the learning tasks the machine is taken apart. All of the gears are removed from the base, and the peripheral parts are removed from the three middle gears. Participants are asked to reconstruct the machine in exactly the same way they saw it before and make it work in the *reconstruction task*.

Data from this experimental study provide evidence that the benefits of explanation are selective; children who explain learn more about the causal mechanisms in the machine and less about noncausal information (i.e., memory for causally irrelevant, peripheral details such as color). This suggests that explanation may be especially beneficial for causal learning. In our next study, we compared how explanation versus description impact causal and noncausal learning to control for effects of verbalization.

Children were introduced to the same machine as in the previous study, and asked either to describe the machine but not explore it (*describe condition*) or to explain how the machine works without exploring it (*explain condition*). Using the same measures as the previous study, we assessed learning as a function of the type of verbal response, with children's spontaneous utterances coded for the presence of explanations. We also presented children with a *generalization task* to examine children's ability to recreate the causal mechanical function of the gear machine.

We examined the extent to which children understood the machine's functional–mechanical relations, remembered perceptual features of the machine, successfully reconstructed the machine, and generalized the function of the machine in constructing a novel machine. Our findings replicated and extended key findings from the first study. First, we found reliable effects of explanation when comparing the content of children's responses rather than the experimental prompt that they received (i.e., to describe versus explain the machine). Children who explained outperformed non–explainers on measures of causal learning, but not on measures of noncausal learning. This result is important in establishing that effects of explanation do not derive solely from the use of language, as all children produced verbal responses. That effects of explanation were not eliminated when compared with alternative kinds of verbalization is especially striking in the context of our two studies given that the noncausal properties that we tested (e.g., color) were, if anything, easier to express linguistically than the causal properties (e.g., gear shape).

Across two studies, children who provide an explanation performed better on measures of causal than noncausal learning. In our study comparing explanation to description, we found evidence that children who explained also engaged in more generalization. Thus the effects of explanation are both selective in that they benefit causal more than noncausal learning, and unique from other kinds of engagement, such as observation or verbal description. These results also indicate that self-explanation can benefit young children's learning, even in the absence of feedback from others.

In other lines of research, members of the CCD Lab have demonstrated that explaining and exploring are not mutually exclusive in spontaneous conversation and play, but instead may operate in tandem (Legare, 2012, 2014). Explanation allows children to generate, constrain, and evaluate hypotheses. Exploration allows children to test hypotheses. Explanation and exploration are thus connected in the context of causal learning and allow children to move beyond concrete appearances to reason about abstract causal structure.

We have also demonstrated that explaining inconsistency guides exploratory behavior. For example, the kind of explanation children generate for inconsistent outcomes differentially predicts (a) the kind of exploratory behavior children engage in, (b) the amount of hypothesis-testing exploratory behavior they engage in, and (c) the extent to which they modify their hypotheses when confronted with disconfirming evidence.

Museum Practitioners' and Researchers' Perspectives on the Partnership

In constructing the partnership, researchers at the CCD Lab and practitioners at the Thinkery constructed a set of objectives for the partnership. We endeavor to more effectively deliver activities and exhibits that promote science learning to the Thinkery, based on cutting edge research on children's learning. This learning can best occur when we engage museum staff in the research process in order to build a better understanding of the research process, what learning research looks like, and how to incorporate it into the museum environment. In doing so, we promote broad thinking from many different perspectives, which informs how to apply insights about parent–child learning to the wide variety of activities, spaces, and educational programs. We also aim to demonstrate the "nature of science" to staff, visitors, and program participants. Public outreach serves to inform the community about learning research by making the research visible and accessible to the public.

Researcher Perspective on Collaborating With Practitioners

The partnership with the Thinkery provides a variety of unique opportunities to enrich the research conducted in the CCD Lab. For example, working in the Thinkery allows us to examine learning in context; examining parent–child interaction in the context of meaningful science learning experiences would not be possible inside the walls of the laboratory. Collaborating with the Thinkery also provides us with the challenge of translating our data about causal reasoning and scientific reasoning in early childhood into information that science practitioners can use to inform and improve museum visitors' learning experiences. Another advantage of working with museum practitioners at the Thinkery is to learn more about how to modify the design of our research to provide insight into questions about learning in context.

The CCD Lab has also assisted the Thinkery with a visitor research project that informed the development of the Thinkery's new early learners' programs. Research assistants have worked with staff to develop formative evaluation surveys, collect and analyze data, and make programmatic suggestions. This increased the Thinkery's capacity immensely in this area and guided decision-making around core programming before the museum transitioned into the new space. This is not a project that the staff would have had the capacity to accomplish without assistance from the CCD Lab. The commitment of time and expertise was key in enabling the museum to approach the project with a more research-based strategy.

In the new Thinkery facility, the CCD Lab has continued their work of collecting data on early science learning. As this partnership has matured, great improvements have been made in the presentation and professionalism on both the part of the Thinkery and the CCD lab staff. Museum visitors are becoming more accustomed to participating in research during their visit to the museum. Museum staff at all levels have also bought into this partnership, with the result that staff are more receptive to visitor feedback and using data to inform decisions. Moving forward, this partnership has great potential to become a true collaboration. Funders are increasingly holding informal learning institutions more accountable in terms of impact on visitors and educational outcomes, not to mention numbers of people served. Anecdotal evidence is no longer sufficient—museums must now demonstrate their impact with quantifiable measures. Gathering these data presents several challenges for museum professionals. First, few institutions allocate funds to keep academically trained researchers and evaluators on staff. Those museums that can are often at the mercy of grant funding, and the number of researchers on staff will ebb and flow with the uncertainty of the funding.

Second, because a single museum professional at a small institution often juggles many responsibilities, such as content area expertise, pedagogical influence, fundraising, grant writing, and marketing, it is very difficult to maintain an objective point of view when tasked with evaluating learning outcomes. It is our hope that through building a more collaborative relationship with the CCD Lab that the Thinkery staff can work alongside university researchers to see excellent research practices in action, and bring that experience to their work in the museum. Another benefit from this collaboration will be access to CCD Lab researchers for internal planning meetings for new exhibits. Exhibit planning and design is currently collaboration between several departments at the Thinkery. Many voices contribute to the process, but often decisions are made based on emotion or aesthetic rather than on research. Bringing CCD Lab researchers to the table for such discussions will demonstrate the Thinkery leadership team's commitment to using research to inform design, creating a new model for exhibit development at the museum.

The next step in this already rewarding partnership between the Thinkery and the CCD Lab is to work even more closely and focus in on research topics that can be directly applicable to the museum's mission of developing child learning activities, staff training programs, and models for family engagement. The Thinkery hopes to apply the research done by the CCD Lab into decision-making about exhibit design, exhibit prompts (graphics, literature, web applications), exhibit facilitation, curriculum, and engagement goals.

Practitioner Perspective on the Research

Partnering with the CCD Lab brings a skill set in research methodology—and the human capital to execute the research—that the museum does not have. The research proposed in this project will provide the Thinkery with credibility in the museum field, particularly as the museum incorporates findings from the research into exhibit refinement, program development, and staff training. The research will be most helpful to the museum if the university researchers maintain open communication with museum staff about their process. This dialogue will not only ensure museum staff understand the intent and methods of the research, but will also model this type of academic endeavor for the staff. Meetings and presentations about the stages of the research process will highlight its significance to the museum, so staff will feel ownership of the project.

Designing the new facility for the Thinkery afforded museum staff the opportunity to rethink the visitor experience in terms of exhibits, programs, and staff interactions. With this fresh perspective, the Thinkery staff have been able to draw from experience and research to design new exhibits that not only engage visitors in STEAM learning, but also provide flexibility for open-ended use. This flexible "platform approach" allows museum staff to quickly and easily switch out exhibit components so that visitors might have new experiences with each consecutive visit. This fluidity also supports an attitude of ongoing refinement; with the ability to modify exhibits and experiences without incurring huge costs, the museum can be receptive to feedback from visitors and input from researchers.

The studies conducted by the CCD Lab provide insight into how parent interaction affects children's causal learning and scientific reasoning; although the museum cannot control parent interaction, museums can provide guidance for parents in the form of verbal suggestions, signage, handouts, and modeling best practices during staff-led programs. Thinkery staff will incorporate findings from these studies into staff training sessions on effective facilitation and program development. Furthermore, as the Thinkery continues to refine existing exhibit experiences and design new components, findings from these studies will inform the style and purpose of exhibit text. This research partnership between the Thinkery and the CCD Lab will not only yield empirical evidence to support program, exhibit, and staff development but will also increase the credibility of the museum in the field of informal education.

Discussion of Mutual Benefit

The spirit of the Thinkery is one of adaptability, flexibility, and responsiveness. The staff prides itself, and the facility, on its ability to reflect on successes and challenges and to quickly make changes for improvement. With this attitude, Thinkery staff welcome feedback from guests to improve the visitor experience, from suggestions to offer sensory-friendly hours for children on the autism spectrum to providing waterproof smocks for the water exhibits. The findings from the proposed research projects will provide information that can immediately benefit the programs and the staff who deliver them. As the CCD Lab shares its data analysis with the museum, the staff will be able to make adjustments to program facilitation and program content that incorporate the suggestions from the research. The CCD Lab research will provide a critical step in the feedback loop for exhibit and program refinement at the Thinkery.

Challenges of Partnerships Between Museum Practitioners and Researchers

There are a number of challenges associated with this partnership. The foremost of these challenges is the pace with which each entity can conduct and achieve their stated goals. The Thinkery prides itself on being a nimble and fast-paced organization that can respond quickly to the desires of its members. This means that when new ideas, concepts, or ways to improve the museum are developed, they can be implemented quickly. The scientific research process, on the other hand, is much more methodical and time consuming. The CCD Lab strives to conduct cutting-edge research that is informed by theory and utilizes rigorous and creative methodologies, a process that by its nature takes time. Thus, both partners in this collaboration must acknowledge the pace at which the other entity can operate and must work to find a common ground upon which new strategies can be implemented in the museum without compromising the integrity of the research. New researcher–practitioner partnerships will benefit from close collaboration and frequent communication to ensure that both parties construct shared goals and maximize mutual benefits.

Another challenge to the partnership has been integrating the participation in CCD Lab studies into the overall museum experience. One of the goals in this partnership has been to make science accessible to museum visitors, not only through the exhibits, but through participation in ongoing empirical research being conducted through the CCD Lab. When researchers from the CCD Lab approach families about participating in a study, we do not want them to feel as though we are pulling them away from the fun of the exhibits, rather that we are providing an additional, exciting opportunity to engage with science. We think this can be better achieved by fully integrating information about the CCD Lab into museum literature and promotions.

Conclusion

The CCD Lab and the Thinkery's overlapping and overarching goals are to better understand how science learning happens in the informal learning setting so that we can more effectively impact our visitors and community. We also intend to integrate the findings of the research into the museum programs and staff trainings through communication with learners, teachers, and parents. We aim to communicate this research to parents in order to engage them more effectively in their children's learning. We also intend to use the research from this partnership as a case for how to most effectively develop family and adult/child learning environments. We are well on our way to achieving these goals and are eager to strengthen our ongoing collaborative partnership.

References

Amsterlaw, J., & Wellman, H.M. (2006). Theories of mind in transition: A microgenetic study of the development of false belief understanding. *Journal of Cognition and Development*, 7(2), 139–172. http://eric.ed.gov/?id=EJ830967

Baldwin, D.A., Markman, E.M., & Melartin, R.L. (1993). Infants' ability to draw inferences about nonobvious object properties: Evidence from exploratory play. *Child Development*, 64(3), 711–728. doi: 10.1111/j.1467–8624.1993.tb02938.x

Bonawitz, E.B., van Schijndel, T.J.P., Friel, D., & Schulz, L. (2012). Children balance theories and evidence in exploration, explanation, and learning. *Cognitive Psychology*, *64*(4), 215–234. doi: 10.1016/j.cogpsych.2011.12.002

Cook, C., Goodman, N.D., & Schulz, L.E. (2011). Where science starts: Spontaneous experiments in preschoolers' exploratory play. *Cognition*, *120*(3), 341–349. doi: 10.1016/j.cognition.2011.03.003

Crowley, K., & Siegler, R.S. (1999). Explanation and generalization in young children's strategy learning. *Child Development*, *70*(2), 304–316. doi: 10.1111/1467–8624.00023

Gelman, S.A., Brenneman, K., Macdonald, G., & Roman, M. (2010). *Preschool pathways to science: Ways of doing, thinking, communicating and knowing about science.* Baltimore, MD: Paul H. Brooks Publishing.

Keil, F.C. (2006). Explanation and understanding. *Annual Review of Psychology*, *57*, 227–254.

Legare, C.H. (2012). Exploring explanation: Explaining inconsistent evidence informs exploratory, hypothesis-testing behavior in young children. *Child Development*, *83*(1), 173–185.

Legare, C.H. (2014). The contributions of explanation and exploration to children's scientific reasoning. *Child Development Perspectives*, *8*(2), 101–106. doi: 10.1111/cdep.12070

Legare, C.H., & Gelman, S.A. (2014). Examining explanatory biases in young children's biological reasoning. *Journal of Cognition and Development*, *15*(2), 284–303. doi:10.1080/15248372.2012.749480

Legare, C.H., Gelman, S.A., & Wellman, H.M. (2010). Inconsistency with prior knowledge triggers children's causal explanatory reasoning. *Child Development*, *81*(3), 929–944. doi: 10.1111/j.1467–8624.2010.01443.x

Legare, C.H., & Lombrozo, T. (2014). Selective effects of explanation on learning during early childhood. *Journal of Experimental Child Psychology*, *126*, 198–212.

Legare, C.H., Wellman, H.M., & Gelman, S.A. (2009). Evidence for an explanation advantage in naive biological reasoning. *Cognitive Psychology*, *58*, 177–194. doi: 10.1016/j.cogpsych.2008.06.002

Lombrozo, T. (2006). The structure and function of explanations. *Trends in Cognitive Sciences*, *10*, 464–470.

McEldoon, K.L., Durkin, K.L., & Rittle-Johnson, B. (2013). Is self-explanation worth the time? A comparison to additional practice. *British Journal of Educational Psychology*, *83*(4), 615–632. doi: 10.1111/j.2044–8279.2012.02083.x

Nicolopoulou, A. (2010). The alarming disappearance of play from early childhood education. *Human Development*, *53*(1), 1–4. doi: 10.1159/000268135

Rittle-Johnson, B., Saylor, M., & Swygert, K.E. (2008). Learning from explaining: Does it matter if Mom is listening? *Journal of Experimental Child Psychology*, *100*(3), 215–224. doi: 10.1016/j.jecp.2007.10.002

Schulz, L.E., & Bonawitz, E.B. (2007). Serious fun: Preschoolers engage in more exploratory play when evidence is confounded. *Developmental Psychology*, *43*, 1045–1050. http://psycnet.apa.org/journals/dev/43/4/1045.pdf

Schulz, L.E., Bonawitz, E.B., & Griffiths, T.L. (2007). Can being scared cause tummy aches? Naive theories, ambiguous evidence, and preschoolers' causal inferences. *Developmental Psychology*, *43*, 1124–1139.

Siegler, R. (1995). How does change occur: A microgenetic study of number conservation. *Cognitive Psychology*, *28*, 225–273.

Singer, D.G., Golinkoff, R.M., & Hirsh-Pasek, K. (2006). *Play = Learning: How play motivates and enhances children's cognitive and social-emotional growth.* Oxford, UK: Oxford University Press.

Stahl, A.E., & Feigenson, L. (2015). Observing the unexpected enhances infants' learning and exploration. *Science, 348*(6230), 91–94. doi: 10.1126/science.aaa3799

Walker, C.M., Lombrozo, T., Legare, C.H., & Gopnik, A. (2014). Explaining prompts children to privilege inductively rich properties. *Cognition, 133*(2), 343–357. doi: 10.1016/j.cognition.2014.07.008

Walker, C.M., Williams, J.J., Lombrozo, T., & Gopnik, A. (2012). Explaining influences children's reliance on evidence and prior knowledge in causal induction. In N. Miyake, D. Peebles, & R.P. Cooper (Eds.), *Proceedings of the 34th Annual Conference of the Cognitive Science Society* (pp. 1114–1119). Austin, TX: Cognitive Science Society.

Wellman, H.M. (2011). Reinvigorating explanations for the study of early cognitive development. *Child Development Perspectives, 5*, 33–38.

Williams, J.J., & Lombrozo, T. (2010). The role of explanation in discovery and generalization: Evidence from category learning. *Cognitive Science, 34*, 776–806.

SECTION 2
Discussion of Partnerships

9

COLLABORATION IS A TWO-WAY STREET

Suzanne Gaskins

The Author

Suzanne Gaskins is professor emerita of psychology at Northeastern Illinois University. Her research focuses on how cultural beliefs and practices structure children's everyday lives and how they influence their learning and development. She has worked in and with children's museums for three decades, studying how families collaborate during their museum visits and how museums can best support learning and social interaction for visitors from all backgrounds.

Seen from the outside, most successful university–museum collaborations often appear to be effortless and rewarding. Having been on the inside of two such collaborations, and having talked to many academics and museum staff about their experiences (often unsuccessful attempts to establish or maintain a connection), I have learned that no collaboration is effortless, and every successful one grows out of a lot of mutual effort and goodwill. Even for those collaborations that are productive, I believe that often the two collaborating parties have very different understandings about exactly what of value their partnership has produced. In this chapter, I will describe my own experiences as an academic collaborating with museums, then discuss the partnerships represented in two of the chapters of this book, analyzing specific examples of what each member of the partnership gained. Finally, I will identify some of the potential difficulties and rewards of university–museum collaborations, drawing from the chapters reviewed, my own experiences, and what I have seen in other collaborations. The bottom line from my perspective as a researcher: Great rewards can be reaped through complex and long-lasting collaborations, but only if the cultural differences between academia and the museum world are respected and taken seriously so that they can be bridged through open-mindedness and patience on both sides.

My Perspective on University–Museum Collaborations

I am a cultural developmental psychologist. I received my Ph.D. in education from the University of Chicago, and until I retired recently, I taught at Northeastern Illinois University (in Chicago) in the Psychology Department. I do research from a sociocultural perspective, studying how children's everyday activities, in collaboration with others, influence their development and their learning. In particular, I study how the cultural organization of their everyday worlds and their interactions with others structure their experiences, leading to culturally specific developmental outcomes.

For the last 35 years, I have done ongoing fieldwork focused on children and their families in a small Mayan village in the state of Yucatan, Mexico. I have studied Mayan children from infancy through middle childhood, looking at their play and exploration (Gaskins, 2013; Gaskins, 2014a, 2014b), their work within the family (Gaskins, 2014c), and their social relationships (Gaskins, 2006). I also have studied how social practices (based on broader cultural beliefs) (Gaskins, 1999; Gaskins & Paradise, 2010) and the structure of their language (Lucy & Gaskins, 2001) influence their learning and development.

My work is aimed at problematizing some of the claims about universal processes and outcomes of children's development and learning that have been made in developmental psychology based on studying primarily middle-class, non-Hispanic white families in the United States and similar European cultures. This argument about cultural variation in everyday activities is especially relevant in approaches to learning and development that argue that learning and development occur during shared activity, situated in particular contexts, such as Vygotsky's sociocultural theory. Whenever differences in caregivers' style of interaction are found (e.g., in museum-based research, Callanan et al., this volume; Friedlieb & Gaskins, 2007), one important question is whether cultural understandings are contributing to those differences.

There is nothing about this intellectual agenda that directly suggests that I would be particularly interested in museums. However, since I am interested in how children's everyday social experiences are structured and how they help them learn and develop, I have found it very useful for my research in the United States to conduct studies in children's museums where natural family interactions are public and plentiful. In particular, I have especially focused on how such activities differ across cultural groups who come to visit the museum (Gaskins, 2008a, 2008b, 2009a). Museums often assume that all visitors will approach their visit and interact with exhibits in the same way. Museums that base their exhibits on play and exploration often see these activities as universal and natural (culture-free). However, if one assumes that children learn while embedded in social context, then it is not difficult to imagine that families from different backgrounds will bring distinct habits of interaction to informal learning environments based on their beliefs about children's development and learning and their social roles in the family—habits that lead them to have distinct patterns of behavior as visitors to museums, where they are learning through interaction with others. And the role of play may differ across cultures as well, especially in cultures that invest in children working alongside family members (Gaskins, 2014c) and in observational learning (Gaskins & Paradise, 2010).

I first became interested in how children and their families learn in museums when I worked at the Please Touch Museum in Philadelphia in the late 1980s as their "child development specialist." I was moving to Philadelphia as a "trailing spouse" and had mailed a letter with my resume to a wide range of institutions and professionals in the area in hopes of finding a job. Something about my outreach attracted the attention of the new director of the museum, Nancy Kolb, and after a few conversations, she decided to create a position for me. I am not entirely clear why she made this decision (one that I suspect was not universally applauded by the staff at the time); perhaps it was because, while she was experienced in the museum world, she was new to working in a children's museum and thus knew little about young children's learning. She may have felt she needed someone new on the staff who could provide that perspective for her.

Working at the museum was a wonderful experience. Because my position was a new one in the institution, and somewhat under-defined when I started, I was invited to advise in almost every department of the museum—exhibit development, evaluation, program development, collections, the museum store, and community outreach. In addition, I offered the staff mini-classes about children's development, the role of play in childhood, and research methods. I was very impressed with the talent and energy of the staff, but I was also amazed how few people outside the Education Department knew much about children's development and how children learn. As an academic, I was also surprised by how many decisions were made *not* on the basis of systematic data about visitor behavior or learning outcomes, but rather on the assumptions, instincts, and biases of the staff. In these respects, the museum did not differ much from other similar institutions at the time.

As more people took my mini-classes about children and research, and as they had concrete experience in observing visitors in unbiased ways, I felt that the staff posed more informed questions than they had before, and that they became used to using higher standards of evidence in answering them. More often, an exhibit design committee, formed of people from the departments of Exhibits, Education, and Collections, would go out on the museum floor and observe visitor behavior when they could not agree about some detail during the design process. From my perspective, this was a vast improvement over their former abstract arguments about whether a certain component would be engaging or support learning. These changes in how the work of the museum was done evolved slowly through continued conversations with an academic colleague (me) across a wide range of activities. It serves as a good example of how exposure over time to a scholarly perspective can influence museum practice.

For my part, I found it intellectually useful to have to articulate abstract and theory-driven research findings to an applied setting. When pushed by the realities on the ground, I often found holes in my knowledge or in the research itself. For example, I found little research at the time looking at what caregivers do spontaneously to support learning in everyday interactions (*not* observed in a laboratory setting), how circumstances effect their engagement, and whether or not their engagement influenced children's learning. I also found the museum floor to be wonderful laboratory-in-the-real-world for conducting research. Not only was it easy to get participants from the endless stream of visitors, but because the museum exhibits and programs were already artificially constructed experiences, it was relatively easy to compare exhibits or modify them on some dimension that was theoretically interesting. For example, for one study done at Please Touch Museum, we observed visitor behavior across the several exhibits in the museum and described the kind of learning we saw and whether or not it occurred during interaction (Puchner, Rapoport, & Gaskins, 2001). We also conducted a study that looked at whether the kind of interaction offered by an adult influenced children's understanding of a component that involved mechanical physics. Children interacted with research assistants posing as museum staff who were trained to vary their interactions across children, either giving them direct instruction about how to achieve the goal of the component, scaffolding content information (asking targeted open-ended questions), or providing encouragement. Children who interacted through scaffolding were more able to solve a new problem using the same principles than those who received direct instruction (Puchner & Gaskins, 2002; see also Haden et al., 2014, for another study that varied visitor experience in an exhibit).

Finally, I began to teach an applied developmental psychology research course for undergraduate psychology majors at the University of Pennsylvania that conducted research at the museum, a course originally developed by Rochelle Gelman. I discovered that such applied research is a powerful opportunity for undergraduates, making what is often a dull class (research methods) exciting and meaningful. A requirement for all of the course research was that it had to be theoretically motivated but also of direct interest to the museum. Many of the projects considered gender or age differences in visitor engagement (and sometimes how to erase them by providing new props, etc.), but they also included projects looking at how exhibit characteristics influence family interaction. For example, in later research classes held at the Chicago Children's Museum, we compared the effect on interaction of exhibit characteristics such as seating (Gaskins, Barbosa, & Obirek, 2007), signage (Gaskins, Flores, Gonzalez, & Ursetto, 2007), and explicit goals (Cole & Gaskins, 2007). This work, at both the Please Touch Museum and the Chicago Children's Museum, was of practical value to the museum, but it also helped staff come to understand the power of using research to inform their practice.

The Value of Complex and Long-Lasting Collaborations

Most museums do not have a "house academic" on staff, but many often work with academics in a variety of ways. How these partnerships work and what they produce is the topic of all the chapters in this book. If the partnerships are deep and long-lasting, they approach the position I had at Please Touch Museum. Since that chapter in my life, I have had the privilege and pleasure of participating in partnerships with two other children's museums in Chicago. At Kohl Children's Museum in the 1990s, I brought students to conduct research on visitor behavior and learning for several years, but my involvement in the museum was otherwise limited. Following that partnership, I worked for over a decade with the Chicago Children's Museum as an advisor and a research collaborator for a National Science Foundation (NSF) grant, and I also regularly taught my research class there.

The depth of that relationship came close to that I had valued at the Please Touch Museum for its multiple layers and longevity. I got to know most of the senior staff, and I was invited to participate in and advise on many projects, so I became more aware of the museum's perspective and goals and what kind of information would be useful for them to have. On the other side, I conducted several research projects through my research class, through a shared NSF grant, and for my own independent research purposes, and the goals and outcomes of those projects was regularly communicated not only to the leadership staff but to the entire staff at general staff meetings.

On the basis of my own experience and my observations of other collaborations, I have come to believe that the richest partnerships—those that will have the biggest impact on both the researchers and the museum staff—are those that establish a strong partnership through complexity and breadth (i.e., academics involved in a number of roles) and depth (i.e., lasting over time). Such relationships are evident in many of the chapters in this book. As an academic, I come to any problem with a certain set of goals and assumptions, and I have learned over the years that museum staff not only does not always share them, but they do not fully understand them, just as I do not always fully understand their goals and assumptions. Developing key partnerships between individuals and being known by a wide range of staff are great helps in getting past such roadblocks.

The two chapters I will comment on here both share this kind of long-term, in-depth partnership between academics and museum staff, and as a result, their work is exemplary in showing how valuable collaboration can be. However, they represent different kinds of researchers whose partnerships with museums can potentially lead to mutually beneficial knowledge: researchers who focus on how specific content is best learned, especially at different ages, and researchers who focus more generally on how informal learning occurs, especially during interaction with others (peers, families, etc.). The Evans et al. chapter (this volume) is about collaboration at the New York Hall of Science that exemplifies the first kind of partnership; the Callanan et al. chapter (this volume) is about collaboration at the Children's Discovery Museum of San Jose that exemplifies the second kind of partnership (and is more similar to my own experience). (Note that this distinction excludes examples of using researchers as advisors rather than research partners, a relationship that perhaps is more common. For example, many museums call upon content specialists to learn about a specific topic when designing an exhibit, or they call upon psychophysicists to determine the best physical characteristics of a display for effective use.)

Taken together, these two chapters, because of their slightly different perspectives, provide a rich source for understanding how researcher–practitioner partnerships develop and what they can produce. Both are strong examples of how such collaborations can be especially useful when they endure over time and when the academics are centrally involved in all aspects of a project, allowing both sides to become comfortable with the working assumptions and goals of the other. Yet because the role of the academics are somewhat different, their experiences are not identical because the ways in which such partnerships contribute to the primary goals of the researchers and the museums are influenced to some degree by the researcher's primary interest, even while some of the obstacles are the same. For instance, the project at the New York Hall of Science could use the researchers as content specialists but had evaluators on the team as well, while the project at the Children's Discovery Museum of San Jose had content specialists on the project, but the researchers could serve as evaluators.

Collaboration at the New York Hall of Science

The project at the New York Hall of Science illustrates the "push me–pull you" nature of collaborations, with each side of the collaboration producing something better and more creative because of the tensions growing out of not fully aligned interests. Evans and Weiss characterize their team's academic interest as "investigating science learning," and their museum interest as creating "a compelling informal learning experience" (p. 38, this volume). Their approach of how to use academics differs from the more common content specialist who is an academic called in to help practitioners understand the basics of some content area (e.g., some topic in physics, biology, history, or economics) because they decided it was important to have their content specialists involved in the actual design of the exhibit and to do dedicated research to answer issues that arose during that process.

Their "spiral model" for exhibit design integrates research, exhibit development, and evaluation in an iterative process. By including the academic researchers in addition to evaluators doing front-end evaluation, the design process was shaped more deeply by their knowledge about how children learn about biology in general and evolution in particular. This integration was practically achieved by having all members of the team attend all planning meetings. How their spiral model shaped the exhibit is described in detail in their chapter, but two examples will be discussed here to show the impact it can have for both sides of the team.

The first example illustrates the value for the museum members of the collaboration when the researchers pushed them early on. Existing research by Evans and colleagues had shown that there was a significant change across the target ages in children's understanding of biological concepts, with younger children showing more "intuitive" understanding and older children showing more "informed" understanding, and a period of transition from one kind of understanding to another. And five key concepts about evolution were already defined by a previous collaboration by the academic researcher and an exhibit designer. While this information was clearly useful and promised to help the museum conceptualize an informative and accessible exhibit, it posed a design problem because it identified too many topics to present to three different audiences (younger, transitional, and older children). And yet, the academics on the team felt it was important to keep this complexity intact in the exhibit.

The team solved this problem together, which illustrates how the project differs from one that just consults content specialists, and the important value of enduring collaboration. The two "bottom lines" that had been in conflict were resolved by narrowing the exhibit to one kind of animal. Their solution to focus on birds allowed the practitioners to feel like the exhibit would have a single focus (Serrell's *Big Idea*), while it satisfied the researchers because it preserved the multiple and complex factors involved in evolution and allowed them to be addressed at several developmental levels. If the researchers had not been at the table, perhaps their concerns about content would have lost out to those of the museum practitioners about interest and accessibility. But because they were there, an integrative solution had to be found, one that satisfied both parties. It is a testament to both groups that each respected the other's concerns enough to work toward a solution that both could be happy with. Evaluators also made a key contribution: They conducted front-end research about children's knowledge of and interest in birds; this research confirmed that birds would provide a good example to work with, one that could be usefully connected to their dinosaur ancestors and that would allow children to generalize to humans. Undoubtedly, the exhibit retained more important and integrated information about evolution because of the researchers' concerns than it would have if museum staff had developed the exhibit on their own after listening to a content specialist explain the important concepts in evolution.

The second example illustrates how the researchers were led to extend a line of research in response to a problem that arose during the exhibit's development and the museum staff's insistence for more information. A major issue was whether to use anthropomorphic metaphors in the narrative to help children understand the content. While the researchers were fairly sure (based on previous research on adults and older children) that anthropomorphic content would interfere with children's understanding of the basic concepts about evolution, the museum professionals were hesitant to abandon a compelling tool for telling a story to young children without better evidence.

So new research was done to figure out whether anthropomorphism was an aid or a deterrent in learning about evolution for primary school aged children. They found that, while the youngest children were inclined to adopt an anthropomorphic retelling of the stories (describing what animals "wanted") no matter what kind of story they originally heard, for slightly older children, a "want-based" story (i.e., the animals changed because they wanted to) did not support their subsequent understanding of evolution, while need-based stories and those using explicit evolutionary concepts did. Both of these kinds of reasoning were ultimately used in the exhibit's narrative, while anthropomorphic, want-based reasoning was eliminated from it. In addition to producing a more effective exhibit, this research produced academic publications about the developmental trajectory of children's reasoning about evolution (Evans, 2013; Evans, Rosengren, Lane, & Price, 2012; Legare, Lane, & Evans, 2013)—research that might not have been done without the urging of the museum staff to provide better evidence about how anthropomorphism interfered with children's learning about evolution.

These kinds of mutual benefits could not happen without a long-term, complex partnership, one that developed to include open communication, sympathetic listening, and patience to work together to find a solution to each problem that would lead to both a compelling learning experience in the museum and to a better understanding of how children most effectively learn new scientific concepts. Not all exhibit development has the time or the resources to foster such a partnership, but when both are available, such collaboration based on the "spiral model" can produce a win–win experience for the researchers and the museum professionals involved in the project, producing a more theoretically grounded exhibit and original academic research.

Collaboration at the Children's Discovery Museum of San Jose

The second project, from the Children's Discovery Museum of San Jose, illustrates the second kind of collaboration with academics, which differs from that seen above where the academics are content specialists: the analysis of interaction patterns within visitor groups. This approach focuses on the sociocultural claim that there is "learning-in-progress" (Puchner et al., 2001) and developmental change during shared activities. Since the researchers are interested in how children learn and develop through everyday activities shared with others, the museum offers a favorable environment for studying this by providing shared attention in family groups during natural interaction in a public setting.

Like the partnership discussed above, the Children's Discovery Museum of San Jose and researchers from UC Santa Cruz have worked closely together. Researchers have been part of exhibit design teams, meeting regularly with museum staff from start to finish for a variety of projects across two decades. Because they are always in meetings, they have been able to inform the museum staff during the planning process about relevant research in the fields of child development and learning. In addition, the researchers have filled both the role of evaluator (the first role they were invited to fulfill at the museum) and academic researcher, believing that since there is some overlap between the two roles, it is efficient for one research team to do both. They collect video data to allow them to be able to do the extensive analysis needed for their own research, but they developed a new kind of data analysis for video that they call "blitz coding" that allows them to have a quick turnaround time on data analysis needed by the museum for front-end evaluation. They have also served a role similar to content specialists by conducting front-end evaluation on developmental differences about children's understanding of a particular topic (even though they did not begin as specialists in the content area). Thus, the researchers have made a major commitment to help the museum design and evaluate exhibits. At the same time, the museum has made a major commitment to help the researchers conduct studies about family interaction at the level of rigor expected in their field. Although their chapter is a rich catalog of how they have benefited from their collaboration, two examples from their chapter will be discussed here to illustrate how their collaboration has been mutually informative and beneficial.

The first example from this project shows the value to museum staff of having researchers studying the interaction of families in exhibits. Early on in the partnership, the researchers discovered a systematic difference in how parents were talking to boys and girls in a STEM exhibit; they provided more explanations to boys, even though boys and girls did not differ in their level of engagement with the exhibits nor in how many questions they asked (Crowley, Callanan, Tenenbaum, & Allen, 2001). This finding was obviously of interest (and concern) to the museum, which was not aware of the gender differences in their visitor behavior.

The results of the study prompted the museum and researchers to develop a new STEM exhibit based on *Alice in Wonderland*, to see if they could design a STEM exhibit that would reduce or even eliminate the parents' bias toward providing more information to boys than girls. The researchers determined that the new exhibit had erased the gender difference (Callanan, Frazier, & Gorchoff, 2015), providing evidence for the academics to argue that context influenced parental gender bias in their explanatory behavior, and for the museum to document their success in creating a STEM exhibit that was free from gender bias. The exhibit won the American Association of Museum's Excellence in Exhibitions award.

Because of this experience, the museum staff became more open to the idea that there might be value to having research partners around. They gained new understanding of the methodological tools that the researchers could provide to identify group differences in visitor behavior. (Subsequently, the researchers have looked at differences in cultural groups and in groups of parents using different guidance styles.) By pairing behavioral observation with surveys and interviews, the researchers could also address how visitor behavior is related to past experience and beliefs, things that cannot be directly observed during a museum visit.

The second example from this project demonstrates how the researchers gained a new research line by being exposed to new ideas by the museum staff and other team members. When faced with the problem of how to help children access the difficult field of paleontology, the PI from the museum decided to focus on how children could discover evidence by examining artifacts, supported by a science education researcher from UC Berkeley who had developed a program for teachers and students that encouraged them to understand science not as an accumulation of facts but as a process of "asking questions, evaluating evidence, and revising beliefs."

This new direction led the research team to expand their investigation of interaction beyond their previous focus on explanation to include talk about evidence and evaluation of children's revisions of their beliefs as a result of interaction. Ongoing research is showing that there are connections between how much parents discuss evidence and how likely children are to revise their beliefs. In addition, the researchers have come to realize by looking at talk about evidence (in contrast to explanation) that meaning-making in families may be more collaborative and reciprocal, and not simply initiated by the parents and directed toward the children. This new way of thinking about learning and development on the part of the researchers has grown directly out of the museum staff's searching for ways to help families use evidence from artifacts to understand fossils.

Clearly, this partnership has been highly successful and is valued by both the researchers and the museum staff. After working together for two decades, they are very familiar with each other's needs and goals and can anticipate conflicts and work sympathetically together to solve them. They have each learned a lot from the other and thus approach new projects with mutual respect. Their mutual investment has paid great dividends to everyone in the collaboration.

Five Domains of Cultural Conflict Between Museums and Academics

Even the authors of these two chapters, who have had very successful, long-term collaborations, report that it is sometimes difficult to bridge the gap between the culture of informal education institutions and the culture of academics. In my own work with museums, I have identified five general domains of interaction where this culture conflict has been most troublesome (Gaskins, 2009b).

The first domain, and the most basic, is in the differing priorities of the two groups. Museum staff have as their bottom line the quality of the visitor experience and the financial health of the institution. Researchers have as their bottom line the professional standards and the theoretical logic for doing research or for constructing learning experiences. When these two come into conflict, it is difficult not only because the two groups disagree, but also often because they are not particularly aware of or sympathetic to each other's concerns. Thus, such differences can generate bad feelings.

For example, a researcher may want to have particular characteristics in a component to test a theoretical hypothesis that the design team does not think will yield the optimal visitor experience (an example of which was reported by Callanan et al., this volume). Or more mundanely, research scheduled to take place in a multipurpose room may be bumped to host a revenue-generating birthday party. While the conflicts cannot be completely avoided, those collaborations that are long-standing and are based on close relationships and strong communication can mitigate the fallout from them. Researchers who are working within an established relationship can more effectively persuade museum staff to include the necessary components and work to find a way to make them more visitor-friendly because the museum staff is in general committed to having researchers in their institution doing basic research. And researchers have time to learn to accept that money-making activities are almost always going to trump their research. But they can also push to be informed of last-minute changes in time to avoid having a full research team show up to collect data only to find that their space has been taken over by some other activity. Thus, these basic differences in priorities loom large in new relationships when they are unexpected, and there may be little sympathy for the other side. Their importance and intractability tend to diminish over time even though they may never fully disappear.

A second domain of potential conflict is the time frame that each team is accustomed to. Museum staff are used to very short turn-around time for gathering and analyzing information; the time pressure to make a decision often is so strong that the staff must move forward even though the information available is not complete. Academic researchers have much less time pressure on them; their primary pressure is to make sure that the information is complete and accurate, even if it takes a while to collect and analyze it. The museum is usually working in a time frame of days or perhaps weeks, while the academic researchers are working in a time frame of months, if not years. One solution to this mismatch of time frames is to acknowledge and accept that there are different standards for collecting different types of information. For example, Callanan's "blitz coding" system was developed to give feedback to the design team and that served the museum's need for timely information, but it did not replace their more detailed coding for their research reports (which the museum could wait for more patiently, once their own needs had been met).

A third domain is interaction style. The museums where I have worked were very friendly places. Staff were used to interacting a lot and having long discussions together in a process of joint decision-making. As an academic, I was used to working more independently and was used to being the top of a hierarchy of graduate and undergraduate students who take my classes and work on their research with me. The sociability and egalitarian nature of a museum's way of doing business has often struck me as being inefficient and even unnecessarily socially sensitive. The independent decision-making that I am used to has, on occasion, struck museum staff as being brusque and perhaps even self-important. Conversations I have had with other researchers working in museums and with museum staff receiving researchers in their institutions suggest that my experiences are not unique. Recognizing these differences in styles of interaction and decision making goes a long way toward not rubbing each other the wrong way, and it is especially useful for all parties involved to know each other well. I have found it particularly helpful to have a single person in the museum be identified as the primary museum contact for research. As our sense of shared purpose developed over time, we found it natural for the staff member to serve as my "ambassador" or "cultural broker" to help others in the museum interpret my odd behavior and to smooth over ruffled feathers, and I have served the same role when my students and colleagues have been confused or impatient over some museum rule or some interaction with the liaison.

How one should communicate research results is a fourth domain of cultural difference. Museum staff, by the very nature of what they do, are often very creative in how they want to engage their audiences and communicate information. They may use narrative, props, or games to engage the audience, and usually encourage a lot of audience participation. Academics, in contrast, often stick to formal presentations. They often speak in the specialized language of "acadamese," expressing ideas by using specialized jargon instead of everyday vocabulary, often in convoluted sentences. They also often present research results as statistics and graphs, assuming statistical literacy, with very few words to explain what the numbers and graphs mean. And they may focus more on theoretical implications of the findings rather than applied ones. For them, this approach to presenting their research allows them to be precise and concise. To nonacademics, it just makes them appear obtuse and boring.

As an academic, I am not comfortable wearing silly hats, singing, or batting balloons out to an audience while giving a talk. I feel it is just distracting. But I think it is reasonable to ask me, when speaking to nonacademics, to explain ideas without using jargon, to explain results in words as well as numbers, and to explain what I feel are the practical implications of the research. One of the biggest benefits for academics working in applied research is the pressure to have both their writing and speaking be clear and accessible to a general audience who wants to understand the research. Often, distilling and clarifying ideas allows them to become clearer to the academic as well. Likewise, while museum staff may still want to wear a silly hat or present some hands-on exercise to get the audience engaged, they can come to see that there is communicative value in presenting their information in a more structured and formal manner.

The final domain of difference is the scope of conclusions. During the question and answer period of almost every talk I have given to a museum staff, the questions go far beyond the scope of the research I have presented. It is reasonable for the staff to want to know the answers to their many questions—answers that could have a great impact on their work. But as an academic, I am more circumspect about how far I am willing to speculate beyond the data themselves. If I have done a study that looks at cultural differences in family interaction but have not analyzed gender differences, I will not be able to answer a question about differences between mothers and fathers. The only way I could do so would be to speculate about any differences based on my informal observations during data collection, which takes me beyond the world of reporting results of the research project and would be at risk of being biased by my own assumptions.

And so my answer to most of the questions I am asked is, "I have no idea," or "The research didn't address that question." I am sure from their point of view, it seems like if I spent so much time working on a problem, I should have a lot more answers! I have come to see this difference in expectations about the scope of research findings arising from a naïveté among museum staff about the power of a research project. Research projects usually ask very narrow questions because of the logistical demands of research methods and the desire to be very confident about the conclusions that are reached. They answer the narrow questions very well, but there is little ability to generalize with any confidence. Academics are willing to speculate about interesting questions to address in future research but are less willing to speculate about what their answers might be. For instance, I could easily agree with the staff member asking about differences in mothers' and fathers' behavior that it would be valuable to reanalyze my cultural differences data to include comparing ways of interacting according to parent gender, or, if there were not enough observations to allow me to do the necessary statistical analyses, I could decide to collect data on more families in order to be able to answer this question.

Again, a long-term partnership helps museum staff to recognize not only the power but also the limitations of research in answering their questions. If I am unwilling to answer a question that goes beyond the data collected, in a presentation to museum staff who know me and my research well, the staff member asking the question is more likely to accept my hesitance to answer their question and refocus on the results presented. Research-savvy staff are even less likely to ask such questions but rather focus on understanding the implications of the findings presented. And the partnership helps researchers to be sure, as they develop their project, that they are targeting research questions that will yield results that are not only reliable and valid, but also meaningful to the museum.

How I Have Profited from Collaborating With Museums

Despite all of these domains of cultural conflict, my complex, long-term collaborations with the Please Touch Museum early on in my career, and more recently those with the Chicago Children's Museum, have been fun, exciting, productive, and very satisfying. In closing, I will articulate some of the many ways that I have profited by such collaborations. Callanan and Evans undoubtedly have their own list of what they have gained from their collaborations, but I suspect there would be substantial overlap with mine. Undoubtedly, the length of the list of benefits for each of them, as for me, has grown over time, as their partnerships have become stronger, and they successfully negotiated some of the difficulties listed in the previous section.

First and foremost, I have benefited by doing my research in a museum because it has been a very effective real-world laboratory for my research agenda, producing results that are more likely to reflect families' learning in everyday activities and the resulting changes in children's understanding than those produced in a lab on campus, yet with more control and accessibility that trying to study them at home.

The first way a museum is an effective real-world laboratory is that, because the environment is an artificial one, it can be varied systematically across samples of visitors to see how behavior is shaped by context. True experiments (outside an artificial lab setting) can be done where a single variable is manipulated by making small changes in an exhibit and observing visitor behavior in the various conditions. For instance, I have varied whether a task is presented as having a goal or being open-ended by manipulating the physical characteristics of an exhibit. Or, multiple exhibits can be studied in which some share one characteristic and others share a different one. For instance, I have looked at three exhibits in which there is a goal built into the exhibit compared with three in which the activity is designed to be open-ended. While the data collected in museums is often "messier" than lab data because of the complexity of its real-world setting, the findings are likely to reflect the everyday experiences of children and their families and therefore yield more valid conclusions about everyday learning.

The second way a museum is an effective real-world laboratory is that it provides a wide range of kinds of families, *allowing the study of many kinds of group differences*: cultural differences, economic class differences, age differences, gender differences, and so on. The location of the Chicago Children's Museum at Navy Pier, a very popular attraction for a wide range of Chicago residents and visitors, has unusual amounts of class and cultural diversity in their visitor demographics. The cultural variability in visitors has been particularly valuable to me because of my interest in how cultures shape everyday learning, including the role of play in learning and patterns of family interaction that organize learning through shared activities.

These and many other theoretical topics I am interested in and are amenable to study in a museum context are also central to the museum's general interests as well. These interests include learning more how informal learning works (and how it is different from formal learning contexts), the role of play in learning through discovery, and the role of interaction in learning. That my central theoretical interests are in harmony with central concerns of the museum has made the collaboration especially rewarding for me.

Second, the museum has provided me with a powerful teaching tool. I have provided research experience to graduate and undergraduate students as research assistants and interns, supervised M.A. theses and B.A. papers of students doing original research in the museum, and used the museum as a site for an undergraduate research methods course. In the course, the students have worked in teams to design, conduct, analyze, and report on a research study of interest to the museum that also has a theoretical motivation. I have had the students develop two presentations: they present their findings on campus at a student research symposium and then present them to the museum staff. This underscores for them the importance of taking your audience into account when interpreting research findings. The applied aspect of the research is particularly compelling to undergraduate students. The research project becomes more than just a learning exercise because they understand that the museum staff will want to use the findings to inform their work. Many former students have told me, years later, that it is the one course they remember well.

Third, I value having been able to use my knowledge and my perspective as an outsider to help the institutions I have worked with as a partner or as a consultant to recognize and reflect on unarticulated assumptions. Working so closely with two museums has given me insights into ways to help museums reflect on how they do their work. Most museums make many assumptions—some of which are mistaken and/or interfere with their goals. A major example from my perspective is the assumption that the learning process is universal, and thus, that visitors from different cultural groups will use the museum in the same way—that is, the way the staff envisions it will be used. When nontraditional visitors violate this assumption (e.g., parents from nondominant cultural groups interact with their children in different ways, or objects are used differently by different groups), staff can be judgmental. Helping them see that these visitors are not doing things wrong, but just differently (and based on beliefs that are important to them) can help them be more interested in designing exhibits for all visitors and less judgmental (and more curious) when they see differences in visitor behavior (Gaskins, 2008a, 2008b, 2009a). I would hope that more researchers would include samples of visitors from different cultural groups to add to this body of knowledge so that museums can continue to learn more about how to interpret differences in visitor behavior more open-mindedly and to develop resources that are accessible and valued by all visitors.

It is interesting to note that in the two chapters reviewed above, neither the project at the New York Hall of Science nor the most recent project at the Children's Discovery Museum of San Jose took group differences as a major issue for study. From my point of view, each of their research projects focuses on a topic that ethnographic evidence suggests might have important variation across cultures. While Callanan has consistently done so in her other work with the Children's Discovery Museum (e.g., Siegel, Esterly, Callanan, Wright, & Navarro, 2007; Tenenbaum & Callanan, 2008), in their most recent work on evidence, they have not yet incorporated looking at how different cultural groups use evidence talk, even though they have found individual differences in parents' use of evidence, and there is reason to believe from the literature that parents from some cultural groups might be more inclined to spontaneously ask evidence questions of their children than others. And while Evans has in the past looked at how cultural and religious beliefs influence families' understanding of evolution (e.g., Evans, 2000, 2001), this current project also did not look at cultural differences in how families used different kinds of evidence, even though there is some reason to believe that children in some cultures might be less inclined to use anthropomorphic (intentional) reasoning (e.g., Gaskins, 2013) than children in cultures where animals are regularly assigned personalities and inner states in stories.

Another major assumption often found in museums focused on young children is their unstated model of learning—in particular, whether learning is thought of as primarily an individual activity or a group activity. When children's museums first appeared in the 1970s and early 1980s, they began working with a constructivist assumption about learning—each child takes in information and constructs meaning as an individual (perhaps during interaction with peers). This model of individual learning, based on the writings of Piaget and Montessori, organized exhibit development, programming, outreach, promotion, and more, but it often was never explicitly recognized. More recently, many children's museums have embraced an alternative model of learning that sees learning happening in groups, not individuals, and believes, based on Vygotsky's sociocultural theory, that children's learning happens through communication and shared activity. Sometimes this sea change in an institution's understanding of the nature of learning has happened with no explicit awareness. In some institutions, some staff have shifted their perspective while others have not. Helping staff articulate their operational theory of learning allows them to recognize their differences, to agree on an explicit commitment, and to apply it more effectively and intentionally. For instance, should seating be planned for one child, for a group of children, or for adults and children together? Should signs be nonverbal, aimed at children, and placed down low or include verbal information aimed at adults and placed higher? Should they convey information or promote conversation? Should pictures representing visitors' experiences engaged with an exhibit be of a single child, of a group of children working together, or of a caregiver and child(ren)?

Other assumptions that museums make include assumptions about the kinds of information visitors will extract from the exhibits and their experiences in them. While evaluation can help illuminate how exhibits are being used and where learning is occurring and where it is not, I find that museum staff often optimistically overestimate how engaged visitors are and what they take away from exhibits and programs. It is natural in informal observations, where there is no systematicity in data gathering, to look for confirming evidence and to ignore disconfirming evidence. Putting learning in museums under the (ideally impartial) microscope of research methods can help museum staff become more cautious about assuming that learning is happening and more curious about how to insure that it does.

Fourth, I have enjoyed helping museum staff understand and commit to being consumers and producers of research. In addition to helping museums recognize and reflect on their assumptions, I have been surprised to find how difficult it is for an institution (and individuals within institutions) to use academic research. For most staff in museums, theoretically driven academic research is a bit of mystery and sometimes seen as more trouble to conduct than it is worth. And always, it is seen as a huge consumer of precious resources—time and money. Sometimes one or two people at an institution are interested in doing research that goes beyond evaluation of a single exhibit, but they cannot get their superiors interested in supporting it. And often, those who want to do research do not have the training or resources to execute a project.

Perhaps the first step in getting an institution to become familiar with academic research and commit resources to it is to help them consume existing research that is useful to them. Academics affiliated with museums, even loosely, can serve this useful purpose, both in providing articles and books about topics requested by the museum and by offering access to other research the museum may not even realize exists but may be relevant to their work. The second step might be to identify and invite academics whose research is of potential interest for the museum to come and conduct a small study in the museum, allowing museum staff to see research up close so they can pay attention to what they do, why they do it, and what they find. More serious institutional commitment to research may then be able to follow as a relationship develops: writing a research component into a grant (which the researcher can help draft), constructing dedicated research space in the museum (in an exhibit or as a free-standing space), and modifying exhibits and programs to test research hypotheses (e.g., Haden et al., 2014). For instance, at the Chicago Children's Museum, through an NSF grant, we were able to install audio and video equipment for research purposes, both in an exhibit and in a free-standing space, using the expertise of the Exploratorium to help us conceptualize the project and to guide us in installation.

Academics can facilitate the acceptance of research in a museum by recognizing the cultural clashes discussed previously and respecting the priorities and concerns of the museum. One important understanding is that no research priority should come ahead of visitor experience and revenue-generating activities. Researchers should work to minimize the impact of their studies not only on visitors, but on staff as well. Perhaps the leadership of the museum has committed support for a research project, but a floor staff member may not understand what is happening nor want to accommodate the practical needs of the researcher. A second important understanding is that it is the researcher's responsibility to demonstrate the ways in which research is interesting and useful for the institution and the people who work there—the transparent value of doing research should not be assumed. Asking research questions that have clear practical implications (and ideally, that have been developed in partnership with the museum staff) can make everyone on staff more excited about the project and therefore more patient with the inconveniences. And reporting the findings to the entire staff of the museum sets the stage for the next project.

At the Chicago Children's Museum, for many years, one all-staff meeting a year was devoted to research reports by me and my students. Over time, this significant commitment did a lot to instill an interest in our research—and in research more generally—at all levels of the museum. But there are less "costly" ways of disseminating information that are also effective: researchers sitting in regularly on meetings offering ideas from existing research (theirs and others), electronic dissemination of useful research articles, tips toward useful bibliographic websites, and so on.

Beyond working with a single institution, about five years ago, I organized a locally based network of academics and museum staff interested in promoting research inside cultural institutions called the Chicago Cultural Organizations' Research Network (or CCORN). It has members from most of the major cultural institutions in Chicago, and some smaller ones, coming from departments of exhibit design, education, evaluation, and elsewhere within their institutions. It also has as members professors and graduate students from half a dozen universities in the area and several freelance evaluators. It serves as an online interest group, meets formally two to three times per year for presentations by members of the group or guests (each time hosted by a different institution), and has more informal social networking events throughout the city that help members get to know each other better. The network has helped institutions be more aware of the kind of research that their fellow institutions and academics do (or would like to do), and it has helped researchers become more aware of the institutional interest in research and some of the barriers. For staff from institutions where research is not an active part of their agenda, it has given them an important network of like-minded colleagues and mentors, so that they continue to stay motivated to work to bring research into their institutions.

Conclusion

The chapters in this book and my own experience demonstrate the potential value of collaborations between academic researchers and institutions of informal learning—especially collaborations that are complex and long-lasting. But it would be a mistake to think that every researcher or every institution is going to find the advantages obvious at first or that there will be no bumps along the road to productive collaboration. The thoughtful narratives provided in this book, including the two reviewed in this chapter, richly demonstrate how the process involves the coordination of two ways of viewing the world—two cultures. The goal is not to collapse them into one, but rather to develop a set of "rules of the road" so that the traffic flows smoothly and head-on collisions are avoided. As such, they may provide other researchers and institutions a road map for their own collaborations, or at least helpful suggestions about how to construct a productive partnership, what to expect, and how to avoid pitfalls. But its biggest value may be in inspiring them to try.

References

Callanan, M., Frazier, B., & Gorchoff, S. (2015). Closing the gender gap: Family conversations about science in an "Alice's Wonderland" exhibit. Unpublished manuscript. University of California, Santa Cruz.

Cole, M., & Gaskins, S. (2007). Family problem solving in an exhibit with and without a goal. Poster presented at the annual meeting of the National Association for the Education of Young Children, Chicago, IL.

Crowley, K., Callanan, M.A., Tenenbaum, H.R., & Allen, E. (2001). Parents explain more often to boys than to girls during shared scientific thinking. *Psychological Science, 12*(3), 258–261.

Evans, E.M. (2000). The emergence of beliefs about the origins of species in school-age children. *Merrill-Palmer Quarterly: A Journal of Developmental Psychology, 46*, 221–254.

Evans, E.M. (2001). Cognitive and contextual factors in the emergence of diverse belief systems: Creation versus evolution. *Cognitive Psychology, 42*, 217–266.

Evans, E.M. (2013). Conceptual change and evolutionary biology: Taking a developmental perspective. In S. Vosniadou (Ed.), *International handbook of research on conceptual change* (2nd ed.; pp. 220–239). New York: Routledge.

Evans, E.M., Rosengren, K., Lane, J.D., & Price, K.S. (2012). Encountering counterintuitive ideas: Constructing a developmental learning progression for biological evolution. In K. R. Rosengren, S. Brem, E.M. Evans, & G. Sinatra (Eds.), *Evolution challenges: Integrating research and practice in teaching and learning about evolution* (pp. 174–199). New York: Oxford University Press.

Friedlieb, R., & Gaskins, S. (2007). Caregivers' teaching style and its relation to children's learning of construction concepts in a museum. Poster presented at the annual meeting of the National Association for the Education of Young Children, Chicago, IL.

Gaskins, S. (1999). Children's daily lives in a Mayan village: A case study of culturally constructed roles and activities. In A. Göncü (Ed.), *Children's engagement in the world* (pp. 25–81). Cambridge, UK: Cambridge University Press.

Gaskins, S. (2006). The cultural organization of Yucatec Mayan children's social interactions. In X. Chen, D. French, & B. Schneider (Eds.), *Peer relationships in cultural context* (pp. 283–309). Cambridge, UK: Cambridge University Press.

Gaskins, S. (2008a). The cultural meaning of play and learning in children's museums. *Hand to Hand, 22*(4), 1–2, 8–11.

Gaskins, S. (2008b). Designing exhibitions to support families' cultural understandings. *Exhibitionist, 27*(1), 10–19.

Gaskins, S. (2009a). Parents' understandings of children's learning in museums. Paper presented at the annual meetings of the Association of Children's Museums, Philadelphia, PA.

Gaskins, S. (2009b). Museums as research laboratories for academics. Paper presented at the annual meetings of the American Association of Museums, Philadelphia, PA.

Gaskins, S. (2013). Pretend play as culturally constructed activity. In M. Taylor (Ed.), *Oxford handbook on the development of the imagination* (pp. 224–247). Oxford: Oxford University Press.

Gaskins, S. (2014a). Cross-cultural play and play research. In L. Brooker, S. Edwards, & M. Blaise (Eds.), *Handbook of play and learning in early childhood* (pp. 31–42). London: Sage Publications.

Gaskins, S. (2014b). Yucatec Maya children's play. In J.L. Roopnarine, M. Patte, J.E. Johnson, & D. Kuschner (Eds.), *International perspectives on children's play* (pp. 11–22). Berkshire, UK: Open University Press.

Gaskins, S. (2014c). Childhood practices across cultures: Play and household work. In L. Jensen (Ed.), *The Oxford handbook of culture and development* (pp. 185–197). Oxford: Oxford University Press.

Gaskins, S., Barbosa, A., & Obirek, J. (2007). Caregivers' cognitive matchmaking in a museum exhibit. Poster presented at the Cognitive Development Society, Santa Fe, NM.

Gaskins, S., Flores, Z., Gonzalez, N., & Ursetto, V. (2007). Helping families to interact: Can signage increase family collaboration? Presented as part of a symposium, *Designing Exhibits with Family Collaboration in Mind*, at the annual meeting of the American Educational Research Association, Chicago, IL.

Gaskins, S., & Paradise, R. (2010). Learning through observation. In D.F. Lancy, J. Bock, & S. Gaskins (Eds.), *The anthropology of learning in childhood* (pp. 85–117). Lanham, MD: Alta Mira Press.

Haden, C.A., Jant, E.A., Hoffman, P.C., Marcus, M., Geddes, J.R., & Gaskins, S. (2014). Supporting family conversations and children's STEM learning in a children's museum. *Early Childhood Research Quarterly, 29*, 333–344.

Legare, C.H., Lane, J., & Evans, E.M. (2013). Anthropomorphizing science: How does it affect the development of evolutionary concepts? [Special issue]. *Merrill-Palmer Quarterly, 29*(2), 168–197. doi: 10.1353/mpq.2013.0009

Lucy, J., & Gaskins, S. (2001). Grammatical categories and the development of classification preferences: A comparative approach. In S. Levinson & M. Bowerman (Eds.), *Language acquisition and conceptual development* (pp. 257–283). Cambridge, UK: Cambridge University Press.

Puchner, L., & Gaskins, S. (2002). Scaffolding versus direct instruction: The relationship between type of adult interaction and child learning in a children's museum. Unpublished manuscript, Department of Educational Leadership, Southern Illinois University, Carbondale, IL and Department of Psychology, Northeastern Illinois University, Chicago, IL.

Puchner, L., Rapoport, R., & Gaskins, S. (2001). Learning in children's museums: Is it really happening? *Curator, 44*(3), 237–259.

Siegel, D., Esterly, J., Callanan, M., Wright, R., & Navarro, R. (2007). Conversations about science across activities in Mexican-descent families. *International Journal of Science Education, 29*(12), 1447–1466.

Tenenbaum, H., & Callanan, M.A. (2008). Parents' science talk to their children in Mexican-descent families residing in the USA. *International Journal of Behavioral Development, 32*(1), 1–12.

10

RESEARCH AND MUSEUM PARTNERSHIPS

Key Components of Successful Collaborations

Helen Hadani and Caren M. Walker

The Authors

Helen Hadani is the head of research at the Center for Childhood Creativity. She authors original research on creative thinking and child development and established the center's onsite research lab at the Bay Area Discovery Museum. She has over 15 years of experience conducting research with parents and children for toy and technology companies to develop innovative products at Hasbro, Apple, Leapfrog, and LEGO.

Caren Walker is an assistant professor in the Department of Psychology at the University of California, San Diego. Her research examines children's developing ability to learn and reason about the causal structure of the world.

Children's museums and hands-on science centers are popular destinations for families with young children and have become part of daily life for many of them. Over the past decade, museums that attract millions of children and parents annually across the country have also become "learning laboratories" for academic researchers studying children in natural contexts and those looking for access to participant populations (Callanan, 2012; Knutson & Crowley, 2005a, 2005b). As the number of collaborations between university researchers and museums has continued to increase, it has led to the creation of a number of distinct partnership models. These collaborations provide mutual benefits for academic researchers who seek to advance our understanding of children's cognitive, social, and emotional development and museum educators who aim to create an innovative and inclusive learning environment.

This chapter discusses three key components of successful collaborations between developmental researchers and museums that have emerged as a result of these partnerships: (1) access to participants, (2) mutual professional development, and (3) conducting research in context. To provide some background, we will first describe the Center for Childhood Creativity (CCC) at the Bay Area Discovery Museum and the partnership between the CCC and Professor Alison Gopnik's Cognitive Development Lab at the University of California, Berkeley. We will discuss the three components in relation to the CCC, the Living Lab model (see Corriveau et al., this volume), and the collaboration between the Thinkery and the Cognition, Culture, and Development Lab (CCD Lab) at the University of Texas at Austin (see Legare et al., this volume).

The Center for Childhood Creativity at the Bay Area Discovery Museum

The CCC is a research-focused educational institute within the Bay Area Discovery Museum. The joint mission of the museum and the CCC is to ignite and advance creative thinking in all children. The museum hosts more than 300,000 visitors annually and is located on an unparalleled 7.5 acres at the base of the Golden Gate Bridge in Sausalito, California. Children ages 6 months to 8 years, their caregivers, and teachers engage in open-ended and child-directed activities in which there are infinite ways to play, discover, and create with every visit. The museum has a long history of expertise in the development of creative thinking in children and early exposure to science, engineering, and mathematics concepts. In 2011, the museum launched the CCC—a not-for-profit research and training center exploring the components of creativity—extending its impact beyond the museum. The CCC studies the cognitive, social, emotional, and environmental tools required to support creative thinking, with a focus on children ages 0–12 years. The center's work is informed by a robust advisory board including leading developmental psychologists Alison Gopnik, Andrew Meltzoff, and Carol Dweck, research partnerships with premier academic institutions, and a leadership team with expertise in informal learning, formal academic systems, and child development.

Given the museum and CCC's focus on cutting-edge developmental research, its location in the San Francisco Bay Area close to leading universities, and the museum's access to a large number of young children, one of CCC's first goals was to establish an onsite research program to benefit researchers seeking young study participants. In addition, this program would benefit museum guests and staff by making current research available and accessible. To that end, the Creative Thinking Research Lab was established at the Bay Area Discovery Museum in early 2013, and to date, more than 1,200 children have participated in studies at the museum on topics ranging from language development to causal reasoning and motivation. Some of the research conducted at the lab was recently published in *Psychological Science, The Proceedings of the National Academy of Science, Cognition, The American Journal of Play*, and *Psychological Bulletin* (Cortes Barragan & Dweck, 2014; Gopnik & Walker, 2013; Walker & Gopnik, 2013, 2014; Walker, Lombrozo,

Legare, & Gopnik, 2014), with several more papers currently under review and in preparation.

Partnership With Alison Gopnik's Cognitive Development Lab

Professor Alison Gopnik was an early supporter of the onsite research program at the Bay Area Discovery Museum and joined the CCC Advisory Board in early 2013. Professor Gopnik's Cognitive Development Lab in the Psychology Department at the University of California, Berkeley explores how children develop theories about the world, other people, and themselves. In particular, Professor Gopnik and her research team have been investigating young children's causal reasoning and how an understanding of causal relationships helps children learn about language, concepts, and the behavior of others.

Caren Walker, a doctoral candidate working with Professor Gopnik, was the first researcher to start collecting data at the Creative Thinking Research Lab, and to date has tested over 500 participants at the museum. Broadly speaking, Caren is interested in the nature of children's early mental representations and how they change. Her approach to these questions is a particularly good fit with the goals of the CCC because she focuses on how even very young children are able to go beyond their direct observations to generate ideas by thinking alone. To this end, Caren has conducted research in the lab on a suite of thought-based learning phenomena that are particularly widespread in childhood, including learning by explaining, learning from analogies and thought experiments, and learning though fiction and imaginative play.

The CCC's partnership with Professor Gopnik's lab has been easy from the start because of the mutual interest in exploring how children learn about the world through open-ended play and child-directed inquiry and exploration. The average age of the children who visit the museum is also perfectly matched to the ages that the Gopnik lab recruits for the majority of their studies (i.e., toddlers and preschoolers). Furthermore, the staff at the museum and the CCC have benefited from this successful partnership by learning about cutting-edge cognitive development research through a monthly series of talks given by researchers that collect data in the lab.

This collaboration with Professor Gopnik's lab has been extremely successful for both the CCC and the researchers in the Cognitive Development Lab. For example, as a result of this growing and meaningful relationship with Professor Gopnik's research team, the CCC research staff has worked closely with Caren on research grants, including a successful proposal to the National Living Lab Initiative to launch a Research Toy Program at the museum. These research toys are hands-on activities that help to educate parents about the methods researchers use to study child development and some of the important findings in the field. The Research Toy Program at the museum started in late 2014 and has been very successful in presenting the findings from recent studies on sharing and the benefits of open-ended play to parents and young children. As a second phase in the program, the CCC research staff collaborated with Caren to create a new research toy based on a recently published set of experiments that investigated young children's ability to reason about the abstract relationships "same" and "different" in a causal learning task (see Walker & Gopnik, 2014).

Access to Participant Populations

One of the challenges for developmental researchers in conducting high-quality research with young children is finding a way to reach interested children and parents. Even when an experiment takes only 5 minutes for a toddler or preschooler to complete, researchers can spend countless hours advertising the study to recruit local families to travel to the university lab to participate. With that challenge in mind, a growing number of academic researchers have partnered with museums to provide much-needed access to young participants for their studies. For example, a fruitful partnership between the CCD Lab, directed by Dr. Christine Legare, and the Thinkery began with visitors from the children's museum participating in research studies on the development of children's causal explanations and exploratory behavior (Legare et al., this volume). This partnership has resulted in the publication of more than 10 empirical papers in peer-reviewed journals and, most recently, a collaborative grant funded by the National Science Foundation to investigate cultural diversity in parent–child explanation and exploration. Legare et al. describe how the relationship between the CCD Lab and the Thinkery started with a mutual respect and interest in educational research on children's learning and blossomed into a productive partnership that has advanced our understanding of early science learning.

Corriveau et al. (this volume) describe another successful model for providing access to participant populations—the Living Laboratory model brings academic studies into plain view of the public by having researchers conduct their studies on the exhibit floor. Conducting studies on the exhibit floor allows museum visitors to see research in action and increases the visibility of researchers and their experiments in a museum setting. Parents and caregivers have a unique opportunity to talk to developmental researchers in a relaxed and informal setting, and researchers are able to engage with the public, which is a rare opportunity for young researchers. In fact, researchers often benefit from these interactions by gaining a new perspective on their research topic, which often leads to new directions in their research. For example, Corriveau et al. shared that questions from parents about different types of stories (e.g., fictional versus religious stories) led researchers to consider the effect of religious education on children's judgments of fantasy and reality.

On the other hand, researchers who work within the Living Laboratory model are necessarily limited in the types of studies that they can conduct on the museum floor. That is, procedures that require children to listen carefully to instructions, pick up on subtle cues from the experimenter, require special equipment (e.g., eye tracking), or last more than 10–15 minutes will most likely not work well in a museum setting where children are easily distracted. As a result, Corriveau et al. identified seven minutes as the "sweet spot" for the length of studies in the type of open museum setting used in the Living Laboratory model. While the protocol that is proscribed by the Living Laboratory approach carries clear benefits—facilitating new researcher–museum collaborations—there are also advantages in deviating from the Living Laboratory model. For example, when the CCC established the Creative Thinking Research Lab at the Bay Area Discovery Museum, the main goal was to give local researchers access to a large number of young children, given the challenge of recruiting participants for developmental research. To that end, the CCC converted a storage space into a research lab to provide a quiet, enclosed space for researchers to conduct studies with our young visitors. Although researchers have the option of conducting studies in one of the museum exhibit spaces, the CCC's research partners overwhelmingly prefer using the research lab.

Currently, researchers from the University of California, Berkeley; Stanford University; and Mills College are conducting research in the onsite testing lab. Research participants are recruited from the pool of museum visitors, and the CCC's research partners have been thrilled to find a diverse audience of parents and children, particularly on free admission days, that are willing to volunteer to be part of science. Of the 300,000 annual visitors, approximately 58% of the visitors identify as non-white ethnicity in their households. One of the unique aspects of the Bay Area Discovery Museum is that it caters to a particularly young population (the average age of the museum visitors is around 3 years old). This means that in addition to older children, researchers are able to find a large number of children under the age of 3, who cannot be easily recruited via the typical channels in local preschools.

The CCC research staff anticipates that demand for space and access to the museum's large and young audience will only continue to increase. To this end, the CCC launched the *Distance Research Project* in late 2014 to allow researchers from across the country to collect data at the museum. This project extends beyond the Living Lab model because researchers are not collecting their own data and are not interacting with the visitors and museum staff. Researchers studying all areas of developmental psychology are invited to submit applications, with special consideration given to projects that seek to better understand and nurture creative thinking in children. Successful applicants will be asked to videotape their procedure so that a trained team of research assistants at the CCC can collect data in the Creative Thinking Research Lab or in one of the museum's exhibit spaces. Video of each participant will be made available to the researcher at the completion of the study. Researchers will pay a reasonable fee for this service and agree to acknowledge the museum and the CCC in all discussions and publications of the research. Currently, the CCC team is working with researchers at Yale University in the pilot phase of the project and navigating the process of Internal Review Board (IRB) approval for collecting data at a remote site. One of the most important goals of this pilot phase is to uncover any potential challenges with receiving IRB approval and to establish procedures for working with future research clients to make this process as efficient as possible. As a result, research clients that participate in the pilot phase of the *Distance Research Project* do not pay a fee, and in return have agreed to provide valuable feedback to the CCC research team on the process from beginning to end. This is an exciting addition to the research program at the CCC and museum and a potentially trendsetting innovation in the field of developmental psychology given the limited access to young participants that most researchers face.

Mutual Professional Development

Partnerships between academic researchers and museums bring together seemingly disparate professional audiences, and a key component of a successful relationship is a mutual respect and understanding of the diverse range of talents and experiences of each. The Living Laboratory model is particularly effective in bringing together developmental researchers and museum educators through their philosophy of mutual professional development. Facilitating regular interactions between museum educators and researchers can be challenging given the diverse backgrounds of museum professionals that link to different philosophies about learning and child development. The "daily greetings" that researchers engage in with the museum staff when they arrive at a museum to collect data provide a short and simple way for researchers to practice explaining complex scientific concepts in accessible and engaging language. These brief exchanges also allow museum educators to interact one-on-one with developmental researchers that are investigating child development concepts often embodied in museum exhibits. In other words, museum educators can gain a different perspective of how to best interact with young visitors and possibly spark ideas for future exhibits.

The Bay Area Discovery Museum and CCC have started to foster mutual professional development between academic researchers and the museum staff by organizing monthly research talks. These informal gatherings give academic researchers an opportunity to present their work to a nonacademic audience and provide an accessible and convenient way for the museum staff to learn about the research studies being conducted in the onsite testing lab. Recently, museum staff has started to invite undergraduate and graduate student researchers to some of the museum's education team meetings to facilitate further dialogue between academic researchers and the museum staff. The researchers provided examples of how they debrief parents on their study procedures and the museum educators provided feedback on how to communicate clearly with parents. In particular, one goal is for the museum educators to help researchers remove jargon that they hardly notice when communicating with colleagues.

Legare et al. (this volume) describe a common challenge for museum–researcher partnerships—the disparate pace with which each institution can set, strive for, and achieve their goals. Academic research adheres to a rigorous and often time-consuming set of guidelines, while most museums strive to implement new ideas and concepts to improve the visitor experience quickly, and often in response to visitor feedback. Legare et al. provide important advice to help alleviate this challenging issue:

> Both partners in this collaboration must acknowledge the pace at which the other entity can operate and must work to find common ground in which new strategies can be implemented into the museum without compromising the integrity of the research. (p. 146, this volume)

At the Bay Area Discovery Museum, the addition of the CCC has provided an effective way to connect academic researchers and museum educators because the CCC staff has experience in both university research settings and children's museums. Specifically, Dr. Helen Hadani, the head of research for the CCC, is a former developmental researcher with a background in cognitive development and years of experience in applied research in the toy and technology industries. Helen's role at the CCC involves establishing relationships with academic researchers, many of which have arisen as a result of her previous connections at Stanford University, where she completed her doctorate. These relationships are part of what makes the CCC a unique institution—a research and training center that is incubated within a children's museum with strong ties to the academic community.

Conducting Research in Context

By conducting scientific studies in the context of a museum, researchers have the unique opportunity to study children in a natural setting that is usually more child-driven and open-ended compared with a lab or school context. From a sociocultural approach, studying children in a natural context, such as a museum, could have important implications for how children respond to a researcher's questions and support new insights about development (Callanan, 2012). The chapter by Legare et al. (this volume) provides some clear ideas for taking the museum–researcher partnerships a step in this direction. In particular, the authors highlight the potential for work that is designed to use the informal learning environment in the museums as the setting for studying the interaction between explanation and exploration. Indeed, children's museums are generally interested in this sort of child-directed and playful learning and particularly in methods for using play to maximize children's engagement in informal learning contexts. However, there are important questions surrounding the best way to study these phenomena outside of the laboratory, and whether they are indeed effective in promoting a variety of cognitive and social skills "in the wild."

Like the researchers in Legare's Cognition, Culture, and Development Lab (CCD), the CCC also hopes to explore ideas that better capitalize on the unique museum context. Many of the research projects that have been conducted at the CCC to date are not currently capitalizing on the museum setting, although the research topics overlap significantly with the museum's goals. In the near future, the CCC hopes to establish a "blended model" in which some of the studies are conducted in the lab and others are conducted on the exhibit floor. This would allow the CCC to continue to support their research partners without limiting the types of studies they can conduct at the museum, and also provide opportunities to study children's learning within social contexts. One goal of the blended model is to encourage our research partners in collaboration with the CCC staff to develop research projects that examine how children learn through interactions with parents, caregivers, and other children in a natural context (Callanan & Jipson, 2001; Callanan & Valle, 2008; Crowley et al., 2001).

In an effort to explore best practices for transitioning into this type of research, the CCC is beginning several projects (using different techniques) to study cognitive development in the natural setting of the museum. In each of these cases, findings from studies first conducted in the lab are being reevaluated in the context of the museum. For example, CCC Advisor Carol Dweck and Rodolfo Cortes, a CCC research fellow, have found in a series of studies conducted in a lab setting that when preschoolers play reciprocally (i.e., interactively) with an adult, they are more likely to trust this adult than if they had played in a noninteractive, individualistic way (Cortes Barragan & Dweck, 2014). As a next step in this research, Dweck and Cortes will be investigating if playing reciprocally in an activity that is part of a museum exhibit will enhance learning, facilitate innovation, and promote intellectual risk-taking. In addition, Caren and Professor Gopnik have been working on developing a set of ideas relating the prevalence of pretend play in childhood to early learning and reasoning skills (e.g., Walker & Gopnik, 2013). A challenge when considering how children learn from pretending is that pretense, by its very nature, is spontaneous and child-directed. Given the unique environment provided by the museum, the CCC is currently collaborating with the Gopnik lab to capitalize on the museum's established summer camp program to create an intervention to nurture this type of spontaneous pretend play in children aged 3–5 years.

In addition to creating new research paradigms that seek to exploit the museum setting to answer novel questions in context, there are also a variety of ways that the research currently being conducted in the museums may be incorporated into the museum exhibits and activities. For example, given the findings highlighted in Legare et al.—that simply generating explanations during learning constrains exploration and provides a means to optimize scientific learning, reasoning, and problem-solving (e.g., Legare, 2012; Legare, Gelman, & Wellman, 2010; Walker et al., 2014)—it is easy to imagine incorporating prompts to explain throughout a variety of museum exhibits. Explanation is a potentially valuable malleable factor (i.e., a variable under the control of the educational system) because simply introducing prompts to explain has been demonstrated to have clear impacts on learning outcomes. As a result, these findings are likely to appeal to a large number of parents and teachers who visit the museum, since they carry implications for informing educational practices and policies both within and outside of the museum. This therefore highlights the possibility of creating a traveling exhibit based on the findings of these studies. This exhibit could potentially visit a variety of children's museums across the country and perhaps target those that are part of the Living Laboratory community. Another way to connect museums across the country, particularly those interested in partnering with academic researchers, is through research collaborations. In fact, given recent collaborations between researchers at UT Austin and UC Berkeley (e.g., Walker et al., 2014), there may be unique opportunities for research projects of this nature that are jointly conducted at the Thinkery and the CCC. In other words, successful museum–researcher partnerships could eventually be leveraged to yield new relationships between different museum sites nationwide.

Finally, Legare et al. (this volume) discuss the success of the Cognition, Culture, and Development Lab (CCD) in assisting the Thinkery with a visitor research project that informed the development of the Thinkery's early learners program. Capitalizing on the data collection and analysis expertise of the researchers involved in these collaborations allows the museum staff to better evaluate their own programming efforts. This may be a benefit of the museum–researcher relationship that is currently under-utilized in the Living Laboratory model. Given that museums are always looking for new ways to improve visitor experience, but often suffer from limited resources, this idea may be a wonderful way for the researchers to further contribute to the growth and success of the museum. Researcher participation in decision-making surrounding core programming will likely benefit the research process as well, given that it may be possible to evaluate the museum visitors' attitudes about participating in research activities during their time at the museum. This will be particularly valuable as these relationships work toward a focus on research topics that are directly applicable to the development of museum programs, activities, exhibits, and research toys. Another clear practical use for conducting this type of research in a museum is providing a unique and productive training experience for undergraduate and graduate students. This seems to be a benefit that is common to many different models of collaboration between researchers and museums, whether there are established channels for formal training or not. Simply conducting research in a museum setting gives students the opportunity to see connections between scientific and practical impact and links between psychology and education.

In conclusion, museums see clear benefits as part of a museum–researcher partnership, including access to cutting-edge research that has not been published yet and gaining credibility as a learning institution as opposed to a fancy playground. At the CCC, our university research partnerships started with connections to researchers interested in conducting studies at our onsite testing lab. These partnerships form the backbone of our organization by providing a meaningful connection to some of the most recent, relevant, and innovative research on children's creative thinking and guiding our research platform to ignite and advance creativity in all children.

References

Callanan, M. (2012). Conducting cognitive development research in museums: Theoretical issues and practical concerns. *Journal of Cognition and Development, 13*(2), 137–151.

Callanan, M., & Jipson, J. (2001). Exploratory conversations and young children's developing scientific literacy. In K.S. Crowley, C. Schunn, & T. Okada (Eds.), *Designing for science: Implications from everyday, classroom, and professional settings* (pp. 21–49). Mahwah, NJ: Lawrence Erlbaum Associates.

Callanan, M., & Valle, A. (2008). Co-constructing conceptual domains through family conversations and activities. In B. Ross (Ed.), *Psychology of learning and motivation* (Vol. 49; pp. 147–165). London, UK: Elsevier.

Cortes Barragan, R., & Dweck, C.S. (2014). Rethinking natural altruism: Simple reciprocal interactions trigger children's benevolence. *Proceedings of the National Academy of Sciences of the United States of America, 111*(48), 17071–17074.

Crowley, K., Callanan, M.A., Jipson, J.L., Galco, J., Topping, K., & Shrager, J. (2001). Shared scientific thinking in everyday parent-child activity. *Science Education, 85*(6), 712–732.

Gopnik, A., & Walker, C.M. (2013). Considering counterfactuals: The relationship between causal learning and pretend play. [Special issue]. *American Journal of Play, 6*(1), 15–28.

Knutson, K., & Crowley, K. (2005a). Museum as learning laboratory: Developing and using a practical theory of informal learning (Part 1 of 2). *Hand to Hand, 18*, 4–5.

Knutson, K., & Crowley, K. (2005b). Museum as learning laboratory: Bringing research and practice together (Part 2 of 2). *Hand to Hand, 18*, 3–6.

Legare, C.H. (2012). Exploring explanation: Explaining inconsistent information guides hypothesis-testing behavior in young children. *Child Development, 83*, 173–185.

Legare, C.H., Gelman, S.A., & Wellman, H.M. (2010). Inconsistency with prior knowledge triggers children's causal explanatory reasoning. *Child Development, 81*, 929–944.

Walker, C.M., & Gopnik, A. (2013). Pretense and possibility: A theoretical proposal about the effects of pretend play on development: Comment on Lillard et al. (2013). *Psychological Bulletin, 139*(1), 40–44.

Walker, C.M., & Gopnik, A. (2014). Toddlers infer higher-order relational principles in causal learning. *Psychological science, 25*(1), 161–169.

Walker, C.M., Lombrozo, T., Legare, C.H., & Gopnik, A. (2014). Explaining prompts children to privilege inductively rich properties. *Cognition, 133*(2), 343–357.

11

WANTED

A New Cultural Model for the Relationship Between Research and Practice

Bronwyn Bevan

The Author

Bronwyn Bevan directs the Exploratorium Institute for Research and Learning. Her work focuses on mediating between research and practice to better understand how learning opportunities, across formal and informal settings, can be organized, structured, and brokered to advance equity in education.

Traditional models of the relationship between research and practice position educators with questions and researchers with answers. This model is similar to conventional models of the patient–doctor relationship, the student–teacher relationship, and the child–parent relationship. It reflects transmission-based models of knowledge and education—one party has the knowledge and the other party needs to absorb and then implement it.

This model creates an unproductive power dynamic between the fields of practice and research. It excuses the research community from needing to think deeply about the uses of its work beyond academic or theoretical circles. It excuses the educator community from the responsibility to make sense of what it is learning in practice in ways that can inform others. Moreover, the model does not account for the deeply social and cultural practices of teaching and learning that vary across contexts (see Nasir, Rosebery, Warren, & Lee, 2006; Rogoff, 2003). As such, it is deeply flawed. Finally, the model does a disservice to the rich intellectual practices of both research and practice communities. It tends to position each unfairly (in the extreme, as either ignorant or arrogant), and does not fully leverage the potential of either. The model does not work; as a result, there is little uptake of the insights and concerns of either party by the other. Research results often prove difficult to sustain. Excellent practices are not theorized in ways that can support their uptake.

Productive research and practice collaborations have always existed in pockets (as this volume demonstrates), some flourishing for decades. But at the level of "the educational enterprise"—where researchers are trained in graduate programs or where educational policy that guides practice is set—they have been almost entirely absent. In these settings we have the doctor–patient model; just switch out the stethoscope for a microscope (or, these days, make it a video camera).

But recently, after decades of calls for the need to "get more research into practice," we are beginning to hear calls to "get more practice into research." Over the past handful of years, several federal agencies and private foundations, concerned about the intransigence of educational disparities despite significant parallel investments in both research and practice, have created new calls for research and practice partnerships. In the field of science education, new projects and resources are being developed that integrate perspectives from both communities (e.g., see http://stem-teachingtools.org, http://relatingresearchtopractice.org, or http://wtgrantfoundation.org/rpp). This may signal that a new and more productive cultural model of the relationship between practice and research is beginning to emerge. Indeed, this volume and the project that generated it may be evidence of this emergence.

Leveraging Perspectives to Make Change in the World

In 2013, with funding from the National Science Foundation, several colleagues and I formed the Research+Practice Collaboratory. The Collaboratory's work is to develop and test new models for integrating research and practice perspectives for the improvement of science and mathematics education. Fundamentally, we are testing the conjecture that by working across research and practice communities, we will develop new and better ways of thinking about and addressing persistent problems of practice: The problems themselves will be reframed, the questions we ask will be different, the strategies we use in practice will shift, and the results we develop will be more relevant and useful to both research and practice.

At the heart of this work there is a deep concern for the need for more expansive and equitable science learning opportunities for young people today. By expansive we mean more intellectually and socio-emotionally rich and meaningful to learners. By equitable, we mean implemented in ways that (a) recognize (see, hear, and honor) the cultural and personal resources young people bring to the learning experience, and (b) leverage those resources to deepen each young person's social and intellectual participation. This concern for advancing expansive and equitable learning opportunities plays out across many levels: From design and instruction to professional learning and practice to policy and advocacy. It involves different combinations of collaborating researchers and educational practitioners (meaning educators, administrators, and support providers for science learning in both school and out-of-school settings) in what we call research–practice partnerships.

Identifying a "persistent problem of practice" that both communities are equally invested in addressing is the critical first step to developing a productive collaboration. But the "identification" process is not simple, and is potentially burdened with the historical power dynamics between research and practice that serve to stymie full collaboration and ownership of "the problem." As Penuel and colleagues note, identifying a productive problem requires negotiating language, meaning, values, and priorities (Penuel, Fishman, Cheng, & Sabelli, 2011). Several groups are developing innovative strategies to support the negotiation and definition of problems in ways that take into account historical power dynamics between researchers and practitioners. For instance, in community research partnership projects, Megan Bang and colleagues engage participants in creating what they call "a river of life" to document the varied historical and cultural events that have created the context or contributed to the problem that the collaboration has been formed to address (Bang, Faber, Gurneau, Marin, & Soto, in press). This process both fully honors and leverages community and practitioner knowledge, and also refines the problem space to take into account invisible (perhaps historical) factors that might later affect the uptake of research results. At the Carnegie Foundation for the Advancement of Teaching, research and practice partnerships are using "driver diagrams" (see Figure 11.1) to engage practitioners in conversations and analysis that make explicit the improvement project's theory of action and help the team identify the full range of relevant sectors and actors whose work impinges on the identified problem (Bryk, Gomez, & Gunow, 2010).

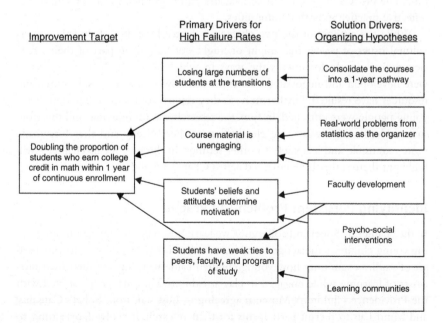

FIGURE 11.1 Example of driver diagram (from Bryk, Gomez, & Gunow, 2010).

In the California Tinkering Afterschool Network, my colleagues Molly Shea and Jean Ryoo have developed a "value-mapping exercise" that surfaces shared and disparate goals, assumptions, and values of both researchers and practitioners in ways that create shared understanding and excitement about the work and that can later guide the collaborative research–practice project's questions, coding schemes, and data analysis. It was through this process that our initial shared question of "What does it take to expand tinkering to after-school programs?" began to morph into a research question that more directly reflected concerns of practice and became "What does it take to support equity-oriented facilitation in after-school tinkering as it expands?" (Bevan, Ryoo, & Shea, 2015). In Chapter 2 of this volume, Callanan and colleagues describe an interesting power dynamic from the other direction when they discuss how sharing data that revealed unexpected patterns of visitor behavior (namely, gender-biased parent–child conversations) increased their legitimacy in the eyes of museum staff who had been skeptical of working with researchers. Making visible the invisible patterns of exhibit use equalized a power dynamic in which the role of researchers had been seen as suspect.

In our research, we have also noted the importance of iterative design work as a context in which research and practice collaborations can flourish (Penuel et al., 2011). It is in the creation of concrete resources, practices, or strategies that the ideas, synergies, or tensions between practice and research perspectives can be revealed and addressed. Iteratively testing ideas in practice acknowledges that practical issues must shape theoretical ideas if the ideas are to be sustainable over time. The process of design, test, reflect, and refine also helps to forge cultures of reflective practice in both communities.

While the authors of the two chapters I discuss here do not directly address cultural issues of power that might or might not have been part of their experience, their work documents the ways in which shared problems of practice were developed and negotiated over time, and how new practices, routines, and resources have resulted. Furthermore, as they report, educational experiences for young people were enriched. In sum, the research was more usable and therefore sustainable. Practice was more clearly framed theoretically and therefore made more extensible and adaptable to other settings. In the rest of this chapter I will highlight themes that have emerged across Chapters 6 and 7.

Identifying Persistent Problems of Practice

In the chapter by Sobel and colleagues, we learn how a mutual interest in supporting young children's metacognition led, over the course of a decade, to a focused set of studies examining how young children came to recognize their own processes of learning while engaged in play at exhibits. The partnership started with the Providence Children's Museum agreeing to host staff from Sobel's Causality and Mind Lab to recruit participants for their research. It evolved, over time, to creating a dedicated lab space for Sobel to conduct ongoing studies and, ultimately, as reported in their chapter, to the production of new museum exhibits, exhibit labels, and other communication tools that reflected issues and findings related to this line of inquiry.

The studies conducted by Sobel and colleagues in the museum's Mind Lab investigated how children think about the process of learning and when they begin to reflect on their own learning. They found that students who defined learning as a process were more likely to reflect metacognitively on their strategies for learning. Responding to this research, the museum wanted to design experiences that could promote children's metacognition about their own learning processes. They also wanted to make those processes of learning more transparent to adults and to provide caregivers with tools they could use to advance children's learning. The research lab wanted to deepen understanding and theory of how children conceptualize the process of learning, including scientific reasoning. They also wanted to enrich their work through inclusion of more naturalistic settings.

In the example shared by Rhodes and Bushara, the parties similarly began their partnership primarily with the Children's Museum of Manhattan serving as a site for research activities that "belonged" to the researchers. In this case, from the beginning, the museum created a dedicated lab space, Play Lab, for the research team. This space raised caregivers' awareness of the role of the museum as an educational institution and of its pedagogy of play as a part of learning and development. It also created a physical proximity that deepened the relationship between the university and museum teams. The shared interest was in children's learning and in particular their socialization as learners. However, through conversations afforded by the proximity of researchers and practitioners in the museum, where the research team observed frequent use of "generic language" (p. 111, this volume) in staff interactions with young children, Rhodes and Bushara became curious about how such language might affect children's relationship to science. Generic language suggests that there are fixed traits. It is the difference between framing an activity by saying "Let's be scientists today!" versus "Let's do science today!" In the former case, one essentializes science by attributing it to "being" versus "doing." Together, the teams developed a shared research question about whether generic language had negative effects for children's engagement in science activities. As it turns out, the study revealed that the use of generic language ("You are going to be scientists today") had negative consequences for girls when they hit [planted] stumbling blocks in the activities, possibly because of the intersection with larger cultural stereotypes of science as male activity. More activity-based language ("Let's do science today") had no negative effects when girls faltered, as planned, in the activities.

In both of these cases, it is notable that the development of a shared research focus on core, persistent dilemmas of practice (such as activity design and facilitation strategies) emerged over time. The relationships started out as something of a quid pro quo: Researchers gained lab space and access to the public, while museums gained a kind of "program" that communicated to their adult visitors the role of the museum as an important site of learning. Over time, these respective individual benefits were negotiated into shared intellectual pursuit of issues at the core of teaching and learning in the children's museum.

Developing New Professional Routines and Resources

Both chapters provide accounts of how new tools or routines were developed through the partnerships. The researchers note that partnerships with the museums provided them access to more economically and culturally diverse research participants, thus enriching their studies. Additionally, in New York, the research partnership led to new professional learning opportunities for the NYU graduate students, who were able to build their capacity to talk about their research with the public. The graduate students also developed a newsletter communicating key ideas and research findings, and the museum benefitted from having a new communication tool for their adult audience.

The creation of a joint research appointment in Providence was an especially productive move. The researcher (Susan Letourneau) was a partner on both lab-led studies and museum-led studies. She was able, by virtue of her ongoing physical presence in both sets of studies, to pick up on possible connections, misunderstandings, or productive lines of inquiry that could advance the work in both groups.

The children's museums benefitted both physically and programmatically. Both museums designed and built a permanent research space on the museum floor. In Providence, it also led to new exhibit labels that could prompt caregivers to recognize and support learning processes of their children. In New York, the authors describe how they have developed a new project that will produce a resource manual for other museums that contains STEM learning activities and training materials that reflect their research around generic language.

In Providence, the authors also detail how the partnership has led to a growing culture of intellectually-rich reflection and inclusion. They describe how they began a study of children's exhibit-based learning by engaging museum staff in reflective discussions about what they knew and had seen in their work with children at exhibits. Thus, the staff knowledge and experience became the basis for the development of an observation tool. This is a good example of shifting power dynamics where the knowledge of practitioners is recognized and integrated into the research. Furthermore, the authors note that the observational research they conducted "contributed to a culture of observation and reflective practice among museum staff and volunteers" (p. 128, this volume).

Theorizing Practice and Using Research

The most important result of integrating research and practice perspectives is that research findings are more relevant and usable (and therefore sustained) and practice is more clearly theorized in ways that can inform others, be adapted into new contexts, and even potentially scaled. I would posit that there is a dialectical relationship between theorized practice and usable research, that it emerges through reflective practice, and that it is critical to the sustainability of educational improvement efforts.

In Providence, the museum moved from a theoretical commitment to play as a powerful process and context for learning to a more deeply theorized design approach that, through play, could help children come to experience, understand, and articulate learning as a process. Thus play became not only a context for learning, but a means for supporting children's developing theories of learning and self. The research helped the museum to identify the kinds of messages and tools adult caregivers needed both to recognize their children's processes of learning and to advance it without disrupting their play. This theorized practice now provides a space for Sobel's lab to conduct more naturalistic studies, and, as the authors report, is serving as the basis for a scale up in design and studies to other museums.

In New York, the museum moved from prioritizing play as a context for learning to theorizing facilitation strategies that could engage or disengage children in that playful learning. Further, the museum is developing related professional materials and training products for broad dissemination to the field. Rhodes's lab intends to study and test whether other museum staff can be trained to avoid generic language to support children's, and especially girls', engagement in science.

I find both of these cases to be powerful examples of the productivity of research–practice partnerships. Not only have they directly effected change in the participating museums, but they are both scaling to inform the field at large. These are excellent examples of the dialectic between theorized practice and practice-oriented research.

Closing Thoughts

Both of these chapters provide important accounts of how research–practice partnerships are developed and what happens as a result. The research itself, on children's metacognition and on generic language, is extremely interesting and relevant to work in museums.

It is notable that first authorship of each of these accounts of research–practice partnerships is the lead researcher. In general, writing is not a part of the schedule or professional routines of most educational practitioners. In my experience, practitioners are generally ecstatic that their story is getting out at all, especially when they have had a chance to contribute to the storytelling. But we must acknowledge that authorship frames the story. While these chapters were primarily written by scholars for a scholarly audience, it will be important for the practitioners to lead the development of accounts of their partnerships that speak more directly to practitioner audiences. Until then, we (all of us) do not have the full story.

Finally, neither of the chapters explicitly addresses the need to integrate data collection activities into the normative culture of the museum. Typically, data collection takes on school-like or lab-like attributes wherein the process (such as test taking or interviewing) becomes the main activity. As Callanan and colleagues note in Chapter 2, families will often agree to participate in lab-like activities, but it is not their first choice, and they tend to end the sessions earlier than they do in a university lab. Many have argued for the need in informal settings such as museums to use assessment or data collection methods that do not distort or interrupt the normative learning experience (Michalchik & Gallagher, 2010; NRC, 2009, 2015). At both museums, the creation of the lab spaces actually changed the physical nature of the museum and the routinization of research activities changed the nature of the museum "program" for visitors. I would be interested to understand how these changes, which have been increasing in museums over the past few years, affect the overall museum experience for children or adults.

On this note, Providence provides an interesting example of how a museum might seamlessly integrate research activities (data collection) into the museum's main activity (exhibit-based play) when it describes its development of a circuit board exhibit. The research-based activity, signage, and other communications materials have been designed to inform caregivers about their children's learning processes and how they can prompt them to support their thinking. The authors note that researchers from Sobel's lab are considering using this naturalistic activity in the museum to study young children's cognition. This is an interesting example of how the child's experience may remain playful, while the adult is encouraged to value play as a context for learning, and the research and practice teams can continue to explore and deepen their lines of inquiry.

References

Bang, M., Faber, L., Gurneau, J., Marin, A., & Soto, C. (in press). Community based design research: Learning across generations and strategic transformations of institutional relations towards axiological innovations, mind, culture, and activity.

Bevan, B., Ryoo, J., & Shea, M. (2015). *Equity in out-of-school STEM learning: Professional development needs and strategies.* San Francisco: Exploratorium.

Bryk, A.S., Gomez, L.M., & Grunow, A. (2010). *Getting ideas into action: Building networked improvement communities in education. Carnegie Perspectives* (p. 19). Stanford, CA: Carnegie Foundation for the Advancement of Teaching.

Michalchik, V., & Gallagher, L. (2010). Naturalizing assessment. *Curator, 53*(2), 209–219.

Nasir, N.S., Rosebery, A.S., Warren, B., & Lee, C.D. (2006). Learning as a cultural process: Achieving equity through diversity. In R.K. Sawyer (Ed.), *The Cambridge handbook of the learning sciences* (pp. 567–580). New York: Cambridge University Press.

National Research Council [NRC]. (2009). *Learning science in informal environments.* Washington, DC: National Academies Press.

National Research Council [NRC]. (2015). Identifying and supporting productive programs in out-of-school settings. Washington, DC: National Academies Press.

Penuel, W.R., Fishman, B.J., Cheng, B., & Sabelli, N. (2011). Organizing research and development at the intersection of learning, implementation, and design. *Educational Researcher, 40*(7), 331–337.

Rogoff, B. (2003). *The cultural nature of human development.* New York: Oxford University Press.

12

EXPLORING MODELS OF RESEARCH–PRACTICE PARTNERSHIP WITHIN A SINGLE INSTITUTION

Two Kinds of Jointly Negotiated Research

Sue Allen and Joshua P. Gutwill

The Authors

Sue Allen is director of research at the Maine Mathematics and Science Alliance. Her current research focuses on strengthening the connections in out-of-school STEM education ecosystems, and on remote-coaching systems that provide professional development for afterschool providers in rural settings.

Josh Gutwill is director of visitor research and evaluation at the Exploratorium, a science museum in San Francisco. His work includes research on learning in informal environments as well as evaluation of exhibits and programs to improve visitors' experiences. In close collaboration with museum practitioners, he focuses on fostering and studying learners' self-directed inquiry in science museum settings.

Introduction

How can researchers increase the probability that the results of their studies actually affect practice? In the field of formal education, academic researchers are increasingly looking for ways to achieve this by collaborating with teachers and school administrators to co-develop questions, assessment methods, and interpretations of results. Such work can be extremely challenging (Coburn, Penuel, & Geil, 2013) because researchers and school-based practitioners have different goals and operate within disparate reward structures, driving them to prioritize different activities and value distinct sets of outcomes. The same issues are faced by university scholars studying learning in informal environments such as museums. To conduct meaningful research that improves practice, they need to gradually build new relationships with curators, exhibit developers, and educators (Callanan, 2012; Crowley & Knutson, 2005).

In this chapter, we describe the kinds of deep professional partnerships that can develop when both the researchers and practitioners belong to the *same* organization. We are Ph.D.-trained learning researchers who have spent years working closely with exhibit developers, educators, and curators at the Exploratorium, the museum of science, art, and human perception in San Francisco. The first author founded an in-house Visitor Research and Evaluation (VRE) group in 1994 and left the museum in 2008; the second author currently directs the VRE group. Few museums in the world have an in-house evaluation group (and even fewer have a learning sciences research group). From our relatively unusual vantage point, we hope to highlight some key affordances and common challenges of deep intra-institutional research–practice collaborations that may be relevant to cross-institutional partnerships as well.

When the first author started at the Exploratorium, the museum's exhibit group was already an active and creative center with 25 years of international acclaim, a long history of successful grants from the National Science Foundation (NSF), and a staff of perhaps a dozen highly skilled exhibit developers. Frank Oppenheimer, the museum's founder, had established an enduring and powerful hands-on pedagogy, emphasizing deeply engaging phenomena, observable mechanisms, and artistic inspiration (Oppenheimer, 1968, 1972, 1974). Exhibits were considered "working prototypes," meaning they could always be improved (Oppenheimer, 1986). Toward that end, exhibit developers often informally observed visitors when iteratively changing or creating an exhibit, but such observations were usually not recorded or systematized.

Over the course of a few years, through embracing a practitioner-centered approach that intentionally focused on trust building, the VRE group developed strong relationships with several of the exhibit developers. Ultimately, our group became fully integrated into the exhibit development practices in the Exploratorium, with many developers even saying they could not build a successful exhibit without incorporating feedback through evaluation. In this chapter, we describe the culmination of this approach, which we call *jointly negotiated research* (JNR). We go on to describe two variations of this methodology, which have emerged for us as sufficiently different to warrant characterization as sub-types of JNR.

Why Conduct Learning Research in Museums?

Much of our research has focused on exhibit design principles as they impact learning in museums. This is not accidental: We view public learning at museum exhibits as a surprisingly under-studied subdomain of the learning sciences, with great potential for increased involvement by learning researchers from many fields. For researchers who may be less familiar with museums as learning environments, we briefly list some of the benefits of conducting research on the public floor of a museum:

Museums are authentic learning contexts. Many of the learning-related phenomena of interest to the learning sciences community are readily observable in the museum setting, as they occur naturalistically over a range of social groups: collaboration and peer learning, conceptual change, embodied and situation cognition, motivation-engagement-identity, scientific reasoning and metacognition, and so on. In addition, many museums—especially science centers and children's museums—utilize features of contemporary learning practices: intriguing phenomena, interactive participation, assumption of group learning, multiple modes of engagement, wide array of choices, hierarchies of salience, small modular text, and multi-sensory experiences (e.g., Allen, 2004; Borun et al., 1998; Humphrey & Gutwill, 2005). In this sense, exhibits support the kinds of modular, self-directed learning that is increasingly dominating 21st century learning opportunities, so they are excellent test-beds for motivational and conative as well as cognitive approaches to learning. Because visitors are entirely free to explore the space moment-by-moment, museums represent a quintessential anywhere-anyone-anytime learning environment, offering an array of interactive experiences to people of all ages and backgrounds.

Museums are designed to promote learning. By contrast with naturally occurring informal learning environments, such as forests and beaches, museums are *designed* to promote enjoyment and learning. Exhibits can be seen as physical embodiments of exhibit developers' educational theories, and the inherent temporal separation of design (in the machine shop) and use (by visiting families) makes them quite similar to the carefully designed objects developmental psychologists often use to tease out children's understandings of the world. But exhibits are also worthy of study as complex motivational objects: To be successful in facilitating learning, they need to support visitors' agency while guiding discovery in particularly fruitful directions, subtly provoking conversations that advance learning in particular content areas. As Michael Spock says, "Exhibit design *is* rocket science" (McLean & McEver, 2004, p. 2).

Museum exhibits afford experimental manipulation. Exhibits make especially powerful micro-settings for studying learning because they are typically used in "stand-alone" mode, without a professional teacher to mediate. This makes them adaptable for detailed comparative experiments of the kind commonly designed by developmental psychologists in a setting with very large numbers of participants using them in short time scales. In addition, the in-house teams of designers, builders, editors, and graphics experts make it possible to test a broad set of design variations. There are, of course, significant nuisance variables at play in museums, but these can be ameliorated to some degree with careful design (Allen et al., 2007). The combination of these experimental affordances, along with the previous two attributes (authentic and intentional environments for learning), make museum exhibit spaces rich "contexts for studying cognitive development" as well as "settings for conceptualizing, designing, and evaluating interventions" (Callanan, 2012, p. 140).

Researchers are developing context-appropriate assessments. Over the past few decades, researchers in museums have developed observational methods for assessing learning in ways that avoid making participants feel tested (e.g., Allen, 2002; Barriault & Pearson, 2010; Borun et al., 1998; Callanan, 2012; Crowley & Callanan, 1998; Gutwill, 2003, 2005; Serrell, 1998; Van Schijndel, Franse, & Raijmakers, 2010). More recently, advances in mobile phone technology, indoor positioning, embedded cameras and microphones, and software for automated audio, facial, and gestural analysis show near-term promise for conducting high-speed, anonymous tracking of large numbers of visitors as they move, interact, and speak together (ByteLight, 2013; Ma, 2014; Rowe, 2015).

Jointly Negotiated Research

Having described some of the advantages of studying learning in museums, we return to the question of how to conduct such studies in ways that maximize their impact on practice. We use the term "jointly negotiated research" to refer to research that engages both researchers and practitioners in deep and meaningful partnerships where decision-making power is shared. To characterize such research, we start with the definition that the second author and his colleagues at the Exploratorium have been developing (Bevan, Gutwill, Petrich, & Wilkinson, 2015, p. 4), based upon work in formal education (Coburn et al., 2013). In this view, JNR incorporates the following principles:

1) *Negotiate problems of practice* that are of equal interest and importance to both researchers and practitioners.
2) *Advance both theory and practice.*
3) *Engage in collaborative design work* to explore and test new practices.
4) *Build capacity to sustain change* beyond the immediate term of the research project.

By definition, JNR gives equal priority to the goals, perspectives, and professional needs of researchers and practitioners. In our experience, such equality takes time to develop fully, but builds institutional capacity through trust, mutual understanding, and common purpose.

One of the key features of JNR is that it does not need to be translated into practice because it is already grounded in practice. We would argue that the prevalent notion of late-stage, one-way "translation" from research to practice harkens back to transmission metaphors of learning that pre-date constructivist and socio-cultural perspectives, and that such metaphors are quite limiting to the formation of true partnerships. We see practitioners as creative professionals who have highly valuable expertise based on their knowledge and experience of creating engaging educational experiences for public audiences. Because of this, they can contribute significantly to the usefulness and applicability of the research by helping researchers to ask better, more relevant questions.

Two Forms of Jointly Negotiated Research

We further subdivide JNR *based on the degree to which researchers and practitioners retain their separate roles as they collaborate*. Our experience has shown that these two subtypes of JNR tend to differ in terms of characteristics (3) and (4) of JNR: the nature of power-sharing in the collaboration, and the potential for organizational capacity-building.

a) JNR-D

In jointly negotiated research with differentiated roles (JNR-D), researchers and practitioners share design-making power as they design and implement research studies, but retain their traditional roles throughout the process, "passing the baton" of decision-making back and forth as the research evolves. The researchers' role is to observe practitioners' practices long enough to identify candidates of theoretical interest and potential for generalizability (making them research rather than evaluation), and to work with the practitioners to choose a particular design decision that will be of immediate use to them before the end of the project. Timing is critical here: too early and the study may be irrelevant to the actual design challenges, but too late and it may inform the field but not the immediate project. Typically, in our context, these studies are principled comparisons between plausible design alternatives. They are often difficult to write into project proposals ahead of time because it may be difficult to anticipate which design dilemmas will dominate a particular development process; in this sense, JNR-D is usually opportunistic in nature. Because of the alternating phases of decision-making, this type of research builds institutional capacity by surfacing different perspectives and allowing researchers and practitioners to better understand each other's language and practices.

b) JNR-I

In jointly negotiated research with integrated roles (JNR-I), research and practice are built simultaneously by a single collaborative community of researchers and practitioners working toward a common goal. The researchers and practitioners collaborate deeply from the earliest stages of a project to the very end, and jointly characterize both the desired learning impacts and the means of achieving them. JNR-I requires periodic deep negotiation of goals, key constructs, assessments, and inferences. Typically this happens when a project attempts a bold and innovative objective (e.g., having learners drive their experiences for themselves instead of following the museum's instructions). The discussions can be challenging, as teams wrangle between the research goals of coherent constructs and the practice goals of optimal design. If the project succeeds, a compromise is reached where practitioners are truly guided by the research data, but retain a large enough design space to create effective learning offerings on an individual level. By the end of such a process, there is full ownership of all, intimate familiarity with the final designs and their learning impacts, and a side effect of powerful bonding within the team. We characterize this as the highest level of institutional capacity-building.

What Do JNR-D and JNR-I Look Like?

To illustrate the two types of jointly negotiated research, we offer brief vignettes from our own experience working in these two genres with Exploratorium practitioners.

Vignette 1: JNR-D

As an example of JNR-D, we describe a small, focused study on alternative designs for exhibits featuring living microscopic organisms. Practitioners and researchers contributed equally to the shaping of the study, but in different ways that reflect their professional training: Practitioners primarily contributed their exhibit-development experience, while the researcher primarily contributed her experimental design expertise.

Roughly one year into an NSF-funded Exploratorium project to develop biology exhibits with living organisms (*Traits of Life*), the researcher, who also acted as the evaluator conducting formative evaluation on early exhibit prototypes, made a list of approximately ten design dilemmas that seemed to be arising repeatedly in evaluation studies. They seemed generalizable enough to warrant systematic study, yet specific enough to the domain of *Traits of Life* to justify conducting them with project resources. The researcher shared the list of design dilemmas with the development team, and the practitioners ranked them in terms of what they found the most useful and relevant to their current work on the project.

In this case, the team selected the design issue of *how much user interactivity to build into exhibits with microscopes used to examine live organisms*. This constituted a genuine dilemma of practice, not a trivial detail, because the practitioners were grappling with an inherent trade-off in terms of the learning outcomes that different degrees of interactivity afford: Including more interactive features allows visitors to explore more variations of the exhibit but actually makes it more difficult for them to rapidly locate a well-focused, well-positioned sample. The team's research question became: "What is the optimal level of physical interaction we should give visitors using live specimens under a microscope? Do more interactive features contribute to visitors' learning, or not?"

The researcher then developed a randomized block design study to answer this research question (see Table 12.1). She created a 3x2 matrix of exhibit versions,

TABLE 12.1 Final study design of JNR study on levels of interactivity in microscope exhibits.

	Interactivity: Multiple Features	Single Feature	None
Live Specimens	X	X	
Video-recordings			X

to allow for testing three levels of interactivity (multiple interactive features; one interactive feature, or none), and two variations in the presentation of worms (live or previously recorded).

At this point, the practitioners were again key to the research design: they identified which of these six exhibit variations were worthy of study and which would be unrealistic. For example, exhibit developers would not go to the bother of putting interactive features on a video-recorded phenomenon, which was seen as wasteful and disingenuous; nor would developers put all the expense into a living sample without giving the visitor at least some interactive features. These cultural norms allowed us to simplify the study to only three exhibit variations.

Ultimately, the study findings showed that visitors were more engaged by, and learned more from, the exhibit version that had live worms and interactivity, but that a single interactive feature was as effective as multiple features.

This vignette illustrates several aspects of JNR-D, with the researchers and practitioners maintaining their respective roles. The researcher's role was to frame the questions, design the experiment, and analyze the results, while practitioners offered important constraints, made key choices throughout that process, and built ingenious physical devices to enable quick rotation among the different exhibit versions to reduce the confounding influence of nuisance variables during the study.

Vignette 2: JNR-I

An example of JNR-I was the NSF-funded project called *Going APE*. In this project, the primary goal itself—active prolonged engagement (APE)—was a construct jointly negotiated between the practitioners and the researchers. When the project began, all team members agreed that "prolonged" referred to visitors spending more than typical time at exhibits. But the term "active" was much harder to operationalize, and ultimately formed the driving issue behind the entire project for both researchers and practitioners.

In the first year of the project, the researchers pushed to define APE as prolonged *scientific inquiry*, where visitors would ask questions, conduct systematic experiments, and make observations and interpretations. The practitioners, in contrast, felt that such investigative inquiry was far too narrow a definition. They proposed including free-form *exploration*, in which implicit questions (e.g., "What happens if I push this?") would lead to trying different things.

After months of argument, consensus finally came when the group adopted the practice of joint video analysis. Ground rules were set such that any team member could nominate an existing exhibit for the researchers to videotape. Then, when viewing the videos together, team members would "call out" moments of interest, trying to identify the kinds of interactions that would illustrate their view of APE. Rather than simply trade opinions, the group sought evidence for their claims and examples to demonstrate their ideas.

Over the next few months, exhibit developers and researchers brought videos home, watched them, and then showed their curated call-outs to the rest of the team. By viewing and discussing together, and by both groups keeping an open mind about the meaning of APE, a jointly agreed-upon definition emerged: Active engagement meant that exhibits would allow visitors to "drive the experience" for themselves. Intentionality was key—in the new definition, visitors were "active" when they decided for themselves what to do next, rather than following instructions from the museum. The goal of the project became building exhibits that were open-ended enough to foster a self-authored experience that could involve exploration *and* investigation, as well as other interactions like construction and observation (Humphrey & Gutwill, 2005). This represented a profound shift in outcome goals for exhibits that resonated with museum practitioners and researchers in the greater museum field (e.g., Hein, 2012; Horn et al., 2012; Szechter & Carey, 2009).

The jointly negotiated definition of APE was only the beginning of the deep collaboration; every exhibit the developers created was videotaped and analyzed by the researchers for (prolonged) time at the exhibit and self-driving behaviors. Roles blurred as the practitioners watched the videos for themselves, saying they "couldn't tell if it was an APE exhibit" until they had seen and heard multiple visitor groups use it. The researchers also switched roles, building an exhibit prototype to test one of their own ideas. Together, the team implemented three quasi-experimental studies, using video, interviews, and real-time observations to make comparisons among conditions.

The APE project exemplifies JNR-I in that the very goal of the project was jointly negotiated and required both development and study to achieve. Roles were malleable, with developers learning to demand evidence and researchers learning about the intricacies of design. The project advanced both theory and practice in the realm of designing learning experiences in museums. Although the process was time-consuming, with much disagreement and emotion, the deep commitment to consensus-based decision-making resulted in acclaimed contributions to theory and practice, and a remarkable degree of joint ownership.

Comparisons With Other Types of Museum Research

In Table 12.2, we give a simplified summary of the key characteristics of the two kinds of JNR we have described above.

TABLE 12.2 Properties of jointly negotiated research in relation to other types of museum research.

Dimension	Sub-Dimension	Independent Research	Collaborative Research	JNR-D	JNR-I
1) Research Focus	Source of inspiration	Learning theories	Learning theories	Problems of practice	Problems of practice
	Perspective on the museum as learning environment	Source of subjects for experimental studies	Source of objects and practices to be incorporated as props into relevant research	Source of malleable educational interventions	Source of malleable educational interventions
2) Field Advancement	Knowledge-building contributions	Builds theory, no significant impact on practice	Builds theory, implications for practice	Builds theory and advances practice ("reciprocal innovation")	Builds theory and advances practice ("reciprocal innovation")
3) Collaboration and Power	Research questions	Predetermined by researcher	Determined by researcher with input from practice or embedded in current objects/practices	Emergent through joint negotiation	Emergent through joint negotiation
	Principal decision-maker	Researcher	Mostly researcher	Alternating	Fully shared
	Researcher's role	Conducts all aspects of research	Conducts research that incorporates authentic elements of the museum	Identifies potentially generalizable practice–based issues, designs study with input from practitioners, analyzes and disseminates findings	Conducts inclusive research and participates in practice

		Risk Sensitivity	Colored Shadows	Microscope Interactivity	Active Prolonged Engagement
3) Collaboration and Power (Continued)	Practitioner's role	Gives researcher consent to use the space, recruit, collect data	Provides access to suitable objects and practices, with minor tweaks as needed	Opens practice to scrutiny, identifies realistic interventions, creates variations for study	Includes researcher in practice, participates in research
4) Capacity-Building	Capacity to sustain change over time	Negligible	Low	Medium	High
5) Implementation Issues	Key challenge	Recruiting, sampling, collecting data outside a controlled laboratory environment	Identifying objects and practices that allow research questions to be addressed	Finding theoretical construct of genuine interest to practitioners	Achieving convergence in time to impact research and practice
	Timing within an R&D project	n/a (independent of development)	n/a (independent of development)	Phased: early and late in a project, majority of research activity follows majority of development	Throughout a project, constantly iterative, research and development drive each other
	Efficiency	High	Medium	Low	Very low
Example Study		*Risk Sensitivity*	*Colored Shadows*	*Microscope Interactivity*	*Active Prolonged Engagement*

For comparison, we include *Independent Research* that is conducted in a museum setting, but is not significantly connected to the work of the practitioners. For example, a psychologist might use a space in the museum because it is a convenient place to recruit and study participants for a study of risk sensitivity, and debrief them afterwards (e.g., Kunreuther, Novemsky, & Kahneman, 2001). Such research is typically, but not necessarily, conducted by university-based researchers, and was already well-established (by Sally Duensing and others) before we arrived at the Exploratorium. It is growing in popularity and quality, thanks in large part to the Living Lab project at the Museum of Science, Boston (Museum of Science, Boston, 2010; Corriveau et al., this volume). In the Living Lab model, practitioners create a space within the museum for researchers to use to recruit and study participants (often children), either singly or in dyads or groups doing specified activities.

Drawing from Bevan (Bevan et al., 2015), we also include in the table *Collaborative Research*, which we elaborate in several key dimensions. We see this as research conducted with help and advice from practitioners or using the educational offerings that practitioners have created. However, the researcher's role is primary, driving the process with a well-defined initial theoretical question and making all major decisions regarding study design, implementation, analysis, write-up, and dissemination. An example is Allen's (1997) study of an exhibit called *Colored Shadows*, which was used for a study of inquiry skills: The existing exhibit (created by skilled exhibit developers) provided an intriguing phenomenon, and the researcher created labels that embodied different inquiry tasks to be used in a mediated way with visitors in a randomized block-design study.

The dimensions in the table begin with those related to the four principles we used (previously) to characterize JNR. Specifically:

1) JNR is initially inspired by a *problem of practice*, rather than a theoretical question, as would be typical of other kinds of research. Also, the museum setting is seen not just as a source of subjects (as in Independent Research) or as a convenient source of exhibits and programs to be used as props (as in Collaborative Research), but as a collection of educational interventions that can be assessed, studied, and changed (c.f. Callanan, 2012).

2) JNR goes beyond the goal of having "implications" for practice and instead *advances practice as it advances research*. Typically this happens through a process we call "reciprocal innovation," where creative explorations in research and practice drive each other in ways that build both.

3) In JNR, the design and research work is *extremely collaborative*, so that neither the researcher nor the practitioner can fully anticipate what will be learned. Even research questions emerge through joint negotiation. Responsibility for the research is shared, either through a process of alternating responsibility (in JNR-D) or a blurring of roles (in JNR-I).

4) JNR *builds capacity to sustain change* in the museum as well as the research team. Changes in practice happen throughout the project because the innovations driven by research questions are aligned to established practices and involve practitioners in the design process. Because of the merging of roles in JNR-I, this represents the type of research with the greatest potential to impact practice in a sustained way, while it also builds capacity in the sense of maximizing professional development of researchers and practitioners in relation to each other's work.

Aside from these four principles, we include in the table some implementation issues: key challenges, optimal timing within a project, and overall efficiency of each type of research.

Getting to JNR

Callanan (2012) and Crowley and Knutson (2005) point out that early evaluation of exhibits served as key early stages in their research–practitioner partnerships. For us as in-house researchers, the same has been true. Through formative evaluation of individual exhibit prototypes, our VRE group was able to move from independent and collaborative research (with relatively low impact on practice) to JNR studies, which are now our most common form of research.

In some cases the evaluation identified general issues that could be studied more rigorously across multiple exhibits. For example, early evaluation of one of the *Going APE* exhibits, *Spinning Blackboard*, led to an exhibit developer thinking creatively about ways to design for independent yet sharable strategies by visitors using an exhibit; this in turn led to a whole series of studies of "multi-station exhibits" and inclusion of this concept in the theoretical framing of APE behavior. In other cases, we formatively evaluated exhibit use and visitor interactions by recording videos of learners, which were later analyzed more carefully to answer a research question.

A key point is that it took the exhibit research and practice team several years to fully establish the two forms of JNR described above. They were not immediately embraced by practitioners, even when more traditional formative evaluation practices had permeated all team projects. Practitioners raised (and still raise) legitimate concerns about the extended times involved and the significant budgetary resources required to do research as rigorous as that which the researchers wanted to conduct. Not every question deserves the kinds of deep dives that characterize JNR, and our in-house staff still conducts the full range of research types listed in Table 12.2, as well as a great deal of formative evaluation. Luckily, we have found that these studies inform and cross-pollinate frequently. For example, a decade-long focus on deepening inquiry at exhibits interwove the threads of extensive evaluation work, JNR-I studies in *Going APE* (Humphrey & Gutwill,

2005), and JRN-D studies on programming interventions in a project called *Juicy Question* (Gutwill & Allen, 2010).

Reflections on Haden, Cohen, Uttal, and Marcus

Our examples have been from our research work as museum-embedded researchers. We now turn to consider Chapter 5 as an example of JNR, in this case conducted across institutions by in-house practitioners and university researchers. Based on our previous framework, we would classify this work as JNR because it meets all four of the defining principles:

1) *Negotiate problems of practice* that are of equal interest and importance to both researchers and practitioners.

   The authors very intentionally identified an issue of importance in museum practice (viz., how to enhance learning through narrative reflection), and framed it with an appropriate theoretical lens (parent–child conversations and memory development). In doing so, they also addressed two more general recurring issues of great interest to museum practitioners: how to extend the museum experience over time and across settings, and how to infuse science content (in their example, the role of triangles as effective structural supports) into interactive experiences without making it didactic. In other words, they successfully identified a very fruitful area of focus of central interest to research and practice.

2) *Advance both theory and practice.*

   The authors' choice of focus—narrative reflection—was not only of joint interest to research and practice, but was of a sufficiently large grain-size to warrant multiple studies and the development of innovative extensions to existing practices.

   The work advanced *research* by showing specific ways that "narrative reflection can be an integral part of the learning process, providing possibilities for extended encoding . . . beyond the duration of the activity itself" (p. 88, this volume). This connects strongly with the concept of "preparation for future learning" of Bransford and Schwartz (1999, p. 68) and addresses the essential theoretical question of how learning experiences build over time.

   Methodologically, the use of time-lapse cameras and prompts for narrative construction provides a wonderful example of ecologically valid embedded learning assessments in informal settings, something researchers continue to call for (e.g., NRC, 2009). In addition, it showcases how relatively minor adjustments (such as small changes to an exhibit or a simple framing suggestion to visiting families) can allow the researching team to explore many variations and find intriguing results relatively quickly.

   In terms of *practice*, this research addresses the well-known museum challenge of extending the learning experience from a typically engaging, hands-on interaction to something with a more reflective component that might be remembered over time and applied in other settings. The study series also generated a useful set of principled, explicit probes, helping caregivers facilitate their children's learning by connecting it to future experiences.

Finally, the studies' results—that amount of STEM talk was increased only by combining engineering principles with prompts to ask questions—were immediately implementable into museum programs.

3) *Engage in collaborative design work* to explore and test new practices.
A particular strength of Haden et al.'s work is the way their research questions and development practices interweave and inform each other, as is typical of JNR. For example, the team's wish to understand the effects on memory of the commonly observed phenomenon of "reunion narratives" led to the development of an experimental orientation experience that was later incorporated into the museum's regular exhibit and related programming.

Importantly, this kind of tight interweaving was maximized through the team's deliberate choice of research interventions that are variations of existing practices in museums. Haden et al. give several other examples:

- "Narrative reflection" is based on a well-documented behavior that families already engage in following museum-based experiences: telling others about their visit when they get home.
- "Inspector Sturdy" imitates the role-playing programs that are common in museums.
- Even the suggested question prompts and connections to prior experience are what skillful families tend to do as they learn together in museums (e.g., Allen, 2002; Borun, Chambers, & Cleghorn, 1996; Gutwill & Allen, 2010), so it is not surprising that families who get to practice it, do it later spontaneously.

As the authors suggest, all of these are ways to scaffold facilitation for caregivers who may not know how to support their children's learning, and all are based on the spontaneous practices of skilled caregivers in the same setting. We agree that the fruits of this entire partnership would have been much weaker without the intentional connections to established practices of staff, parents, and children.

4) *Build capacity to sustain change* beyond the immediate term of the research project.
Haden et al. describe research that extends beyond a single study or even series of studies to relationships that continue to grow and cross-pollinate over time. The research team now includes multiple research faculty and a number of research assistants and students, such growth that the museum has felt compelled to create "a system for thinking about and responding to different kinds of requests" (p. 86, this volume). Perhaps most tellingly, the authors report that

research has become "part of the culture" (p. 98, this volume) at the museum, bringing new tools and perspectives that have been readily embraced.

JNR-D or JNR-I?

It is difficult to tell whether Haden et al.'s research was JNR-D or JNR-I because the authors focus on the whole team's process, rather than the roles played by different members. Nevertheless, we might speculate that the work leans toward JNR-I because the authors promote "practitioners and researchers who are willing to . . . *determine together* interventions and methodology that can advance research and practice" (p. 101, this volume).

Either way, we see their work as a beautiful model of JNR across institutions.

A Causal Account of JNR

In Chapter 1, the editors of this volume note that it contains a variety of frameworks, names, and criteria for different levels and types of collaboration. They also note several likely causal mechanisms. Below we propose our own interpretation of the causal relationship among three levels of partnership principles, incorporating those suggested by Haden et al. where possible, and drawing on our own experience as well as the experiences of others described later in this chapter (e.g., Maureen Callanan, Kevin Crowley, and Karen Knutson). In brief, we propose that a single driver is supported to a greater or lesser extent by nurturing factors, leading ultimately to emergent properties that characterize JNR.

Driver. We resonate with Haden and colleagues' recognition of the key significance of having "one dedicated, even passionate person on each end of the partnership who can make the time to find common ground" (p. 101, this volume). In fact, we see such a partnership as the only essential driver of JNR. We would argue that partners need to be *curious, flexible, and committed to advancing practice* (JNR principle 3 on collaborative design). Flexibility is essential because no matter how aligned their interests seem to be, there will always be a need to learn from each other and adapt to the stream of incoming findings as the research unfolds.

Nurturing factors. There are several nurturing factors that significantly support the partners as they build their JNR partnership. Four of the most salient are proximity, time, institutional support, and a fruitful domain of inquiry. (1) By *proximity*, we mean easy communication that allows for frequent exchanges of ideas. Ideally, partners are physically near each other, but frequently used videoconferencing tools may allow for something similar with a remote presence. (2) Prolonged *time* for the partnership, preferably in decades but at least in years, builds empathy, common language, and joint goals. Usually this also means that stable funding is required. (3) JNR is also nurtured through *institutional support*, particularly from the museum side, that values and welcomes the deep involvement of a researcher. (4) Finally, JNR thrives within a *practice-based subdomain of the right grain-size* to afford multiple directions of exploration for both research and practice (JNR principle 1 on finding problems of practice; similar to Haden's "degree of alignment," p. 86, this volume). We think of this as a nurturing factor rather than an essential driver because we believe two curious and open-minded partners with enough time and support will almost invariably find an area of overlapping interest in the study of practice; at the same time, if there is already an articulated subdomain of mutual interest (such as narrative reflection), then this may accelerate, extend, or simplify the relationship-building process.

Emergent properties. When enthusiastic research–practice partners have the time, proximity, and support they need to unearth and pursue jointly negotiated questions, several properties of JNR emerge naturally: (1) Both partners *relinquish some individual control* and adjust what they are fundamentally willing to explore, based on the perspective of the other partner. (2) As partners gradually learn to think more like each other, there may be *increased role-blurring.* (This is the issue that distinguishes JNR-D from JNR-I and relates to JNR principle 3 on collaborative design.) (3) The *researchers gain greater permission* from practitioners to intervene. (We see this in Haden's correlation of research method with seniority of research personnel.) (4) Both *research and practice advance* via "reciprocal innovation." This means that the partnership spins off a series of innovations in practice that are interwoven with discoveries in research, neither of which could be fully anticipated at the outset (JNR principle 2 on advancing both theory and practice). (5) Finally, *long-term capacity increases for both sides,* as more researchers become interested in the domain, and as practitioners incorporate the innovative practices into their regular repertoires (JNR principle 4 on capacity-building).

Of course, the emergent properties further reinforce the driver and nurturers, so the linear causality is ultimately cyclical.

Other Cross-Institutional Examples

That Haden et al. were able to conduct cross-institutional JNR is a major feat; this kind of deep partnering is not easy even within an organization.

It has also been achieved by Maureen Callanan, a developmental psychologist at UC Santa Cruz, who has worked for many years in an equal partnership with the practitioners at the San Jose Children's Museum (Callanan et al., this volume; Crowley & Knutson, 2005). During her research studies, Callanan also conducts formative evaluation for the museum, serving practitioners' needs in parallel with her own. She uses an evaluation approach called "blitz coding," originally developed by her then-post-doc, Kevin Crowley. In this approach, the researcher helps practitioners by employing students to quickly code videos of visitors so as to give exhibit developers timely feedback (Crowley & Knutson, 2005; Knutson & Crowley, 2005). The videos then also serve the needs of the research later in the project.

In his own right, Kevin Crowley has conducted JNR by setting up a partnership between his academic institution—the University of Pittsburgh—and the

Children's Museum of Pittsburgh, studying learning within the museum. Crowley and his colleague, Karen Knutson, report that they first conducted research independent of practice, then gradually started helping the practitioners by offering small evaluations of exhibits, and finally began conducting jointly negotiated research (Crowley & Knutson, 2005; Knutson & Crowley, 2005). Interestingly, after a few years of working in partnership with practitioners from the Children's Museum, Kevin founded the museum's Department of Visitor Research and Evaluation and became its first director, all the while working as a professor at the university. By becoming in-house researchers while maintaining academic appointments, Crowley, Knutson, and their colleagues created a hybrid of Callanan's model and ours.

A Potential Model for Cross-Institutional JNR-I

The Exploratorium is currently exploring a cross-institutional model for research–practice partnerships that might allow academic researchers to engage in the most deeply collaborative of our models, JNR-I, without being on staff. The project, *Exhibits for Social Science Research*, involves university-based social science researchers working closely with exhibit developers to create engaging exhibit experiences for visitors. Simultaneously, the exhibits will be structured so as to collect useable data for the outside researchers. The project has already garnered interest from behavioral economists, social psychologists, and developmental psychologists. In essence, we wish to create a social science laboratory on the museum floor, populated with interesting, educational exhibit experiences that simultaneously gather data for research. Our hope is that this laboratory will give academic researchers the opportunity to truly co-design exhibits at the same time as it offers exhibit developers the chance to contribute significantly to methodological design, blurring the disciplinary boundaries in the service of exhibits that achieve multiple purposes simultaneously.

Closing Thoughts

As a process, JNR has some particular challenges. For example, it is often difficult to identify fruitful research questions within a complex design process (e.g., those that are interesting, generative, tractable, at an appropriate level of abstraction). In this sense, the process is similar to the practice of asking fruitful questions in scientific inquiry (either in a classroom or at an exhibit), but with the additional constraint that the question should be considered worthy of study and not already answered by both practice and research communities.

At the same time, we would argue that JNR is worth the additional challenges because the potential impacts on practice and institutional capacity-building are much greater than with the other types of research. JNR generates long-term, simultaneous professional development for both researchers and practitioners in an authentic context of advancing actual current practice. Researchers come to appreciate the norms, complexities, and constraints of a design environment, while practitioners come to appreciate the norms, complexities, and constraints of conducting systematic inquiry through a theoretical lens. In a successful JNR project, both researchers and practitioners gain credibility through their joint ownership of the work, and they tend to disseminate more often and across a much broader set of professional communities.

References

Allen, S. (1997). Using scientific inquiry activities in exhibit explanations. [Special issue]. *Science Education, 81*(6), 715–734.

Allen, S. (2002). Looking for learning in visitor talk: A methodological exploration. In G. Leinhardt, K. Crowley, & K. Knutson (Eds.), *Learning conversations in museums* (pp. 259–303). Mahwah, NJ: Lawrence Erlbaum Associates.

Allen, S. (2004). Designs for learning: Studying science museums exhibits that do more than entertain. *Science Education, 88*(Supplement 1), S17–S33.

Allen, S., Gutwill, J.P., Perry, D., Garabay, C., Ellenbogen, K., Heimlich, J., . . . Klein, C. (2007). Research in museums: Coping with xomplexity. In J. Falk, L. Dierking, & S. Foutz (Eds.), *In principle, in practice: Museums as learning institutions* (pp. 229–246). New York: Rowman & Littlefield Publishers.

Barriault, C., & Pearson, D. (2010). Assessing exhibits for learning in science centers: A practical tool. *Visitor Studies, 13*(1), 90–106.

Bevan, B., Gutwill, J.P., Petrich, M., & Wilkinson, K. (2015). Learning through STEM-rich tinkering: Findings from a jointly negotiated research project taken up in practice. *Science Education, 99*(1), 98–120.

Borun, M., Chambers, M., & Cleghorn, A. (1996). Families are learning in science museums. *Curator: The Museum Journal, 39*(2), 123–138. doi: 10.1111/j.2151–6952.1996.tb01084.x

Borun, M., Dritsas, J., Johnson, J.I., Peter, N.E., Wagner, K.F., Fadigan, K., . . . Wenger, A. (1998). Family learning in museums—The PISEC perspective. Philadelphia, PA: Philadelphia-Camden Informal Science Education Collaborative (PISEC).

Bransford, J., & Schwartz, D. (1999). Chapter 3: Rethinking transfer: A simple proposal with multiple implications. *Review of Research in Education, 24,* 61–100.

ByteLight. (2013). ByteLight illuminates the Museum of Science. http://blog.bytelight.com/post/40011523606/bytelight-illuminates-the-museum-of-science—.VUL-6mZXUqg

Callanan, M.A. (2012). Conducting cognitive developmental research in museums: Theoretical issues and practical considerations. *Journal of Cognition and Development, 13*(2), 137–151.

Coburn, C.E., Penuel, W.R., & Geil, K.E. (2013). Research-practice partnerships: A strategy for leveraging research for educational improvement in school districts (p. 24). New York: William T. Grant Foundation.

Crowley, K., & Callanan, M. (1998). Describing and supporting collaborative scientific thinking in parent-child interactions. *Journal of Museum Education, 23*(1), 12–17.

Crowley, K., & Knutson, K. (2005). Museum as learning laboratory: Bringing research and practice together (part 2 of 2). *Hand to Hand: Association of Children's Museums, 19,* 3, 6.

Gutwill, J.P. (2003). Gaining visitor consent for research II: Improving the posted-sign method. *Curator, 46*(2), 228–235.

Gutwill, J.P. (2005). Observing APE. In T. Humphrey & J. Gutwill (Eds.), *Fostering active prolonged engagement: The art of creating APE exhibits.* Walnut Creek, CA: Left Coast Press.

Gutwill, J.P., & Allen, S. (2010). Facilitating family group inquiry at science museum exhibits. *Science Education, 94*(4), 710–742.

Hein, G. (2012). *Progressive museum practice: John Dewey and democracy.* Walnut Creek, CA: Left Coast Press.

Horn, M., Leong, Z.A., Block, F., Diamond, J., Evans, E.M., Phillips, B., & Shen, C. (2012). Of BATs and APEs: An interactive tabletop game for natural history museums (pp. 2058–2068). Proceedings of the 2012 ACM Annual Conference on Human Factors in Computing Systems. New York: ACM.

Humphrey, T., & Gutwill, J.P. (Eds.). (2005). *Fostering active prolonged engagement: The art of creating APE exhibits.* Walnut Creek, CA: Left Coast Press.

Knutson, K., & Crowley, K. (2005). Museum as learning laboratory: Developing and using a practical theory of informal learning (part 1 of 2). *Hand to Hand: Association of Children's Museums, 18*, 4–5.

Kunreuther, H., Novemsky, N., & Kahneman, D. (2001). Making low probabilities useful. *Journal of Risk and Uncertainty, 23*(3), 103–120.

Ma, J. (2014). *Using an indoor positioning system to automate visitor tracking.* Paper presented at the Visitor Studies Association, Albuquerque, NM.

McLean, K., & McEver, C. (Eds.). (2004). *Are we there yet? Conversations about best practices in science exhibition development.* San Francisco: Exploratorium.

Museum of Science, Boston. (2010). Living laboratory materials [Brochure]. Boston: Museum of Science, Boston.

National Research Council [NRC]. (2009). *Learning science in informal environments: People, places, and pursuits.* Washington, DC: National Academies Press.

Oppenheimer, F. (1968). A rationale for a science museum. *Curator, 11*(3), 206–209.

Oppenheimer, F. (1972). The Exploratorium: A playful museum combines perception and art in science education. *American Journal of Physics, 40*(7), 978–984.

Oppenheimer, F. (1974). The study of perception as a part of teaching physics. *American Journal of Physics, 42*(July), 531–537.

Oppenheimer, F. (1986). Working prototypes: Exhibit design at the Exploratorium. San Francisco: Exploratorium.

Rowe, S. (2015). Free-choice learning lab. http://oregonstate.edu/freechoicelab/

Serrell, B. (1998). Paying attention: Visitors and museum exhibitions. Washington, DC: American Association of Museums.

Szechter, L.E., & Carey, E.J. (2009). Gravitating toward science: Parent-child interactions at a gravitational-wave observatory. *Science Education, 93*(5), 846–858.

Van Schijndel, T.J.P., Franse, R.K., & Raijmakers, M.E.J. (2010). The exploratory behavior scale: Assessing young visitors' hands-on behavior in science museums. *Science Education, 94*(5), 794–809. doi: 10.1002/sce.20394

SECTION 3
General Discussion

13

CURATING EXPERIENCE

The Role of Learner Agency in Museums and Schools and the Development of Adaptive Expertise

Tina A. Grotzer and S. Lynneth Solis

The Authors

Tina A. Grotzer is an associate professor at the Harvard Graduate School of Education and a senior researcher at Project Zero. She directs the Causal Cognition in a Complex World Lab. Her research focuses on: 1) how reasoning about causal complexity interacts with our decisions in the everyday world and public understanding of science and; 2) how causal understanding develops in authentic but supported contexts and interacts with science learning (toward the goal of developing curriculum to support deep understanding). She is the author of *Learning Causality in a Complex World* (Rowman Littlefield, 2012) and lead author of the *Causal Patterns in Science* series.

S. Lynneth Solis is a doctoral student in human development and education and a researcher in the Causal Cognition in a Complex World Lab at the Harvard Graduate School of Education. Her research involves the study of conceptual development and the cognitive processes that lead children to evermore complex conceptions of the world. She is particularly interested in the role of the sociocultural and pedagogical environment in supporting young children's learning in both formal and informal settings. Her current work investigates young children's exploration of scientific phenomena through object play in cross-cultural settings and the unique play experiences of children growing up in indigenous contexts in Latin America.

"Did you see lots of things at the museum?" "No, I just saw two." "You went on a field trip for hours to the air and space museum and just saw two things?" "Well, Theo and I were trying to figure out how to overcome gravity in Kerbal Space Program [a rocket-launching computer game]. So we studied the design of a rocket and drew it in our

212 Grotzer and Solis

journals. Then we found another one that was really different, so we drew that one. Then we compared them and how their features worked. When we tried it out, we landed on the moon and went up ten levels!"—Dialogue between the first author and her 13-year-old son.

This volume is full of wisdom about collaboration between museum educators and researchers and what each can learn from the other. The partnerships are at different levels; in some cases, the goals are co-generated, resulting in integrated aims and outcomes, while in others, the relationship is newer, and their collaborations are at the level of helping to serve each other's goals. Even so, there are clear benefits to be gained for each set of partners and these are elaborated in the various chapters. In this discussion chapter, we aim to take a different approach; we look at the curating of experience and ask "for whom" and "by whom" are experiences designed? We consider how characteristics of children's learning in museums—elucidated through the research partnerships detailed in this volume—inform notions of learner agency and how museums and families can provide the supporting social contexts for learning. We offer examples of innovations in formal education that exemplify these characteristics in school practices and ask how these models might inform our notions of curriculum more broadly. We propose that supporting learner agency in museums and schools can promote the development of adaptive expertise.

A vision of the learner is a critical component of informal and formal settings for learning; each attributes different levels and types of agency to learners. Here we argue that these attributions shape and inform much of the experience that learners have. Ultimately, what happens in museums and schools is about curating and providing opportunities to make sense of experiences. The ways in which each institution plays a guiding role and the ways in which they encourage agency on behalf of learners inform the key features of what each does. The research in this book focuses largely on children's museums and the learning of young children. Children's museums offer affordances—opportunities that can be leveraged toward certain goals—for developing learner agency, as discussed below, that are available to a varying extent in other museums. In addition to informing formal educational contexts, these affordances may offer a vision for the role of learner agency in museums for older children, young adults, and adult visitors.

Why is a vision for learner agency so important? A changing world requires a dynamic notion of expertise. Adaptive expertise refers to the ability to orient to and respond to novel problem spaces (Hatano & Inagaki, 1986; Hatano & Oura, 2003). In contrast to more traditional notions of expertise, which refer to learning something very deeply in terms of recognizing the deep structure and patterns (Bereiter & Scardamalia, 1993; Chi, Feltovich, & Glaser, 1981) and continuing to display those specific understandings, adaptive expertise requires being able to set learning goals at the edge of one's competence. Adaptive experts engage in a form of progressive problem-solving and hold the cognitive and affective mindsets that enable them to deal with ambiguity, push forward despite partial knowledge, and ask the kinds of questions that lend insight into the problem space. Developing adaptive expertise is an important type of learning how to learn. Learners who are delivered a curriculum that has been digested for accessibility and sequenced in a neat progression of lessons are unlikely to develop the skills to persist at the edge of competence and to engage in progressive problem-solving. Enabling learner agency in designing and redesigning their learning experiences and facilitating the supporting familial and social structures is imperative to developing adaptive expertise.

Museums have traditionally served the purpose of collecting, preserving, and archiving artifacts; an important socio-historical role within society (Alexander & Alexander, 2008). Increasingly, however, museums have placed greater emphasis on the visitor experience and what they take away from their visit. Visitor agendas are a primary focus of how museum experience is conceptualized and attention is paid to how the social, physical, and personal contexts interact (Falk & Dierking, 2011). Just as museums have moved away from a vision of curating and archiving objects, encouraging the development of adaptive expertise in museums may require moving away from a vision of heavily curating opportunities for knowledge gain toward one of cultivating learners with their own agendas. Similarly, schools that have relied upon determining what the most important knowledge is and in transmitting that knowledge to students may need to consider how to invite learners to actively co-construct the curriculum in response to questions that they hold. The demands of our dynamic, complex, and interconnected world might well necessitate it. Below, we outline how research in children's museums, especially that of the research partnerships in this volume, offer an important advance in that direction.

A Focus on Play and Agency in Museums

Children's museums have especially focused on visitor initiative in terms of play; demonstrations and models are less common and a focus on play experiences and provocations are more prevalent (Henderson & Atencio, 2007; Mayfield, 2005). In these exhibits, the self-initiated nature of play is honored and provocations can encourage certain kinds of play. The curated space becomes a "laboratory of the possible" (Henricks, 2008, p. 168) where learners can question, discover, invent, and evaluate content at their own pace following their own roadmap through a playful disposition. Play, thus, is employed as a vehicle for learning in designing museum experiences (Anderson, Piscitelli, Weier, Everett, & Tayler, 2002). An essential characteristic of play is that it is not driven by external goals but is inherently reinforcing and intrinsically driven (Pellegrini, 2009; Rubin, Fein, & Vandenberg, 1983). While it is not motivated by articulated questions, research has demonstrated that inherent puzzles, such as the confoundedness of the causal mechanism (Schulz & Bonawitz, 2007), ambiguity about the causal pattern (Solis & Grotzer, in press), or inconsistency with current knowledge (Legare, 2012), can invite wonder and drive engagement in play.

The research in this volume also emphasizes the agency and cognitive processes that learners can exercise within flexible contexts, placing them in the role of sense-maker and theory-builder (Rhodes & Bushara, this volume). For instance, Sobel, Letourneau, and Meisner (this volume) view the child as actively thinking and initiating discovery. Their research on how children understand the acquisition of knowledge invites consideration of how this thinking and developing metacognition supports a notion of learner agency. By quantifying these behaviors and helping museum staff and parents to observe them, the research encourages development of new scaffolds to support self-driven learning.

Conversations between museum educators and researchers can also support museums in building upon a rich legacy of existing research findings in addition to those that grow out of their collaborations. This research can inform exhibit development. For instance, Needham, Barrett, and Peterman (2002) in their "sticky mitten" study found that infants who experienced sticky mittens that allowed them to pick up objects before their grasping skills enabled them to do so persisted with greater exploration than controls after the mittens were removed. Sobel, Letourneau, and Meisner (this volume) in their Mind Lab research invited children to reflect upon themselves as learners who control their play and make decisions. Making children's learning visible to themselves and their family unit, as was the case in this research, may support learners in adopting a view of themselves as an agent in curating their experiences. Research such as this illustrates how provocations can be effective even with the youngest of learners in helping to shape future learner agency and related behaviors. Learning about affordances, or provocations, inherent in different experiences and materials through research provides fruitful inspiration for creative and productive ways of engaging visitors in museums.

Yet, a well-developed collaboration extends far beyond being able to apply research to museum contexts. In considering the relationship between research and practice, Stokes (1997) introduced the following concepts that address possible relationships between the two: 1) Bohr's Quadrant as a focus on basic research that is theory-driven, informs theory, and may eventually inform practice but is not predicated on doing so, as in research on atomic structure; 2) Edison's Quadrant as a focus on use-inspired research that attempts to impact practice directly, as in the research that led to the invention of the lightbulb; and 3) Pasteur's Quadrant as a focus on research that informs both use and basic research for which the questions are often use-inspired, as in pasteurization and microbial theory. Questions at the intersection of research and museum practice can inform studies in ways similar to how Stokes (1997) imagined basic and applied research in the sciences interacting within Pasteur's Quadrant (i.e., use-inspired basic research). In contrast to schools, where prescribed curricula typically guides learning, studies in museums can seek to understand how learners and their families initiate and engage with opportunities as well as how they take advantage of affordances to drive their own agendas.

An important question is how to maintain this sense of self-initiated questioning as children grow older, particularly by elementary and middle school age. Research shows that young children are more likely than older children or adults to engage with interactive exhibits (Hein, 1998); without their own questions or a least a sense of wonder and intrigue, older children are less likely to approach demonstrations and models with the same sense of play (Griffin, 2004). Art museum educators talk about the tendency to "wall-cruise" (LaSenna, 2010, 189) rather than to invest deeply in anything (in referring to a pattern of spending less than 30 seconds in front of an artwork) which has been found to be prevalent (e.g. Falk, 2009; Hein, 1998; Smith & Smith, 2001). A similar dynamic of minimal engagement was found in a broad range of museums as demonstrated through a series of tracking and timing studies reported in a meta-analysis by Serrell (1998) supported by the National Science Foundation.

Rethinking the Curating of Experience in Schools

What might schools borrow from how children's museums engage visitors in play experiences? Curriculum is a form of curation of experience in schools. Often it is rigidly structured rather than aimed at inviting opportunity. A static curriculum will not work in a changing world and is unlikely to result in adaptive expertise. However, there are ways of thinking about the curriculum that more closely align with the self-initiated play that is honored and studied in children's museums—ones that more likely will support the development of adaptive expertise.

"The living curriculum" is a concept put forth by a small group of schools (Wilmot, 2010). These schools encourage the students' role in curriculum development—a negotiated, dynamic process in which the learner and a teacher set understanding goals together and operationalize the questions that learners have. This is a significant departure from the concept of "backwards design," which involves determining a set of understanding goals that are the expected outcomes of the curriculum and then designing instruction to them. Backwards design has been, in recent years, considered the gold standard of instructional design and is an inherent part of many well-respected, research-based forms of curriculum development, including Teaching for Understanding (e.g. Wiske, 1998) and Understanding by Design (Wiggins & McTighe, 2005). In these models, educators often set understanding goals for learners far in advance of students' interaction with the curriculum and without their questions and learning goals in mind.

The living curriculum is not the first model of instructional design to argue that curriculum should grow from learners' agendas. The Organic School movement (Johnson, 1938/1974), for instance, focused on learning that "organically emerges" from what children were interested in, both from a developmental perspective and in terms of their expressed interests. Children's questions of all kinds motivated learning and the activities at the school. A key difference is that curriculum was still designed *for* children with their interests in mind. The living curriculum invites learners into the design process and subsequently helps them understand how learning goals can be advanced. In this way, schools can incorporate the self-motivated, self-sustaining flexible learning exhibited in museums to foster adaptive expertise. Below, we discuss how other curriculum models, such as Reggio, also depart from a rigid stance of backward design.

Considering the Importance of the Surrounding Social Context

This consideration of learner agency above is intentionally not framed as learner autonomy. This is in recognition that social context is a critical aspect of learning communities and those that reveal adaptive expertise. The importance of surrounding social context has been recognized as an essential feature in developing expertise and pushing people to work at the edge of their competence (Baroody, 2003; Smith & Semin, 2004). Historical examples of communities of creativity and innovation exist, from the Renaissance to the Concord authors group in the mid-1800s that included Emerson, Hawthorne, Thoreau, and Alcott. The view of learning within a social-historical context (Vygotsky, 1978) provides balance to Piaget's focus on the individual mind. It fits with notions of distributed cognition (Salomon, 1993) and "a view of knowledge as socially constructed and distributed among individuals, groups, cultural tools and artifacts" (Krechevsky & Mardell, 2001, p. 285).

The research in children's museums discussed in this volume embraces the importance of the social and cultural context of learning interactions. Much of the work is strongly embedded in sociocultural theory (e.g., Rogoff, 2003). For instance, Callanan, Martin, and Luce (this volume) analyze natural and spontaneous family conversations to reveal how caregivers' questions interact with children's play in ways that build upon and support understanding. The research offers insights into ways that parents can support children's inquiry and learning and explains resulting shifts in how exhibits were framed, such as in the rotating skull example offered in their chapter. Further, Haden, Cohen, Uttal, and Marcus (this volume) focus on the interaction of the physical environment of the *Skyline* exhibit and family conversations as essential mechanisms for memory and transfer of concepts. Studying the narratives that children develop in their visits, reunion narratives with a caregiver who was not present, and memory narratives once they return home focuses beyond the museum walls and on the context of the family in supporting learners.

The research partnerships offer an important avenue for helping parents and the broader community support and recognize new visions for learning. The Mind Lab research discussed by Sobel, Letourneau, and Meisner (this volume) helps parents to develop views of their children as being thoughtful, in pursuit of questions that can compel further learning, and as having learning agendas, albeit unarticulated. They help caregivers understand scaffolds that interact with and further children's learning, for instance, the effectiveness of certain kinds of questions in the *Build and Talk* exhibit, described by Haden and colleagues (this volume).

What might schools borrow from the strong focus in children's museums on the social context surrounding children's learning experiences? Adaptive expertise can be supported by visions of what is possible and working at the edge of one's competence can be scaffolded within Vygotsky's zone of proximal development (Vygotsky, 1978). Visions of what next steps might look like can be generated by more advanced peers and teacher guides. The burden of teachers to support the agency of individual learners is balanced against the distributed cognition of the group members.

The Making Learning Visible (MLV) Project, a collaboration between Project Zero of Harvard University and the municipal preschools of Reggio Emilia, Italy, helps to exemplify how this vision can be realized in schools (Project Zero & Reggio Children, 2001). Given the strong focus on documenting the learning of groups in contrast to individuals in the Reggio Emilia framework, a central focus of the MLV Project was to examine group learning and how to define and understand it. The resulting principles emphasize the social context of the learning group and the inclusion of learners, their peers, teachers, and parents. Research questions in the resulting MLV model generate from different members, including parents. Documentation is undertaken to help the community engage in careful, thoughtful looking and to allow patterns to surface and reveal themselves that otherwise might not. It is aligned with emergent, qualitative analyses (e.g. Charmaz, 2006; Strauss & Corbin, 1998). This work has inspired adaptations for schools in general and extending beyond the preschool years through 9th and 10th grades (available at the Making Learning Visible website, www.mlvpz.org/index22aa.html). What can be seen in this work is the synergistic relationship between the individual and community and the sociocultural milieu that upholds the interactions between various members of the learning community. With their focus on carefully documenting the learning process within the social context, museum–research partnerships can shed further light on factors that facilitate (or hinder) the productive communication and interchange of ideas among learners.

Possibilities, Puzzles, and Lingering Questions

While the research partnerships between cognitive scientists and children's museums offer models and important affordances for how schools might rethink learner engagement, there are also a number of distinctions between the environments that raise puzzles. Most predominant is the longer-term view of the learner that schools can adopt; one that is coherent and continual. This enables new possibilities for developing and supporting the growth of learner agency. Schools have the luxury of time, while museums may only have one visit to engage visitors.

An extended view makes it possible to know the individual learner more deeply and to support agency across time—at a level not possible in discrete visits—and supports the possibility of emergent curriculum co-constructed with students and guided by teachers. This may also be a double-edged sword, making it harder for schools to maintain the flexible mindset that is possible in museums. Cognitive scientists working at the intersection of education, curriculum, and the learning sciences bring significant knowledge to bear about the challenges of learning specific content and what learners need to understand first before they can grasp other concepts deeply. Recent research has focused on learning progressions (e.g., Carraher, Smith, Wiser, Schliemann, & Cayton-Hodges, 2009; Mohan, Chen, & Anderson, 2009; Wiser, Smith, Doubler, & Asbell-Clarke, 2009) across numerous topics, particularly in the sciences, from astronomy (Plummer & Maynard, 2014) to the water cycle (Gunckel, Covitt, Salinas, & Anderson, 2012) to energy (Jin & Anderson, 2012). The result of careful task analyses and considerable research on learning, learning progressions offer possible pathways into topics. This invites questions about how the long view is handled in ways that support learner agency and still benefit from this wealth of findings.

A further set of questions relates to how museums for older learners can respond to agency. If schools enable a stronger sense of learner agency, such as that exemplified by the student in the opening paragraph, learners will come equipped with questions, peers, and an operationalized understanding of how to interact with provocations and artifacts in museums that further their learning aims. Can learners with agency bring their own questions into the museum? How well does the museum respond to this agency and sense of possibilities? How might museum–school partnerships allow for fostering of ideas and questions that can be explored in the museum setting but also brought back to inform a dynamic curriculum in schools? If schools did more to enable learners to hold questions and to curate their own experiences in their learning, they could complement these efforts with actively encouraging a view of museums as places to explore and test ideas, much as the learner in the opening quote used the museum to learn about rocket design. Museums might also provoke puzzles that students can then bring back to school to investigate deeply over time and through the resources there.

Museums offer a vision of the learner as the curator of one's own experience, albeit highly scaffolded by exhibit materials and family in the early years. By offering provocations for learning, visitors are enticed into finding, developing, and exploring questions that they have control over. This is an optimistic view that features the best case scenario for the role that museums can play and the ways that families will respond. There are cases in which this ideal could fall short in museums, just as it does in schools; it hinges on many things, such as the specific exhibits, the museum policies for engaging visitors, and the goals, attitudes, and inclinations of the families who visit, for a few examples. But the model of promise is important as a picture of possibility that can motivate future goals and aspirations. Ultimately, we all are curators of the experiences of our lives. Keeping this in mind as we explore possibilities for learning in museums and schools should help us to develop affordances in formal and informal settings that invite learner agency and the development of adaptive expertise.

Acknowledgments

The authors express their appreciation to Dave Sobel and Jennifer Jipson for their thoughtful guidance and framing for the development of this chapter and for the opportunity to contribute to this volume and the conversations leading up to it. Thank you to Rosemarie Sese for assistance with the literature review. This chapter is dedicated to Malcolm O. Campbell; as a student of the Organic School who went on to live a long, loving, and productive life, he understood the value and importance of its approach.

References

Alexander, E.P., & Alexander, M. (2008). *Museums in motion: An introduction to the history and functions of museums*. Lanham, MD: AltaMira Press.

Anderson, D., Piscitelli, B., Weier, K., Everett, M., & Tayler, C. (2002). Children's museum experiences: Identifying powerful mediators of learning. *Curator: The Museum Journal, 45*(3), 213–231.

Baroody, A.J. (2003). The development of adaptive expertise and flexibility: The integration of conceptual and procedural knowledge. In A.J. Baroody, & A. Dowker (Eds.), *The development of arithmetic concepts and skills: Constructing adaptive expertise* (pp. 1–34). New York: Routledge.

Bereiter, C., & Scardamalia, M. (1993). *Surpassing ourselves: An inquiry into the nature and implications of expertise*. Chicago: Open Court.

Carraher, D., Smith, C., Wiser, D., Schliemann, A., & Cayton-Hodges, G. (2009). *Assessing students' evolving understandings about matter*. Paper presented at the Learning Progressions in Science (LeaPS) Conference, Iowa City, IA.

Charmaz, K. (2006). *Constructing grounded theory*. London: Sage.

Chi, M.T.C., Feltovich, P.J., & Glaser, R. (1981). Categorization and representation of physics problems by experts and novices. *Cognitive Science, 5*(2), 121–152.

Falk, J.H. (2009). *Learning in museums*. Walnut Creek, CA: Left Coast Press.

Falk, J.H., & Dierking, L.D. (2011). *The museum experience*. Walnut Creek, CA: Left Coast Press.

Griffin, J. (2004). Research on students and museums: Looking more closely at the students in school groups. *Science Education, 88*(Supplement 1), S59–S70.

Gunckel, K.L., Covitt, B.A., Salinas, I., & Anderson, C.W. (2012). A learning progression for water in socio-ecological systems. *Journal of Research in Science Teaching, 49*(7), 843–868.

Hatano, G., & Inagaki, K. (1986). Two courses of expertise. In H. Stevenson, H. Azuma, & K. Hakuta (Eds.), *Child development and education in Japan* (pp. 262–272). San Francisco: W.H. Freeman.

Hatano, G., & Oura, Y. (2003). Commentary: Reconceptualizing school learning using insight from expertise research. *Educational Researcher, 32*(8), 26–29.

Hein, G.E. (1998). *Learning in museums*. London: Routledge.

Henderson, T.Z., & Atencio, D.J. (2007). Integration of play, learning, and experiences: What museums afford young visitors. *Early Childhood Education Journal, 35*, 245–251.

Henricks, T. (2008). The nature of play. *American Journal of Play, 1*(2), 157–180.

Jin, H., & Anderson, C.W. (2012). A learning progression for energy in socio-ecological systems. *Journal of Research in Science Teaching, 49*(9), 1149–1180.

Johnson, M. (1938/1974). *Thirty years with an idea: The story of organic education*. Tuscaloosa, AL: University of Alabama Press.

Krechevsky, M., & Mardell, B. (2001). Four features of learning in groups. In Project Zero & Reggio Children (Eds.), *Making learning visible: Children as individual and group learners*. Reggio Emilia, Italy: Reggio Children.

LaSenna, D. (2010). Adults, appreciation, and participatory arts education. In E.P. Clapp (Ed.), *20Under40: Reinventing the arts and arts education for the 21st century*. Bloomington, IN: AuthorHouse.

Legare, C.H. (2012). Exploring explanation: Explaining inconsistent information guides hypothesis-testing behavior in young children. *Child Development, 83*, 173–185.

Mayfield, M.I. (2005). Children's museums: Purposes, practices and play? *Early Child Development and Care, 175*(2), 179–192.

Mohan, L., Chen, J., & Anderson, C. (2009). Developing a multi-year learning progression for carbon cycling in socio-ecological systems. *Journal of Research in Science Teaching, 46*(6), 675–698.

Needham, A., Barrett, T., & Peterman, K. (2002). A pick-me-up for infants' exploratory skills: Early stimulated experiences reaching for objects using 'sticky mittens' enhances young infants' object exploration skills. *Infant Behavior and Development, 25*, 279–295.

Pellegrini, A.D. (2009). *The role of play in human development*. New York: Oxford University Press.

Plummer, J.D., & Maynard, L. (2014). Building a learning progression for celestial motion: An exploration of students' reasoning about the seasons. *Journal of Research in Science Teaching, 51*(7), 902–929.

Project Zero & Reggio Children (Eds.). (2001). *Making learning visible: Children as individual and group learners*. Reggio Emilia, Italy: Reggio Children.

Rogoff, B. (2003). *The cultural nature of cognitive development*. New York: Oxford University Press.

Rubin, K.H., Fein, G.G., & Vandenberg, B. (1983). Play. In E.M. Hetherington (Ed.), *Handbook of child psychology: Socialization, personality, and social development* (4th ed.; vol. 4; pp. 693–744). New York: Wiley.

Salomon, G. (1993). *Distributed cognitions*. New York: Cambridge University Press.

Schulz, L.E., & Bonawitz, E. (2007). Serious fun: Preschoolers engage in more exploratory play when evidence is confounded. *Developmental Psychology, 43*, 1045–1050.

Serrell, B. (1998). *Paying attention: Visitors and museum exhibitions*. Washington, DC: American Association of Museums.

Smith, E.R., & Semin, G.R. (2004). Socially situated cognition: Cognition it its social context. *Advances in Experimental Social Psychology, 36*, 53–117.

Smith, J.K., & Smith, L.F. (2001). Spending time on art. *Empirical Studies of the Arts, 19*(2) 229–236.

Solis, S.L., & Grotzer, T.A. (in press). They work together to roar: Kindergarteners' understanding of an interactive causal task. *Journal of Research in Childhood Education*.

Stokes, D.E. (1997). *Pasteur's quadrant: Basic science and technological innovation*. Washington, DC: Bookings Institute Press.

Strauss A., & Corbin, J. (1998). *Basics of qualitative research—Techniques and procedures for developing grounded theory: Second edition.* London: Sage Publications.

Vygotsky, L.S. (1978). *The mind in society: Development of higher psychological processes.* Cambridge, MA: Harvard University Press.

Wiggins, G., & McTighe, J. (2005). *Understanding by design.* Alexandria, VA: Association for Supervision and Curriculum Development.

Wilmot, B. (2010). The living curriculum. http://www.tremontschool.org/livingcurriculum.php

Wiser, M., Smith, C., Doubler, S., & Asbell-Clarke, J. (2009). *Learning progressions as a tool for curriculum development: Lessons from the inquiry project.* Paper presented at the Learning Progressions in Science (LeaPS) Conference, Iowa City, IA.

Wiske, M.S. (Ed.). (1998). *Teaching for understanding: Linking research with practice.* San Francisco: Jossey-Bass.

14

TWO MISSIONS IN SEARCH OF A SHARED CULTURE

Kathy Hirsh-Pasek and Roberta Michnick Golinkoff

The Authors

Kathryn Hirsh-Pasek is the Stanley and Debra Lefkowitz Faculty Fellow in the Department of Psychology at Temple University. Her research examines the development of early language and literacy as well as the role of play in learning and she is deeply interested in how we can optimize informal learning environments for children and families.

Roberta Michnick Golinkoff is the Unidel H. Rodney Sharp Professor of Education, Psychology, Linguistics and Cognitive Science at the University of Delaware. She has won numerous awards for her work, including the 2015 James McKeen Cattell Fellow prize (with Kathy Hirsh-Pasek) for lifetime contributions to applied psychological science. She travels worldwide to speak to academic as well as lay groups. She is an expert on language development, playful learning, and early spatial knowledge. Three of her books are directed to parents and practitioners, as she is passionate about dissemination. With Hirsh-Pasek, she co-founded the Ultimate Block Party movement to celebrate the science of learning.

At the turn of the millennium, Jack Shonkoff (2000), speaking to scientists, practitioners, and policy makers, penned a provocative piece entitled "Science, Policy and Practice: Three Cultures in Search of a Shared Mission." The abstract of this paper illuminated a problem that resonates with the collection in this book. Shonkoff wrote, "The capacity to navigate across their borders, to understand their different rules of evidence, to speak their distinctive languages, and to achieve credibility in all three worlds while maintaining a sense of intellectual integrity in each, requires respect for their differences and a commitment to their shared mission" (2000, p. 181). In many ways, this volume represents a sequel to this classic article, but one with a twist. As scientists and museum educators continue to forge a working relationship, they need to take their often separate missions and fuse them into a common culture, or at the least, two cultures that can communicate. Scientists look to museums as a perfect location for collecting data from a diverse sample of children and parents as they examine hypotheses about learning. Museum professionals look to scientists to help them craft or augment exhibits that engage families and help them see the link between playful exploration and learning. Scientists largely have no audience beyond their peers in the academic community. Museum professionals are deeply vested in their audience—the families who frequent the museum and the community that supports them. This volume is testimony to triumphs and challenges that these partnerships encounter as scientists meet face to face with museum personnel and attempt to build that shared culture.

Over the last decade, a number of museums around the United States have established long-term relationships with scientific partners. Moving from virtual newlyweds setting up their first apartment to seasoned young marrieds, these partnerships offer a wellspring of good advice for others following in their footsteps. Across the seven museum–scientist partnerships represented in this book, the advice looks a bit like good marriage counseling. If you want to create a new culture of learning between museums and scientists, it is imperative to 1) respect one another's perspectives, 2) establish and talk about your mutual goals, 3) make sure that the distribution of chores is even rather than imbalanced, 4) ensure that everyone is getting something out of the relationship, and 5) establish a strong sense of trust in one another. The partnerships in this volume are now in a position to offer these nuggets of advice to others, as they were among the first to bridge the two cultures and to learn from their successes and challenges along the way.

Reaping the Benefits and Meeting the Challenges

The benefits to working in tandem have been substantial. The scientists report that access to children and families helps the research move more quickly. And the science has already generated important theoretical and practical results. More on those findings later. Museum personnel find that they have modified their exhibits and offerings on the basis of scientific results garnered from their collaborations. By way of example, The UC Santa Cruz/San Jose Children's Discovery Museum team found that moving from a more traditional science-based set of STEM exhibits to a science exhibit that featured *Alice in Wonderland* removed gender bias in the kinds of conversations parents were having with their children (Callanan, Martin, & Luce, this volume). In the traditional STEM exhibits, parents were more likely to give scientific explanations to sons than to daughters, a result that was nullified when the exhibit became more female-friendly. Findings from NYU scientist Marjorie Rhodes helped to inform the way in which museum staff in New York's Children's Museum of Manhattan (CMOM) engaged with children around "doing science" rather than "being scientists" (Rhodes & Bushara, p. 113, this volume). The change in wording altered both attitudes and behaviors within the exhibits and informed museum practitioners who could change the ways in which they facilitated strategies for child engagement. The Chicago Children's Museum's Inspector Sturdy—a research assistant carrying a triangle-shaped magnifying glass who pretended to be a building inspector—and *Story Hub* were both outgrowths of findings about the importance of reflection and recounting in learning (Haden, Cohen, Uttal, & Marcus, this volume). As we see then, the partnerships between scientists and museum educators have been fruitful. Museum educators profited from hearing a new voice that added to the creation of evidence-based exhibits. The collaborations served as a source of professional development for museum staff and offered a rare glimpse into the science of learning for parents who are happily transformed into participants in the generation of knowledge. The scientists who participated in research within the museum setting also benefited by learning to de-jargonize their work so that they could more easily communicate their efforts and findings with museum staff and the museum visitors.

Partnerships with diverse groups, however, also pose unique challenges. One less emphasized in the current set of papers is that of balancing both the needs of the scientist and the museum staff as they iron out their collaboration. The scientist is charged with collecting clean data and having perfect control groups. The museum staff needs to make certain that the exhibit is accomplishing what it was intended to accomplish. If it does not attract families and if families are not engaging in the expected ways, museum educators need to tweak the exhibit. Thus, the scientist looks to conduct primary research. The museum staff would be thrilled to have strong evaluation research. Sometimes these needs clash, as when a research project is thwarted midstream by a change in an exhibit that is not attracting visitors.

Different models arise to deal with conflicting needs between scientists and museum educators. The Children's Museum of Manhattan (CMOM) with their NYU partner adopted what we might call the "perfect science model" of collaboration: research is conducted in a separate room in the museum rather than in the context of the exhibits (Rhodes & Bushara, this volume). The research question is primary and the hope is that the data, once collected, will inform museum practice. Here the challenge is to ask a research question in a way that can be relevant to museum practice and potentially to professional development for museum staff. This model weighs research purity as primary and thinks less about interfacing with the flux and flow of the museum experience. The museum is a venue for the research. Models like this have been remarkably productive. The CMOM/NYU partnership has already generated 21 publications, two National Science Foundation (NSF) grants, and 25 conference presentations. They are not alone in generating funding and solid research dissemination.

The UC Santa Cruz and San Jose Discovery Museum use several different models, but their first collaboration on the NSF-sponsored *Take Another Look* project represented more of a "perfect evaluation model" (Callanan et al., this volume). It was in this evaluation project that the team discovered how parents gave more scientific explanations to boys than to girls (Crowley, Callanan, Tennenbaum, & Allen, 2001). This then resulted in revision to the museum exhibits, as well as published research articles on parent–child conversations about science.

Finally, there is the *Build It Together*—an example of a balanced model represented by the Chicago Children's Museum team with the University of Chicago. This team adopted a framework in which research is conducted as a more integral part of the exhibit *Skyscraper Challenge* (Haden et al., this volume). Researchers are welcome and have a loud voice in the design of the exhibit, but their research must be conducted on the museum floor as an appendage to the natural exhibit as well as in the lab. When the research is on display on the main floor, noise level and random subject selection is compromised in favor of a more "authentic" context for observation.

The Living Lab group at the Boston Museum of Science endorses a balanced model and provides a set of guidelines for researchers who want to work in the museum climate (Corriveau et al., this volume). Their advice? Design studies that they know will work in short spurts (optimally 7 minutes long) where easily accessible research opportunities exist and where the process of science and the communication about the science provides professional development for museum educators and visitors. Figuring out which model is optimal for a particular partnership is one of the challenges that scientists and museums face when building a solid marriage.

Ancillary to the question of balance is the realization that everyone will probably not get his or her way at least some of the time. The researcher might not get a perfect setting to conduct the research, as children might be noisy, or worse yet, captivated by other activities that are part of the vibrant setting. Further, researchers will need to worry about the selectivity of the families who visit museums, a problem that might slant their answers. For example, the findings that stress increasing explanation and reflection within exhibits might be more potent for children whose parents are more, rather than less, educated. Museum visitors are often drawn from more educated and more well-off families. Indeed, CMOM reported that only 20% of the families that visit are of low income. Further, researchers are limited in the kinds of research they might conduct, as designs that incorporate longitudinal data will not fit the setting.

On the museum educator side, the staff must deal with the inconvenience of having researchers who are on the museum floor working with visitors to ask questions and videotape responses—both potential disruptions to the smooth flow of a museum visit. For scientists and museum educators alike, creating the optimal culture will also involve face-to-face meetings that focus on building strong relationships. Each of the partnerships reviewed in this book are meeting these challenges and grown together.

What Have We Learned?

Taking the papers as a collective, we have learned quite a lot. A review of the six papers suggests several common themes. By way of example, Haden et al. (this volume) report the finding that conversations make direct experience a topic of reflection and abstraction. Those children who participated in a *build and talk* condition asked more questions and could transfer what they learned to a new problem. Legare, Gose, and Guess (this volume), working with the Thinkery in Austin, report a very similar set of findings suggesting that the benefits of explanation to learning may be unique. When presented with a new mechanical toy, children who provided an explanatory response to how the toy worked remembered more about the core causal features of the toy, and were more likely to discover how yet another novel toy worked. Callanan et al., with the Children's Discovery Museum in San Jose, noted that family conversations enrich how children learn. Beyond the natural discovery that accompanies most good exhibits, the conversations about the exhibit illuminate the science behind it and elevate how children reason and think about the exhibit. Finally Sobel et al.'s Mind Lab reports that reflecting on learning—*making the learning visible*—was central to how children learned and understood learning itself. In each, the message is strong. If we talk about or highlight portions of the exhibit rather than just presenting it, we can increase its learning value. Optimal learning happens when we help children discover the learning variables of interest.

These findings underscore a finding that we have had in our laboratory. Discovery and exploratory learning of the type found in museums offers a playful learning pedagogy, but *guided play*, where adults make the learning visible, is key to making the learning stick and to the transfer of learning (Fisher, Hirsh-Pasek, Newcombe, & Golinkoff, 2013; Weisberg, Hirsh-Pasek, & Golinkoff, 2013). Put another way, if a particular exhibit has a learning goal, then finding ways to subtly point children to the relevant dimensions for learning are critical for success. That is, being free range can be fun, but it might not focus children on the dimension of importance to achieve the learning in science, math, or literacy. In a series of studies, we directly tested this assertion by examining the relationship between pure discovery play and learning. One study examined early geometry through the learning of shapes (Fisher et al., 2013). Children were either allowed to play with a set of regular, irregular, or non-triangles and were asked to "feed" Lulu the picky ladybug puppet only the "real" triangles. The children were divided into three groups: 1) a pure discovery play setting in which they interacted with the shapes objects with no adult participation, 2) a guided play setting in which children were asked questions that allowed them to reflect on their play as they discovered the essence of the shapes, or 3) a direct instruction condition in which they were told that the triangle had "three corners and three sides." Children in the guided play condition outperformed their peers in both the free play and the direct instruction conditions. Most impressively, they outperformed children in the direct instruction condition by 30% in deciding whether never-before-seen shapes were category exemplars. A similar finding emerged in a recent vocabulary-learning paradigm (Weisberg, Ilgaz, Hirsh-Pasek, Golinkoff, & Nicolopoulou, 2015). Four- and 5-year-old low income children learned more vocabulary in a read and adult-directed play condition than they did in either a read and flashcard condition (Toub et al., 2015) or a read and play alone condition.

In our experiments, guided play sits midway between the two pedagogical approaches of direct instruction and free play. Free play has been difficult to define (Burghardt, 2011), but generally is considered an activity that is fun, voluntary, flexible, involves active engagement, and that offers an element of make believe (for reviews, see Fisher, Hirsh-Pasek, Golinkoff, Singer, & Berk, 2011; Weisberg et al., 2013). There is no question that free play has many benefits for young children (Hirsh-Pasek, Golinkoff, Berk, & Singer, 2009) and that children prosper from doing free play in the museum context. Yet when there are learning goals for an activity or exhibit, guided play is optimal. Guided play is fun, but also has the advantage of focusing the child on the dimension of interest for a learning objective. Guided play incorporates adult-scaffolded learning while at the same time remaining child-directed and fun.

Guided play can take two forms. In one, the context is set by adults as in a museum exhibit but is designed in ways that will highlight a particular kind of interaction and learning. Montessori schools also use this approach (see Lillard, 2013). The second form of guided play occurs when teachers watch the child-directed play and either question or encourage the children to question, comment, or extend their interest. Guided play, for example, emerges when we help children focus on their discoveries by commenting on ongoing activities (Inspector Sturdy in Chicago's *Skyscraper Challenge*) or by prompting them with open-ended questions of the sort suggested by Haden et al. (this volume). Importantly, guided play augments child's play but is careful not to disrupt it. The construct of guided play is consistent with the research presented in this volume, supporting the idea that adult-enhanced play that remains child directed might have a pronounced role in supporting learning.

Why might guided play activities encourage more learning than either free play or direct instruction? Several possibilities come to mind. One is that playful learning is fun, and as such, children attend more to learning that is set within a playful context. We have suggested that the playful context sets a *mis en place* or a disposition for learning through curiosity and active engagement (Weisberg, Hirsh-Pasek, Golinkoff, & McCandliss, 2014). Second, guided play with adults involves children's social side and heightens their desire to interact and engage with an adult. Third, we speculate that child agency plays a strong role in that when children are the directors of their own learning, they learn better than they do when we both initiate and direct that learning (Alfieri, Brooks, Aldrich, & Tenenbaum, 2011). Finally, through guided play, adults can encourage the use of reflection and explanation that will foster better learning (Sobel et al., this volume).

The chapters in this volume suggest that museums inspire playful learning. For us, playful learning is an umbrella term that includes both free play, which is totally child-directed, and guided play, in which adults scaffold children's interests and learning. Our challenge is to augment the wonderful exhibit designs to make this guided play a rich experience in which the learning is visible, as Sobel et al., (this volume) suggest. Further and importantly, the more visible the links between playful learning and outcomes for children, the more parents will come to understand that museums are both fun and fuel for learning. Mixing what the science has shown us with the creative genius of museum educators can offer a culture of learning that can be a model for education writ large.

Looking Forward: A Challenge for Science and Museum Partnerships

The seven scientist–museum partnerships offer a case in point that two missions can develop a shared culture. We have seen how scientists reap the benefits of working in the museum context and how exhibits are created and tweaked in ways that are sensitive to scientific findings. We have also seen scientists' sphere of influence widen: Scientific findings can impact the museum by offering professional development for museum educators who will forever change, for example, the way they spark parental explanation or the generic use of "being scientists" versus "doing science."

The spheres of influence thus far, however, have been fairly local and contained within the walls of the museum. It would be interesting to see whether the partnerships could also spread to create a community of learning beyond those walls by opening up the wealth of possibilities to those less likely to travel to the museum. In one preliminary study of this kind, my colleagues and I asked whether it might be possible to increase conversations between parents and their young children by transforming supermarkets into museums. Signs, for example, were placed in the dairy section that read, "Question for your child: Where does milk come from?" with a huge picture portraying a cartoon cow and a gallon of milk. When the signs were up, we observed that caregivers in the low-income neighborhoods spoke 33% more to their children than when the signs were down. The signs made no change in middle-income markets (Ridge, Weisberg, Ilgaz, Hirsh-Pasek, & Golinkoff, 2015), as parents were already having conversations with their children. We are working with the DuPage Children's Museum to extend this study in areas of Chicago.

Another experiment in partnership with the Children's Museum of Manhattan was called the Ultimate Block Party (www.ultimateblockparty.com), in which 22 activities born from the science of learning were placed around the Naumberg

Bandshell in Central Park (Zosh, Fisher, Golinkoff, & Hirsh-Pasek, 2013). Over 50,000 people participated in this event that was later repeated in Toronto, Canada and in collaboration with the Port Discovery Museum in Baltimore, Maryland. Evaluations of these community-wide experiments reveal that the more activities that a parent attends, the more they see the relationship between play and learning (Grob, Schlesinger, Pace, Hirsh-Pasek, & Golinkoff, 2015).

Importantly, the latter two projects were conducted in places that families naturally go. The parents did not have to travel to a destination. There is no admittance fee, as families could reap the benefits of learning during the course of their everyday activities (going to a park and shopping). Even more potent is that these kinds of projects allow science–museum partnerships to have greater reach among lower income families who often do not have rich home environments stocked with books and puzzles that stimulate cognitive growth. As we look to the future, it would be wonderful to consider ways to have scientists and community organizations like museums widen their influence into communities.

Conclusion

We are just at the beginning. Ten years ago, developmental scientists sat in their closed laboratories combing the newspaper for birth announcements so that they could fill the data cells in their studies. Their research was written up and sent to high-impact journals for publication. The public rarely saw the results.

Museum educators, on the other hand, worked with designers and architects to create playful environments that were attractive and engaging for families. They had outstanding intuitions about what might attract children and they became a city's hub for a number of families with young children.

Today those two missions can be jointly achieved by understanding that playful environments are learning environments. Museums are houses for playful learning and, thus, are outstanding natural laboratories that are fun and educational for families. By fusing the desire to have imaginative play spaces with the desire to create active learning spaces, the two missions are indeed forming a common culture.

Acknowledgements

We thank Stanley and Debra Lefkowitz for supporting some of the research mentioned in this manuscript.

References

Alfieri, L., Brooks, P.J., Aldrich, N.J., & Tenenbaum, H.R. (2011). Does discovery-based instruction enhance learning? *Journal of Educational Psychology, 103*, 1–18.

Burghardt, G. (2011). Defining and recognizing play. In A. Pellegrini (Ed.), *The Oxford handbook of play* (pp. 9–19). New York: Oxford University Press.

Crowley, K., Callanan, M.A., Tenenbaum, H.R., & Allen, E. (2001). Parents explain more often to boys than to girls during shared scientific thinking. *Psychological Science, 12*(3), 258–261.

Fisher, K., Hirsh-Pasek, K., Golinkoff, R.M., Singer, D., & Berk, L.E. (2011). Playing around in school: Implications for learning and educational policy. In A. Pellegrini (Ed.), *The Oxford handbook of play* (pp. 341–363). New York: Oxford University Press.

Fisher, K., Hirsh-Pasek, K., Newcombe, N., & Golinkoff, R.M. (2013). Taking shape: Supporting preschoolers' acquisition of geometric knowledge. *Child Development, 84*(6), 1872–1878.

Grob, R., Schlesinger, M., Pace, A., Hirsh-Pasek, K., & Golinkoff, R. M. (2015). Playing with ideas: Evaluating a collective experiential intervention designed to enrich perceptions of play. Manuscript under review.

Hirsh-Pasek, K., Golinkoff, R.M., Berk, L., & Singer, D. (2009). *A mandate for playful learning in preschool: Presenting the evidence.* New York: Oxford University Press.

Lillard, A. (2013). Playful learning and Montessori education. *American Journal of Play, 5*(2), 157–184.

Ridge, K. E., Weisberg, D. S., Ilgaz, H., Hirsh-Pasek, K., & Golinkoff, R. M. (2015). Buying language in the supermarket: Increasing talk among lower SES families. *Mind, Brain, and Education, 9*, 127–135.

Shonkoff, J.P. (2000). Science, policy and practice: Three cultures in search of a shared mission. *Child Development, 71*(1), 181–188.

Toub, T.S., Hassinger-Das, B., Ilgaz, H., Weisberg, D.S., Nesbitt, K.T., Collins, M.F., . . . Nicolopoulou, A. (2015). The language of play: Developing preschool vocabulary through play and shared book-reading. Manuscript under review.

Weisberg, D., Hirsh-Pasek, K., & Golinkoff, R.M. (2013). Guided play: Where curricular goals meet a playful pedagogy. *Mind, Brain & Education, 7*(2), 104–112.

Weisberg, D.S., Hirsh-Pasek, K., Golinkoff, R.M., & McCandliss, B.D. (2014). Mise en place: Setting the stage for thought and action. *Trends in Cognitive Sciences, 18*(6), 276–278.

Weisberg, D.S., Ilgaz, H., Hirsh-Pasek, K., Golinkoff, R.M., & Nicolopoulou, A. (2015). Shovels and swords: How realistic and fantastical themes affect children's word learning. *Cognitive Development, 35*, 1–14.

Zosh, J.M., Fisher, K., Golinkoff, R.M., & Hirsh-Pasek, K. (2013). The ultimate block party: Bridging the science of learning and the importance of play. In M. Honey & D. Kantner (Eds.), *Design, make, play: Growing the next generation of STEM innovators* (pp. 95–118). New York: Taylor & Francis.

INDEX

Note: page numbers in *italics* indicate figures and tables.

successful 171–2; Creative Thinking
Research Lab 173; essential elements
69f; Living Laboratory model 174–5;
mutual professional development
176–7; participant populations 174–6;
productive nature of 76; research in
context 177–80; the Thinkery 174
museum–scientist partnerships: benefits
and challenges 223–6; introduction
222–3; lessons learned 226–8; looking
forward 228–9; "perfect evaluation
model" of collaboration 225; "perfect
science model" of collaboration 224

narrative reflection 87–9, 203
National Living Laboratory (NLL) project
78–9. *See also* Living Laboratory model
natural selection 44–5, 59–60
Natural Selection (computer interactive) 52
need-based reasoning 48, 59
Needham, A. 214
New York Hall of Science (NYSCI) 37,
156–8

object manipulation 88
On the Origin of Species (Darwin) 52
Oppenheimer, F. 191
Organic School movement 215–16
Osberg, S. 17–18, 22

Palmquist, S. 37, 38
parent–child conversations 85, 88, 99, 159
participant pools, research 30
partnership. *See also* collaboration;
museum–academic collaboration;
museum–researcher partnerships;
museum–scientist partnerships:
defined 86–7; overview 2–4; process
descriptors 6
Partnership for Playful Learners
(project) 85
Pasteur's Quadrant 214
Penuel, W.R. 183
"perfect evaluation model" of
collaboration 225
"perfect science model" of
collaboration 224
Peterman, K. 214
photo-narrative record 90
photo narratives 95–7
play: learner agency and 213–15; learning
through 186–7, 226–8; *PlayWorks*
(exhibit) 105–6

Please Touch Museum (Philadelphia)
153–4
Prager, M. 38, 46
professional development 176–7
prototyping, *vs.* final exhibits 24–5
Providence Children's Museum 120–1;
proximity, jointly negotiated research
(JNR) and 204
psychological research, with children 71

question prompts 203

Rand, J. 38, 46
randomized controlled trial (RCT) 56
reconstruction task 141
Reggio Emilia framework 217
relatingresearchtopractice.org 20
research, jointly negotiated 193–7
researcher–museum collaboration 77–9
researcher–museum interactions 71–3
researcher–museum partnerships: at CCM
86t; challenges of 145–6; cultural
model for 181–8; mutual professional
development model for 65–81;
participant populations 174–5
researcher–museum relationship
challenges: competing goals 23; diverse
family groups 25–6; mismatches in
expertise 25; practical matters 23–4;
prototyping vs final exhibits 24–5;
visitor perceptions of 24
researcher–visitor interaction 70–1
research findings, and reciprocal influences:
assumptions, systematic test of 27–9;
learning and development 30–31; new
design goals 26–7; participant pools 30;
questions and directions 31–3
research methodology 144–5
research platform 89
Research+Practice Collaboratory 182–3
research–practice interaction: convergence
of goals 6–7; core issues 6–10; discussion
4–6; education and public outreach
10; open questions 8; overview 1–2;
partnership overview 2–4; patterns of
partnership interaction 6–8; practical
matters 8–10
research–practice partnership models:
cross-institutional 206; cross-institutional
examples 205–6; introduction 190–3;
jointly negotiated research 193–7, *196t*,
198t, 201–5; other museum research
types 197–201